East Africa by Motor Lorry:
Recollections of an ex-motor transport driver
by
WW Campbell

Edited by
Anne Samson

GWAA / TSL Publications

The Great War in Africa Association

Published in Great Britain in 2020
By Great War in Africa Association, TSL Publications, Rickmansworth

First edition, 1928 London John Murray
This edition, Copyright © 2020 Great War in Africa Association
Photographs and drawings by WW Campbell.

ISBN: 978-1-913294-43-4

The right of WW Campbell and Anne Samson to be identified as the authors and editor of this work has been asserted by the editor in accordance with the UK Copyright, Designs and Patents Act 1988.

All rights reserved. No part of this publication may be reproduced, stored in a retrieval system or transmitted, in any form or by any means without the prior written permission of the publisher, nor be otherwise circulated in any form of binding or cover other than that in which it is published and without a similar condition being imposed on the subsequent buyer.

INTRODUCTION

It is very gratifying to find a book such as this which relates events in the World War I East Africa Campaign through the eyes and words of a British soldier – in this case a motor transport driver in the Royal Army Service Corps. The author had a keen eye for his surroundings and he illustrated his work with interesting photographs and sketches whilst his narrative is straightforward and very readable.

Although by the end of 1917 nearly every European and Indian infantryman had been posted out of the East African theatre as African Askari took their places, a considerable number of Indian troops remained to run the railway systems in British and German East Africa, now Kenya and Tanzania, and many European troops remained in the theatre working on the lines of communication. The British Royal Army Service Corps supplied motor transport units until the end of the campaign, and in the pages of this book we learn about the activities of that Corps and also about others who supported its efforts such as the Road Corps and the men who constructed and operated light railways.

An important section of this book is the observations on the Allied logistical activities in Portuguese East Africa, now Mozambique, as the military operations in that country during 1918 have not been described elsewhere from a lines of communication perspective. The young British drivers and mechanics whose daily duties and activities are described in these pages may not have been in the front line of military activities but they were at risk, not just from enemy ambushes but also from a far more deadly foe – "fever" as malaria was termed – and also from snakes and predator wild animals. The Commonwealth War Graves Commission cemeteries in Mozambique located at Pemba and Lumbo contain 25 burials of men from the Army Service Corps and Royal Army Service Corps (as it was later titled) as well as several more drivers from the South African and East African Service Corps. Driving on the primitive roads in East Africa, especially during the torrential monsoon downpours that regularly occurred, was not a "cushy" job and a stranded driver had to be ready to use his rifle to protect himself from human as well as animal attackers during the hours of darkness.

Finally I am sure that most readers will value the observations on local African culture that the author encountered on his journeys or when he trained and worked with local men in his transport workshops. A mutual respect is displayed here that helps to make the book pleasing to read.

Major Harry Fecitt MBE TD

About

William Wallace Campbell

The author of this book, *East Africa by Motor Lorry*, William Wallace Campbell was born on 9 or 10 February 1881 in Nottingham.[1] He married "Kitty" Eliza Oliver in 1902 and had four children, Mona 1903, Nora Kathleen 1907, Lorna Doreen 1912 and William Wallace 1913.

Between 1899 and March 1916 he worked as a Commission Agent, speculator and, at one time, had been managing director of a company. He spent 13 months employed by the National Projectile Company, Kings Meadow Road, Nottingham as a machine operator where he was described as "an efficient thorough workman, and good timekeeper." He left to join HM Service. During his time as a munition worker, a role for which he volunteered, William issued two thousand 9.2 shells and had three breakdowns. It was on his third that he enlisted as a driver in the Motor Transport. His doctor recorded his first nervous breakdown in 1909: "although a well built man he is very easily upset and does not stand a strain at all well."[2]

William attested on 8 December 1915 and was placed on the army reserve on 9 December 1915. At attestation, his address was recorded as 32 Priory Road, West Bridgford, Nottingham. He was two months short of 35 years of age.

---

[1] The information in this section is derived from Campbell's military personnel file which is one of the 'burnt documents'. He was 36 years and 24 days when he had his military medical on 5 March 1917. (WO 363/4/007287294; WO 372/3/227268)

[2] Doctor's report August 1917.

On 3 March he passed his Army Medical with an "A" rating and despite a request to be downgraded for health reasons from "fit for general service", it appears this failed. Mobilisation of Private 383866 William Wallace Campbell, Royal Army Service Corps, took place on 15 May 1917 and he served at Home until 9 October of the same year. From 29 May 1917, he was at Grove Park No 1 MT Res Depot, London, with the Sherwood Foresters. Six weeks into his training he was admitted to "Fango Hospital" having had a breakdown and was discharged on 31 July 1917.

On 9 October 1917 he embarked from Devonport on HMT *Port Lincoln*,[3] arriving in Dar-es-Salaam, East Africa, on 18 November 1917. The next day he was posted to 648 MT Co, ASC and on 15 January 1918 transferred to 816 Co.

On 10 February 1918, William was admitted to hospital in Mingoyo for malaria, and transferred to Lindi on 12 February. He was discharged on 15 February and embarked on the *Laconia*[4] the same day for Durban. A report by his Commanding Officer on 12 February 1918, Douglas Fillsell of 618 MT Base, noted that William was a Ford Driver, was Reliable and Intelligent and concerning his Sobriety: Good.

Between 16 February and 19 April 1918 he was in South Africa. He embarked on the *Ingoma*[5] on 20 April for East Africa arriving on 26 April 1918, and disembarked at Port Amelia the next day.

William was again hospitalised for malaria on 30 May 1918 at Ankwabe, being transferred to Monapo on 31 July 1918. On 1 August he was hospitalised in Mozambique being discharged on 7 August, rehospitalised on 23 August and stayed in hospital in Mozambique until 2 September 1918.

[3] Australian transport vessel contracted to Commonwealth and Dominion Line Ltd, London until 26 September 1917

[4] RMS *Laconia*, 18098 ton ship of the Cunard Line, patrolled the Atlantic Ocean until April 1915 when she was used in East Africa. Hit by a torpedo, she sank on 25 February 1917. The date does not tie in with when Campbell travelled.

[5] SS *Ingoma*, 5,686 ton ship of the Charente Steamship Co Ltd converted to a troop carrier for the duration of the war.

William served in East Africa for 290 days, leaving on 11 February 1919 on HMT *Salamis*[6] from Dar-es-Salaam for England where he arrived on 21 March 1919. He remained in service on "Z" reserve until 18 April 1919 when he transferred to Army Reserve.

What follows is William's account of his time in East Africa as he recalled in 1927, ten years before he passed away, aged 57 in 1939. The text has been transcribed exactly as William had it published, containing language which is not generally acceptable today. This has been retained to enable cultural researchers to draw their own conclusions. Despite these few detractors, William provides a rich insight into the life of a driver in East Africa during the First World War and his encounters with the local populations and environment.

Harry Fecitt MBE TD suggested reprinting the text to enable greater access to a little known aspect of the war in Africa and kindly provided copies of the images.[7]

The War Diary[8] of 18th Motor Ambulance Convoy, 1 Feb 1917 to 31 May 1918 covers the period when William was in East Africa and refers to events mentioned in his recollections. It is transcribed here, courtesy of Crown Copyright and The National Archives, UK.

Biographical information, where traceable, has been included.

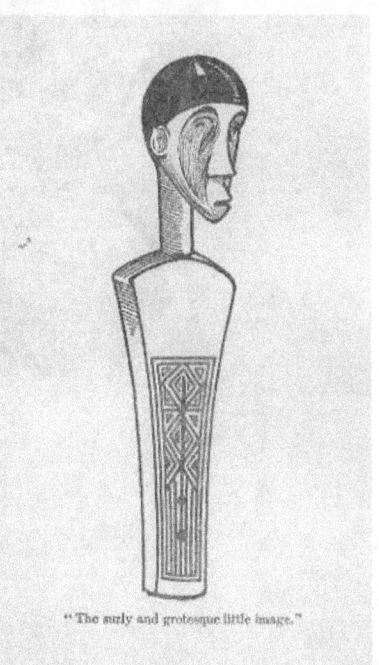

"The surly and grotesque little image."

[6] SS *Salamis*, troop ship served 1899-1924

[7] All reasonable steps have been take to ensure copyright has not been breeched in the reprint of this edition. If you feel an infringment has been committed, please contact the publisher.

[8] WO 95/5371/2

The Author and his "surly and grotesque little image."

Foreword

My object in writing these reminiscences is to place on record a true account of work undertaken in a strange and savage country by inexperienced city men, called out from the comfort of their own homes and from the blessings of civilised surroundings, by the exigencies of war, to a new and little-dreamt-of exploratory campaign the like of which, inasmuch as the motor car played such a unique part, will probably never happen again – at least not as we knew it.

My ambition is to interest all those good fellows who, during those hysterical years that now seem so distant, helped to chase that will-o'-the-wisp, Von Lettow, through the eerie fastnesses of Africa's wilds, and to give to friends and all sufficiently interested an entertaining account of a plain man's simple adventures.

These were less concerned with the powder and shot aspects of warfare than with the difficulties and interests of life in general and motor transport in particular. So I have endeavoured to set down an account of my impressions of the character of the country and its people, their habits and customs, with duly expurgated comments on the climate and the fauna; all linked by the thread of personal experience. In attempting to portray life in this fascinating country – it included a journey through Portuguese East Africa – and to give pleasure to the reader, I hope I have succeeded.

WW Campbell
Nottingham
December 1927

Contents

Chapter 1: All aboard. Through the blockade. Two days' gale. The convoy in the Tropics. On the edge of the Gold Coast. High Jinks. Cape Town.   **13**

Chapter 2: An agreeable change. Up the East African coast. The "Haven of Peace". The parting. At sea again.   **24**

Chapter 3: Lindi. All night in the creek. Mingoya. An optimist. Small life. Off up country.   **31**

Chapter 4: A wild ride. Massasi Boma. Up with the troops. Strenuous days and nights.   **44**

Chapter 5: The Germans cross the Rovuma River. Troops at a standstill. Work on the line. The Rajah, Bell and our menagerie. On the Rovuma River.   **58**

Chapter 6: On Livingstone's trail. Diversions on the road. Ominous signs and preparations. Lions on the Rovuma. A dangerous encounter. Hunting for food. Native superstitions. Christmas. New Year's Eve.   **72**

Chapter 7: A fight. The native element. "Merry and Bright" A disruption. A change of convoy. Transport difficulties. The Lemasuli River. The camp on fire. A native sense of humour. Line abandoned.   **92**

Chapter 8: Mingoya[9]. Inconceivable conditions. Down and out. Evacuation. At sea. Durban.   **108**

Chapter 9: The military situation. A call at Beira. Arrival at Port Amelia. Our camp on the hill. General van Deventer. A night in the bush. Arrival at Ankwabe.   **126**

Chapter 10: The Germans at Medo. In the workshop. The recruiting of natives. Pleasantries in camp. The tsetse-fly. Malaria and the sun. Camp on fire. The bachelors' den. Lions.   **144**

[9] Today known as Mingoyo.

Chapter 11: Blown up. Out of action. Camp on fire. The sick parade. An invasion of ants and an alarming discovery. More fires and two brave men. The tale of a shirt. Germans gone to earth. Chased by a lion. Westward Ho! **160**

Chapter 12: Medo. Bush fires. The Lurio River. Night driving. An unwelcome apparition. The camp in the swamp. Blackwater. Mkonta. Alarming reports. Chasing the devil. Disaster. **177**

Chapter 13: Away from the swamps. Mkonta. Bumping the sick. Strife at Monapo. The fever friend. Down the line. Alarm at Monapo. The fire engine. Lumbo. In hospital. Recreation at Lumbo. The MT Stores camp. The whirlwind. A human alarm clock. Blessings of the YMCA. Fever again. The snake collector. A delicate subject. Birds of a feather. **199**

Chapter 14: The situation reviewed. The jigger and the ant-lion. A merry evening. The *Ngoma* dancers' curse. Man *versus* beast: a battle of brawn and brains. A visit to Mozambique. Empty Lumbo. The agony of a woman. Wonderful news. The beginning of the end. **222**

Chapter 15: Our share of the world epidemic. The beginning of evacuation. Excursions. Adventures with the pioneers. Psychology of the native. Sea View Camp and the joy of the seashore. Von Lettow appears. Christmas in the heat. **236**

Chapter 16: A full day of interest. Speeding to the end. A letter home. Departure. To Southampton via the Cape. Arrival home. The end. **253**

War Diary 18th Motor Ambulance Convoy, 1 Feb 1917 to 31 May 1918 **262**

Motor/Mechanical Transport Companies in East Africa

273

Index **275**

With illustrations and photos

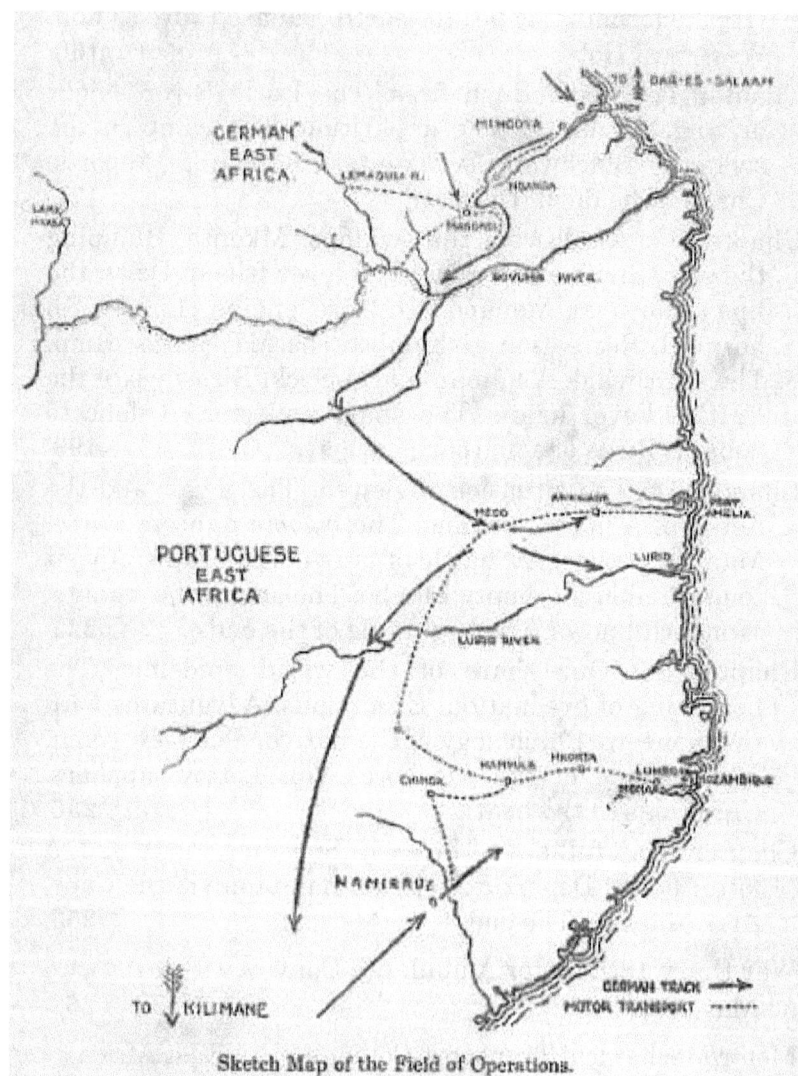

Sketch Map of the Field of Operations.

Chapter 1

Characteristic of the citizen army, with marked variety of human types, reduced for the duration of the Great War to the common denominator of khaki, twelve hundred of us cheerfully adapted ourselves to the slender individual allotment of space in the 'tween decks of HM Transport *Port Lincoln*, one sunny October morning. There were men out of mansions and men out of hovels; workers with brain and horny-handed sons of toil, some thoughtful and silent, and others clamouring and shouting – all now concentrating on securing the maximum of creature comfort under novel and cramped conditions. In the near future loomed the prospect of strange adventure in East Africa.

Our own little party soon settled down to the new conditions: there was Raspin[10] of my own town, well-known for a robust manner, a prominent lower jaw, and a resounding baritone voice; Harris,[11] a little man with a personality, from one of the London music halls, an excellent accompanist for any songs that were going the rounds; Knowles,[12] who had extremely long legs and occupied his time in keeping them out of the way; Wheatley[13] of solemn mien; good-natured, fat-faced, ruddy complexioned Mercer,[14] who was ready to fall in with anything where fun and entertainment abounded; De Bussy,[15] with his whimsical, laughing eyes, and peculiar manner of ejecting witty

---

[10] Edward Raspin, Army Service Corps M/336253 (WO 372/16/151667)

[11] Harris - unable to trace

[12] Knowles - unable to trace

[13] John Wheatley, Army Service Corps, Motor Transport, M2/051218 (WO 372/21/102167)

[14] Mercer - unable to trace

[15] Alexander F De Bussy, Army Service Corps, M/338506 (WO 372/5/138378)

epigrams from the corners of his lips; Mumford,[16] whose name, somehow or other, coupled with the fact that he held his head as if he had a stiff neck, and mumbled his speech, suggested the mumps; Thompson,[17] who always found he had

---

[16] Phillip James Mumford, Royal Army Service Corps, Motor Transport M/323713 (WO 372/14/141226)

Off the East African Coast.

Troops Ashore.

a lot to say when everybody else had finished; a young Len Jones,[18] affectionately known as "Baby"; and last, but not least, Tiny – we never new him by any other name – dapper little chap who appointed himself our bodyguard and general factotum, as if we couldn't look after ourselves, but who was, nevertheless the life of the party. Later, when everybody was down with sea-sickness, it was Tiny who nursed them back to life with happy smiles and optimistic encouragement.

We sailed on a Friday, a sad omen to the superstitious. Seaplanes and stubby-nosed dirigibles swept the surface of steel-grey and menacing waters, floating away from the harbour mouth to recede to mere specks on the horizon; destroyers darted hither and thither, and then, like a modern Goliath defying the hidden peril, a battle cruiser stood up majestically in the gathering gloom of evening and passed out to sea, followed immediately by a convoy of eight transports flanked by two auxiliary cruisers.

Thus as we left the historic waters of Plymouth Sound –

> Visions of old world heroes, wake . . .
> Granville, Hawkins, Raleigh, Drake . . .

were the thoughts begotten by concentration of mind on the present, forcing realisation of the emptiness of time. There was no difference between yesterday and today; only the ships were iron shops of action, steam and smoke, with pulsating mechanical hearts of solid steel, and – how grotesque! – covered all over with multifarious designs of many colours – a poor camouflage, one thought, against detection by prying eyes from man-made monsters of the deep.

Accompanied by destroyers, which never once reduced speed in dashing to and fro and encircling the convoy, the

---

[17] John Lawrence Thompson, Army Service Corps M314648, died 14 November 1918 (WO 372/20/780; CWGC) OR Frederick Thomas Thompson, Army Service Corps M2/156847 died dysentry 12 April 1918 (Rugby Remembers; CWGC)
[18] Emlyn Jones, Army Service Corps, Motor Transport DM2/117672, Dorset Regiment 20020 (WO 372/11/40804)

ships turned slowly into the night on a south-west course, feeling the lift of the on-coming Atlantic rollers, heaving and tossing to the freshening breeze. Before we turned in, it became pitchy dark. Not a light glimmered ahead or astern. The presence of the other ships could only be sensed. Beneath the whistle of the gale playing through the rigging, and the noise of breaking water over the side, the steady throb of the *Port Lincoln*'s powerful engines came half consciously to sleeping forms, and gave a false sense of security.

From my own personal experiences gained in deep water sailing-ships, when we rolled ourselves round the world and traversed the wide waters from the Roaring Forties to north of 'Frisco, the sea in its many strange moods was quite familiar to me; but I must confess that the following two days' horror below decks surpassed all my previous knowledge of how far bad weather could be responsible for misery and wretchedness. For forty-eight hours it blew a full gale; everybody was prostrate, not a morsel of food was fetched or eaten, and during those two long pitiable days and nights hardly a man stirred. On the morning of the third day the conditions below, as sufferers lay about in a state of exhaustion and physical collapse, can best be left to the imagination.

Not included in the mass of suffering men below there was a limited number on deck in the happy position to enjoy the magnificent picture of rolling seas and storm-tossed vessels, in brilliant sunshine, with the air cold and fresh. The heavy metalled battle cruiser encountered difficulty in keeping her position at the head of the convoy as her charges were rolling all over the place. Tempestuous green seas swept right over her nose to the foot of the navigation bridge, and, when she lifted, she thrust them from her in beautiful cascades that fell back hissing into the sea. Ere she could run completely dry she was again wallowing in the trough, repeating her nautical gymnastics. I was surprised to see the destroyers still with us, when they could be seen, for they were hidden by the spray most of the time; but at the height of the gale they suddenly turned about and disappeared astern.

* * *

A week later, everybody had forgotten about the gale. The convoy was in the middle of the Atlantic, a thousand miles from the usual path of traffic, in calm weather, under a hot sun, accompanied by the peaceful conditions that are generally associated with a sea voyage when the human freight has settled down. But, unhappily, about this time the men began to suffer from the monotonous diet of beef and potatoes, beans and porridge, which almost solely comprised their daily fare. Then, too, the heat of the tropics began to assert itself. Small wonder therefore that there was an epidemic of boils among the troops. I had one on the very end of my nose. This the doctor dressed with a piece of sticking-plaster which, by mischance or design, was applied in the form of the letter X. At any rate it made my appearance comical enough for me to become the innocent source of a good deal of amusement. Even so, I was luckier than some who had boils in more inconvenient places.

There were so many troops on board, all cramped, cabined and confined, that much inconvenience and suffering had to be endured. The only guarantee of a comfortable toilet – or a toilet at all – was to be up first, at 4 a.m., and shave in the dark; for soon after everyone was striving for the same thing, at the same time, the lavatory accommodation being utterly and entirely inadequate. It was lamentable to see the bad-tempered, struggling rank and file trying to get near the all too few water-taps together. To add to the difficulties the water invariably gave out and sometimes made it impossible for the men to be properly groomed, or to parade to time. One morning the orderly officer appeared on the scene; it was 7 o'clock; not a drop of water had been obtainable for the last hour and a half, and men stood around half naked and helpless. There was a lack of understanding between the ship's officers and our own which made itself apparent in the remark made by this officer as he looked concernedly about him: "I have talked enough about it, and cannot do any more!" And with that he disappeared.

However, we all scrambled through somehow, and if men appeared on parade looking as if they hadn't had a wash or a shave for a week, "inspection" failed to reveal the "crime".

The facilities available for a sea-water shower bath were taken full advantage of by many. It helped to keep one right, and was something to look forward to every morning as a refreshing tonic – the sea-water in all conscience plentiful enough, but quite useless, of course, for the more important purpose of a wash or a shave.

Pleasantries of a social and musical character helped to soften the asperities of the voyage. Troubles, such as they were, were forgotten in the evenings when the men gathered round, with pipes aglow, to yarn about the past, or discuss the uncertain prospect of the future. Musically, the Harmony Four beguiled the time entertaining an admiring crowd in the waist of the ship, till one night somebody without a soul, but with a raucous voice, yelled from the depths of a dark porthole: "What the 'ell's the row about? For Christopher's sake put a cork in it!" And that naturally fired ambitions!

The formation of a concert followed. As a vocalist of more or less serious pretensions, with a weakness for exciting the boys into roaring the chorus of "Merry and Bright" as it had never been roared before, I duly presented myself to the Adjutant, still unfortunately with the sticking-plaster on my nose – indeed I had forgotten it as I stood strictly to attention and presented my credentials. "Well I cannot judge your qualifications," he declared at last, staring at me with unassumed frankness, "but I should have imagined from your appearance that you were a comedian!"

The Adjutant proved a real good sportsman. He not only organised the concert party, but took a prominent part in it himself. Few among those twelve hundred troops on the *Port*

Lincoln in those days will ever forget the Light Blue Concert Party, as it was called, and the happy times we all had together before reaching our destination. The Adjutant, a young man and quite capable enough, took the part of the one and only leading lady. George Godfrey[19] delighted the audience, especially that section containing the officers, with his skilful impersonation of a commissioned officer in the humorous song: "I'm on the Staff!" and another particularly aesthetic number: "It was the end of my old cigar!" The dramatic Wheatley curdled the blood with "Murders"! Poor Fitzpatrick[20] charmed everyone with "I want the moon", and "They wouldn't believe me!" (pathetic in after-memory as he died in East Africa). Harris, the highly-strung little pianist, as our director-accompanist, was the life and soul of the whole company. White[21] had a tenor voice of exceptional sweetness; and my friend Raspin delighted his audience with sonorous ballads on love in a passion, rich red wines, and fights to a finish. I selected such chorus songs as were dear to the hearts of the boys. Merryweather[22] played on a stringed instrument of uncertain origin; chubby-faced Mercer and young Lorriman[23] took part in the sketches, and Dukes[24] (who also died in East Africa) was the stage manager. Performances were given on deck in fine weather, below when the weather was unfavourable. For those who had eyes to see and a heart to commune with, they were happy yet sad days out there in the peaceful solitude of the

---

[19] George Godfrey - unable to trace
[20] William Arthur Fitzpatrick, Army Service Corps, 648 Motor Transport Compnay M/340632 died 24 November 1918 of influenza (WO 372/7/81061; CWGC)
[21] White - unable to trace
[22] Possibly Horace William Merryweather, Army Service Corps M/340959 (WO 372/13/216541)
[23] Arthur J Lorriman, Army Service Corps M/287238 (WO 372/12/139173) OR Herbert Lorriman, Army Service Corps M/334041 (WO 372/12/139185) OR John B Lorriman, Army Service Corps M2/074239 (WO 372/12/139192)
[24] Horace HJC Dukes, Army Service Corps M/319901 died 26 November 1918 (WO 372/6/110291; CWGC)

vast Atlantic, while in Europe the fires of hatred and vengeance burned . . .

In beautiful tropical weather, under a sky like burnished brass, with a great stillness over the now adjacent land, we moved slowly into the harbour of Freetown (Sierra Leone). The blue waters of the sun-bathed harbour, edged with a strip of golden sand, and the little town spread out toy-like in patches of rich colour on the sloping shore, presented a pleasing picture to sea-weary eyes. Mellowed by distance, a range of mountains could just be discerned, far inland. On the placid waters lay a light cruiser, at rest, her decks deserted, a think wisp of smoke rising lazily from one of her funnels, symbolical of mighty destructive power held in leash. She was HMS *Kent* (of Falklands Island fame)[25] waiting to escort us to Cape Town. There was no other evidence of life on our arrival. The aspect was one of peace and repose under the spell of tropical heat.

But soon there was plenty of noise and activity. Native boats came alongside whose dusky occupants scrambled on board with a tempting variety of fresh fruit with which to barter for whatever they could lay their hands on. In consequence, hurriedly collected from obscure corners of kit bags, out came all sorts of odds and ends. These once prized trifles their respective owners now considered they could well do without, the resultant bartering and excitement becoming highly diverting. From primitive dug-outs diving boys plunged head first into the cool, clear water to recover flung coins, returning to the surface again, repeating the performance so long as coins were available.

After coaling operations we left this corner of Fairyland; for although we were quite aware of its sinister reputation the beauty of the place still appealed to us. HMS *Kent* was now

---

[25] Participated in the Battle of the Falkland Islands end 1914, patrolled South American coast in 1915 and assigned to Cape Station in 1916 for convoy duties until mid-1918 when returned to China Station and then Vladivostock. HMS *Kent* was launched March 1901 and sold for scrap in June 1920.

in charge and led the convoy out of the harbour. The *Port Lincoln*, the last boat to leave, grounded on the bar, and for ten breathless minutes she churned up the sand and water before finally succeeding in backing off. Some little time elapsed before we caught up with the convoy and resumed our proper station.

There were many pastimes of a diverting nature. Amongst the most absorbing games were "Crown and Anchor", "Housey-Housey", and such like. The 'tween decks continuously resounded with such abstruse cries as "Clickety-click!", "Top of the House" and "Kelly's Eye!" Some considerable sums of money were made in this way, and some losses sustained, but in its favour it may be said that everybody seemed thoroughly to enjoy the excitement.

The heat now became intense. We all tried to sleep on deck. When all who could were lying down there was not an inch of space left. Hammocks were brought up and slung, zig-zag, over the heads of the sleepers below. Consequently, late comers drew forth unparliamentary language from those unavoidably trodden on.

So far, so good. But one night a deluge of rain descended with such violence as is only to be met with in the tropics, and in a single moment the scene was changed from one of perfect peace to a chaotic pandemonium. A glorious stampede followed. Vivid flashes of lightening momentarily blinded everybody, and collisions took place – men falling headlong. When the deluge ceased with its usual tropical suddenness a feverish search took place for missing property. A heterogenous mixture of bedding, wearing apparel, pocket wallets and watches lay submerged in decks awash and hammocks waterlogged . . .

The line was crossed with the usual ceremonies. With loud cries of "Ship ahoy! What ship is that?" all hands were astonished to perceive a strangely garbled individual, representing the King of the Watery Main, clamber laboriously over the bow of the *Port Lincoln*. He was old and bewhiskered, with a ruddy complexion of artificial origin. Wearing a tinsel crown slightly askew, he gripped a trident with majestic defiance and proceeded aft followed by a retinue of active satellites. And so the fun began. Thus, many members of the ship's company, including our clever officer-comedians, "Messrs Clap and Trap", were initiated into the mysteries of King Neptune's slippery domain. After a great number, too great to count, had been shaved, doctored, and half drowned, and a few given up for dead, the tormentors tired of their nefarious work and turned the hose-pipe on all and sundry, effectually clearing the decks.

As we neared Cape Town, discipline, which had been relaxed, was applied again. One of the convoy, turning suddenly, went off into the west alone, and disappeared with the setting sun. The next morning another boat, dropping astern, walled in the trough as if disabled, and we wondered what could have happened until we noticed her flag at half-mast, denoting a burial at sea. Then, unfortunately, it was our turn. The *Port Lincoln*'s engines were stopped, and as she lay sluggishly inert, all troops on parade, the body of a seaman was committed to the deep – an impressive

Drivers in the Motor Transport.

ceremony. Curiously, and to the alarm of the superstitious, at the very moment the body entered the water – with a splash that awoke the solemn silence – the heavy plate-glass window of the navigation bridge slammed to with a loud report, shattering it to pieces, the glass falling to the deck below.

The convoy, now closing in on the South African coast, began to feel the force of the strong head-winds, the ships plunging their noses into the heavy seas which broke and hurled themselves across the forecastle heads . . .

At last, in striking contrast to the heaving decks, the throbbing of the engines, and the whistle of the wind, to which we had become so accustomed, was the gentle, gliding motion of the *Port Lincoln* as she slowly entered the calm waters of Cape Town's handsome harbour. To feel the close proximity of Table Mountain's towering side, to gaze with increasing curiosity on the animated scene along with the harbour front, to catch the strong land scents that came to one's nostrils on the hot air, was to make one long to be ashore.

". . . we dubbed the little Ford line 'The Scenic Railway.'"

Chapter 2

Considering we had been obliged to make a wide detour into the heart of the Atlantic in order to reduce the possible chances of meeting with a lurking submarine, and that our pace was governed by that of the slowest boat, we arrived in Cape Town in fairly good time – four weeks.

My first concern on landing was to fulfil an obligation I had contracted before leaving England. This was to cable home the news of our safe arrival so that my message could be despatched to my home circle on a hundred and twenty-four postcards to the relatives of that number of men aboard who had entrusted me with the task. I subsequently heard that the welcome news was distributed within twenty-four hours of the cablegram leaving South Africa.

Cape Town's appeal to the stranger is at once delightful and fascinating. We spent five happy days in this town of sunny streets, stately buildings, pretty bungalows, lovely flower gardens and walks. The broad outlook with its spacious harbour, expansive bay, long sea-fronts, and handsome pier – upon which the Municipal Orchestra performed every evening – are screened from the north-east winds by Table Mountain's great wall of rock, and on the seaward side warmed by a benevolent semi-tropical sun that shines all the year round.

One of the excursions enjoyed was a run up the hill by electric car, through the pinewoods, round the Lion's Head – the name given to a mountainous-like lump of rock towering skyward – thence through the broad cutting on the far side and down a long, gentle slope, with an extensive view of ocean, to Camp's Bay. Here we disported ourselves to our heart's content on the sands, patronising the little tea chalet, and rambling over the great boulders that lay strewn about in all directions as if cast down at some remote period by giant hands from the high peaks close by the while foaming seas broke continuously over the nearer rocks with a dull roar. Approaching darkness made us realise that time had sped only too quickly. Scrambling on board one of the electric cars (a convenient but necessarily belated and infrequent service), in high spirits we returned by the gently undulating coast route, past bungalows nestling by the hillsides, whose homely, lighted windows gave out a friendly gleam as darkness rapidly closed down.

I had often wondered to what extent one's mind would be affected by a sudden rebound from homely affairs to the atmosphere of the mysterious tropics again, to feel once more the delight of youthful irresponsibility, to become again intoxicated with the seductive fragrance of strange and mystic perfumes, to gaze enchanted on more new and fascinating scenes, peeping once more into delectable corners of the world's great Fairy Garden, so limitless, so enchanting, and to break again the health-giving air of ocean and of mountain. And here we were by a strange force of circumstances that few of us ever dreamed of. These were my thoughts as we sat and listened to the orchestral music on the pier, when the fashion of Cape Town mingled with the crowd, sipping cooling drinks and smoking choice tobaccos, amidst the subdued murmur of voices mingling with the music from stringed instruments, while a soft breeze blowing in from the sea wafted relief to a heated brow.

The Light Blue Concert Party gave two performances in the town, and we made many friends. All too soon our stay was over, and when the time came for parting, it was with sad hearts we said "good-bye", so great our welcome, and so kind and hospitable our hosts . . .

As chance would have it, as the distance between the ship and shore widened, and familiar objects became faint to straining eyes, white vapour settled down on to Cape Town's flat-topped mountain and we saw the "tablecloth laid" – a rare privilege. The heliograph's spasmodic flashes became fewer and then ceased. Conscious now only of the rhythmic throb of the ship's engines and the leap of the bows as she charged the on-coming seas, darkness descended, and for the first time since leaving England our navigation lights were burning . . . as we forged ahead – alone . . .

Nearing the tropics again, the 'tween decks became once more a Turkish bath. Men walked about half naked, mopping face and chest, and some of them collapsed – to become inmates of the little hospital.

The question of food was still a serious one for the men, the unsuitable nature of it, and the scant quantity arousing deep-voiced complaint.

However, this did not subdue the natural instinct of the men to make the best of it, and loud uproarious reception was accorded any effort at entertainment. Indeed, so recklessly irresponsible had we all become by this time, that the following doggerel very well illustrates the state of mind we were now in. It was sung as a concerted item and taken up enthusiastically by the men:

> The silliest song that ever was
> We'll now inflict on you;
> There's neither sense nor reason
> In the words or tune, 'tis true!
> But, nevertheless, we'll sing to you
> This lilty, little lay;
> And if you want any more of it, well,
> All you have to say, is,
> "Carry on! – Carry on! –
> And keep on carrying on –
> And on – and on – and on!"

The last night on board was a veritable farewell orgy of mirth. Repeated complaints had brought about an improvement in the feeding, and so, with more contented minds, the diversion was all the more enjoyed. "Messrs Clap and Trap" were responsible for the "orchestra", which comprised almost anything with a "big noise" from the humble piano down to saucepan lids. There were no less than fifty "instrumentalists", ably assisted by hundreds of lusty vocalists, and the row in the 'tween decks till midnight, when the proceedings terminated, can only be likened to what one might fancy would be the state of a great musician's mind when the subject has gone mad.

However, it was all good, innocent fun, and proved a fine stimulant.

Our first impression of the East African coast was that of a long, dark pencil line on the horizon with a string of black dots – palm trees – plainly to be discerned.

In sober silence now, we find ourselves getting ever nearer to the land. Imperceptibly the ship drew right in, passing a lighthouse on a small island to the left, and a solitary hospital ship – conspicuous in fresh white paint and gigantic red cross – lying peacefully at anchor to the right. With pilot aboard we moved through the shallows to the very edge of the palm-covered beach, when to our surprise, a large opening suddenly revealed itself and we passed through. As we did so, the wreck of a steamer was to be noticed lying to the right on its side (an early attempt of the Germans to block the harbour entrance), and grouped about the water's edge were diminutive (by distance) khaki-clad figures. They hailed us as we passed, but we could discern only such words as "Jambo! ... news ... Blightly ... Europe ..."

The next moment we had swung widely into the middle of the harbour, coming to anchor with a noisy rattle of cabin chain. Now, deprived of the slight breeze we had enjoyed while the ship was in motion, the heat was terrific. It struck mercilessly down from a midday sun with fierce intensity, reflected hotly from the shimmering water, and radiated from the shore in draughts of hot air; until, indeed, we gasped at its vehemence and suffered discomfort in the mere act of breathing. From the spacious and landlocked waters around, our gaze wandered to the environs of the harbour. We saw enchanting prospects of delightful walks in the future in the form of shady avenues between palm trees along the harbour front, for the distance of about a mile, to where, half hidden among a greater profusion of palm trees, lay the sleepy little town of Dar-es-Salaam. One or two prominent buildings and a church steeple showed over the tree tops – evidence of an improved state of civilisation. In spaces between the trees could be seen structures of Oriental design, so white as to dazzle incandescent in the glare of the sun, relieved in splashes of vivid blues and reds where a scheme at decoration had been attempted. On the foreshore a number of sailing dhows and smaller native boats lay idly on their sides. There was no sign of life or movement. A solitary rickshaw passed between the trees, and one curious person, strangely garbed, stayed for a moment to gaze upon us – possibly our impressions and his were reciprocal.

This, then, was Dar-es-Salaam, "the haven of peace", as its name implied, appropriately enough, we thought, in the still heat of the midday siesta – a name that leant itself to the thoughtful speculation as to its origin and history, redolent of strange romances of the past. (At one time the capital of German East Africa, it was now under British control, used as a main base for administration purposes. Geographically, it is almost on a line with the island of Zanzibar, which is distant only a few hours' sail, and is but two hundred miles south of Mombasa.)

The general desire to go ashore was not satisfied. Some of the companies were landed, but others, including the one I was in, became transferred to the transport *Salamis*, and within an hour we were at sea again, steaming over the route we had just traversed . . .

Such a heterogenous crowd of human rabble as was congregated in the open well of the forward deck of the *Salamis* it would be hard to find elsewhere. There were African natives of all kinds, half naked, wholly naked, and some clothed to the chin, the whites of the eyes showing one minute and the face screwed up as if in pain the next; there were men from the Orient, sinuous, lithe-bodied, shifty Chinamen; haughty, upstanding Indians, arms upraised as they dexterously twisted wisps of dark, greasy hair, or re-arranged a soiled cotton turban; and many more creatures of a doubtful lineage who emphasised the doubt by looking like nothing on earth. Collected into crowded groups, both confusing and overlapping, they hung their heads over multi-coloured trappings, sorting the various articles into little piles, and picking out their own mean personal belongings, over which they fought, quarrelled, laughed, and yelled alternately.

The British troops were worse off. We were accommodated below in the 'tween decks where the stench was so bad as to force us to the only conclusion that cattle had been there. When the midday meal arrived, two hours late, during which we were not allowed to leave the table, it consisted merely of bully beef and biscuits – dog biscuits the boys called the latter. Incensed at this indifferent treatment, the food was declined, the boys demonstrating by howling and barking their opinion of "dog biscuits" for dinner. We had witnessed the mixed crowd forward taking food into their mouths by the handful, and because the mess was soft and apparently appetising we hungry fellows envied them as they devoured it with noisy relish and avidity. Little consideration seemed to have been bestowed upon us, however, otherwise oppor-tunity would have been taken at Dar-es-Salaam to provide us with more palatable food than bully beef and biscuits.

At any rate, the men barked and howled, gnawed sullenly with grating teeth on the "hard-tack", and lowed like a herd of cattle before rain. Indeed, so terrific did the din become that all the staff officers came tumbling below decks to see what was the matter. They listened attentively to explan-ations and were sympathetic enough, but regretting they could do nothing in regard to the food, readily gave permission for us to regain the open air, setting a good example by getting there first! In the excitement of the rush that followed, men literally fell over one another, coming playfully to fisticuffs in the scramble up the gangways.

In the evening those two humanly sympathetic officers, "Messrs Clap and Trap", did their best to cheer the boys' spirits with a concert.

But what a game it all was! I would not care to live that life again. Of course the experience was extremely novel to most, the scenes around us new and fascinating, and to all, the future was a distinctly absorbing prospect. Perhaps it was these considerations that accounted for the way difficulties were met and successfully overcome.

A day or two was quite enough for us on this wretched transport, and we were glad to fetch the land. The good ship *Salamis* fetched it – fetched it so abruptly that she shook all over with the concussion as she bumped the bottom and came to a full stop.

Responding to the frantic signals that were run up, a string of lighters came out from the mouth of a creek hard by, and into these we scrambled, helter-skelter, with kit-bags, great-coats, rifles and all, and away we went – for the creek and Lindi, our destination.

The shallow East African Strand.

Chapter 3

We found Lindi a dark, damp, and airless settlement, composed only of a few grass huts, situated on the banks of the creek, almost blotted out by a profusion of coconut trees and overshadowed by hills clothed in dense vegetation. On the slopes of the hills behind, dominating the district, stood the white, battlemented walls of an ancient Arab fort, a grim reminder of slave-trading days, silent witness to the departed power of those hoary-headed old buccaneers who bore down and ousted the Portuguese from nearly all their East African possessions. On the other side of the creek, from the very water's edge, the thickly covered banks towered into the high hills, so high as to blot out the southern sky, as if jealous of the light that struggled to penetrate Lindi's dark confines. In the creek, resting on the waters like a bare plank, but as menacing as a dozing crocodile, lay a flat-bottomed British monitor whose scanty crew of bluejackets raised a cheer as we drew alongside the jetty.

Once ashore, and standing by, a few optimists in our party made the ludicrous attempt to obtain milky coconuts by throwing at them – but these grew on trees! Even with the help of a native boy who adopted the less impetuous but more certain method of obtaining a few specimens by climbing for them, they proved far too tough in their remarkably thick coats of fibre for peaceful penetration, much to the astonishment of those who had laboured in vain with jack-knives until reluctantly compelled to realise a knife's uselessness. It would require a native expert, skilful in the use of the *panga* (bush-knife), to overcome the difficulty.

A roll call followed; hot coffee and bully were welcome, if only to stay our hunger. We were then divided into numerous small companies. Eventually the section I was in, comprising about thirty men, marched off on to the wooden jetty, and without further delay boarded an ungainly looking Arab dhow, with its characteristic high stern and rakish prow, and sailed away into the night, up the stream.

We found it a romantic situation: the moon high in the sky, the huge lateen sail blotting out half its magic light. A rascally looking, almost naked savage of enormous proportions – he was probably half Arab and half Swahili – stood on the high poop, his big, course features sharply outlined against the opalescent sky as he looked keenly aloft, grasping the spokes tightly with gnarled, black fingers, giving the steering-wheel a spin, first this way then that. Occasionally his thick lips parted, and his red mouth opened like a cavern to bark rapid orders in a language strange and vivid to our ears, upon which the members of the crew scrambled to different ropes, entangled themselves, and quarrelled furiously.

To what strange adventures were we bound? We had arrived in this outlandish country right enough, were here in this deckles, open boat, sailing serenely up the dark creek. All was apparently peaceful, the still night charged with mystic romance; realism was brought closer by the presence of the dark savages about us, but they, like the night, became subdued and quiet. Without the remotest idea of where we were, what we were doing, or where we were going to, the position was, indeed, full of possibilities. To add to the mysterious nature of our errand we had no knowledge of circumstances ashore, or of the military situation – even if there was one, and of that we were uncertain.

Soothed by the influence of the calm night air and the gentle motion of the boat as it glided along in the moonlight, some of the boys began to sing softly, as humans are wont to do in those heavenly lapses when peace takes the place of worldly care; but even that little break into the stillness died away after a time, and then we heard only the gentle gurgle of the water lapping the bows, and the sigh of the wind in the sail. The "dog-man" in the stern had long since ceased his barking. The black, impenetrable banks on either side slipped astern into obscurity, and thus, in the great stillness of the warm, tropical night, the whole company dozed.

An hour, and the breeze failed altogether, the sail falling back on the mast with a dull thud. The heavy dhow, losing way, and swinging helplessly into mid-stream, stuck on a sand-bank and remained fast.

It was soon evident that, apart from this hopeless position, there was no immediate relief. The scallawag captain, and his equally undesirable but necessary crew, furled the sail, looked aimlessly about for a few moments, muttered a few unintelligible words, curled themselves up in a corner of the boat and went fast asleep. There was nothing else for us but to follow suit, and so, in many uncomfortable positions, the whole company had soon followed the example of their dusky associates.

The tide must have ebbed rapidly, or perhaps time went quickly. Anyway, we all received a rude awakening at 3 a.m. when our vessel suddenly heeled right over, and, with a quiver, lay on her side, the tide having receded. The human cargo went rolling through space in a confused heap of flying legs and arms, and bruised heads. I was more fortunate as it had occurred to me to make an improvised hammock out of a bight of the sail; thus I swung out to the perpendicular when the disaster occurred . . .

At dawn everybody was up and doing, and in spite of the risks, first one and then another of the boys tumbled over the side and sported in the cool, refreshing water. (We afterwards heard that crocodiles measuring twelve feet on length infested these waters, but if that was so it was probably higher up in more secluded parts of the stream.) Anyway, they all came aboard safely, freshened by the limpid water which was so clear that the pebbles could be seen on the bottom as though crystal. This early diversion put a keen edge on appetites which, however, had to remain keen as we carried no rations.

So we waited impatiently for an early release. This did not come, however. During the morning a steam launch came down-stream, and, seeing our plight, made an attempt to tow us off, but the tow-rope broke, the end falling into the water and becoming twisted round the propeller before the engine could be stopped. Two of the crew, stripping naked – not a long operation for them – jumped over board, and for a few minutes together remained submerged, trying in vain to unwind the rope. Finally it became necessary to hack it away with knives, after which they troubled no more about us, but made off.

After this the hours passed languidly by, the hot sun mounting the heavens and scorching us. Never a sign of human life, but only the empty dome of heaven, and the dark, impenetrable banks kept us company.

A happy thought inspired the officer in charge to take advantage of the time at our disposal to give the men some idea of the military situation ashore, and of the mission they were on. This he did in the form of an address. It as a mistake to imagine that the war in Africa was over.[26] A good deal of fighting had taken place, and a good deal of the country had been cleared of the enemy, but there were still several strong companies in the field, including the redoubtable leader, General Von Lettow-Vorbeck, with three hundred white troops and seventeen hundred black. Far from the campaign being over, these forces were very much alive and kicking – hard. Our fighting troops, so it was explained, were following the retiring army into wild and foodless country by long and forced marches, and, because the motor transport system was breaking down, were starving for want of food and

---

[26] An allusion to the statement by Commander-in-Chief Jan Smuts that the war in Africa was "all but over" when he handed over command to Richard Hoskins in January 1917.

support. There were plenty of cars, but the ranks of the drivers had been seriously depleted by the ravaging effects of the disease, the sun and hard work. Unfortunately, malaria fever was rampant, the heat virulent, and the duties – long, trying journeys over roads that were little better than mere tracks through the bush – arduous. So urgently were fresh drivers required to fill up the places of those who had gone down, that it accounted for our obvious haste after leaving Cape Town. In the ordinary way we should have put in at Durban for a spell for the really necessary purpose of becoming acclimatised; but haste was unavoidable if relief was to be brought to those men so greatly in need of it. It was up to us, therefore, fresh from England, to get to work and do our level best to fill successfully the places of those who had done so well, but who were now, through no fault of their own, out of action.

It was apparently the practice of the military to keep men in ignorance of what was going on. Because of this, it is true that on this occasion the officer's friendly and confidential talk had the effect of clearing the air, relieving our minds, and of bringing forth a rousing cheer which must have been very gratifying to one who had broken a convention – we never had such a talk before or after.

It was nearly noon when we floated off with the return of the tide, and, once more to a resumption of barking from the stern of the boat, sail was set and the journey continued.

And ere long, with the help of a good breeze and the rising tide, good progress being made, and bearing right, the waters narrowed so abruptly as to cause a fouling of the rigging by the touch of the lofty trees on either side. Here we sprang ashore on to an improvised landing-stage, to the north, or right, side. And as we did so a small party of German (white) prisoners, and a number of our own nationality (recently prisoners themselves), all wan of countenance and bedraggled, embarked on a steam launch and disappeared down-stream.

Once ashore, I was entrusted with the unloading of the whole of our baggage, yelling natives seizing kit-bags and marching off with them poised on their heads, now laughing and singing as they followed, like a long, black snake, the rest of the company, who had disappeared over the crest of the hill. Meanwhile, and in the hope that I might be obtaining useful information, I conversed with a solitary and reserved-looking individual who was on guard over a piled-up stack of tins of petrol. He optimistically sat on the very edge of it, nonchalantly smoking, and surrounded by burnt match-sticks, in spite of leaking petrol and an atmosphere charged with fumes. To my surprise he informed me he came from my home town, and followed up the information by handing me a copy of our principal newspaper – although useless, proving weeks older than the date of my departure from England. A queer fellow was this! As indifferently as he had talked, so he continued to tell me, striking another match, how the Germans had been on that very spot only a few weeks ago; that they were now but thirty miles away, waiting in ambush for anyone fool enough to intrude upon their preserves; that the country was blasted, that everybody was either dying of disease or starving to death, and that I (looking at me intently) would only last six weeks!

Thanking him, I hurried away to get what satisfaction I could out of a little food and reflection.

I found beyond the crest of the hill a flat plateau cleared of all scrub and trees, with the sun beating down on a hot, dry, sandy surface, upon which, leaving a large space in the centre, stood a number of large *bandas* (native-built huts of bamboo and dry grasses) and tents. A number of double-roofed marquees, invitingly cool, and dazzling white in the sunlight, proved to be the hospital, separated from the rest of the camp by a light bamboo fencing. On the north side of this rather large depot, the slopes, on which was camped a body of Indian troops, led down to the marshes and round to the creek I had just left. On the south side, further slopes, covered in dense undergrowth, led to more marshes which had another outlet in the creek. Straight ahead the ground remained fairly level and from here the high road led up country. Beyond these limits the boundless virgin forest stretched away on either side to the far-distant hills. In the immediate vicinity of the swamps, on the edge of which were to be seen a few solitary native huts, hovered high in the air a dark cloud of vultures (loathsome creatures!), craning their necks in their never-ending quest. In the low, water-sodden marshes thrived in countless millions the insect curse of the tropics, the Anopheles, or malaria-carrying mosquito.

This was a place known as Mingoya. The camp did not appear to be in a good position, and we had every reason to think so at a later period; but where there appeared to be no alternative the best had to be made of a bad situation.

As the first opportunity I made some excuse to enable me to obtain a closer scrutiny of the place. A large number of scantily clad natives were hurrying about in all directions. I tried to gather their business, but as the majority of them simply ran outward and inward, or performed perfunctory, aimless circles round their less energetic comrades, the task was perplexing. Those who were not racing about in this fashion were either laughing and playing together, or fighting among themselves. Making a terrific din, they all jabbered incessantly in Swahili, the coastal language, of which I had no knowledge; but it was good to study their frank, open expressions of countenance varying with every change of thought. In general appearance there was a marked difference between some, who were as black as coal, with incision marks on the face, throwing up into still greater prominence the broad nostrils and thick lips, and others who were real chocolate-coloured coons, free from embellishment of any kind, and distinctly pleasing in character, with smooth, regular features, perfect teeth and laughing eyes.

In the vicinity of the only water supply, in the centre of the open space, a scene of great activity presented itself. About half a dozen natives were pumping at unnecessary and frenzied speed, while they yelled and shouted to others who were fighting and struggling to catch the precious water which, to the consternation of all, but owing to their own stupidity, was all running to waste in the hot sand. Native police arrived on the scene to instil some method and order in the collecting of the water, but their own clumsy and excitable manner of dealing with the matter by hitting out, right and left, with their batons, only added to the general row, which very soon developed into a pitched battle, so hopelessly ludicrous as to cause one to be glad to hurry away from the rumpus.

The next scene was not by any means so amusing. Attracted by a crowd of natives looking on silently at something, I discovered that it was a culprit, stripped and pegged face downward to the ground, receiving corporal punishment from a stalwart native, who seemed to take an unnatural delight in bringing a raw hide down on the man's naked body with sickening regularity. Justified as no doubt this punishment was, one could not help but feel sympathy for the man who had to receive it, especially as he did so manfully, wincing with silent fortitude. The ordeal over, he stood up before his white judges – commissioned officers sitting at a table – listened to the stern words they had to impart to him, wheeled round, drawing his scanty loin cloth about him, and departed, his teeth clenched upon his lower lip, his eyes searching wildly the far horizon as he strode swiftly away.

From observation, it occurred to me that there were very primitive and crude ideas here, and that administration was striving to transform chaos into some sort of order – a difficult proposition.

I had no time – or mind – to linger further, and returned to the petrol dump to find my optimistic friend still sitting and smoking, surrounded by more dead matches and, if possible, stronger petrol fumes. It was now my business to relieve him, and he, with just a nod, walked off and left me alone.

In the stillness of the hot afternoon, as I reflected on the scenes I had just witnessed and the prospects of the future, I became conscious of a curious "clicking" sound that came from the back of the stack of petrol, but when I went round there, there was nothing to be seen. Later, however, the noise was again audible. More cautious this time, investigation revealed a number of horny-backed, long-legged creatures at the entrance to a lot of little holes in the hard, sun-baked mud – fiddler crabs – whose numbers grew as I watched until there must have been a hundred. It was a quaint spectacle: each crab had a claw out of all proportion in size to the other, and this large appendage was waved incessantly in the air by some of them in the most purposeless manner imaginable. As a matter of fact, it was the call of the male to the female, thus creating the "clicking" that had disturbed the silence. It was a curious sight to see them all "clicking" together, and, with increasing confidence, all furiously waving to each other. One clap of the hands was sufficient to send the whole community to earth.

In the course of time the Optimist returned, and not desiring to court any further "information", I returned the nod he gave me and took my leave.

In our little camp, which was pitched on the edge of the depot, preparations were being made to stay the night. Therefore, we should be obliged to sleep on the ground. There were scorpions, ants, centipedes, and innumerable other insects to be found crawling about; and what seemed to be bits of stick, blades of grass, and dead leaves, walked about on legs in this strange country – leaf and stick insects. Spider-like tarantulas, with bodies as big as an egg-cup, darted from one's presence, and slimy, black objects, very much like flaccid sticks of Spanish-juice – and as large – millipedes – were quite common. Eternal warfare seemed to be raging between these denizens of the ground, the need for nature's wonderful scheme of colour-deception and mimicry among them being apparent. Camouflage counted for nothing where a centipede was surrounded by an army of ants. At first the centipede certainly got the best of it in the struggle that ensued, which I happened to witness, seizing the ants as they came on and throwing them into the air, right and left. But the faster they were disposed of in this way the greater they became in numbers, attacking vigorously and with determination. At last, exhausted with the uneven struggle, the centipede sank to the ground, its body was cut up into sections and the victors, triumphant in the fight, carried the pieces underground. To study the habits of the insects was interesting – to sleep with them was another thing!

To prepare a bed on the ground, the first thing laid down was the waterproof ground-sheet; upon this was laid the one and only blanket, and on this a greatcoat for outer covering. It was a good plan to roll oneself in the blanket, before lying down, for better warmth and additional protection against undesirable bedmates, snakes being credited with possessing a keen appreciation for a warm and comfortable human.

A Motor Transport Camp in the Bush.

Sticks cut from the adjacent bush provided excellent uprights from which to suspend the box-shaped mosquito nets. The sight of all these erections gave one the unwelcome impression of a row of coffins, merely waiting to be occupied before being interred. With the bottom edge of the nets tucked in all round, the operation was completed.

Tea was now our next concern. Len Jones ("Baby") and I messed together – the rest of our little party of friends had gone, left behind at Dar-es-Salaam and Lindi – and he and I, anxious that no mishap should occur to spoil the tea we should share together, now seized the precious water that was coming to the boil and spilt the lot. Nothing daunted, off we went to get some more, which we did at the Indians' camp, by paying for it. After that all went smoothly. But those Indians for the ability to strike bargains could take greatest credit: we visited the place again next day and parted with personal belongings and a good deal of our clothing that we considered the warmth of the climate warranted not worth carrying farther afield. Truly, these greedy Orientals would have stripped us altogether; and the clatter of their tongues became so appalling that we fled. They followed at our heels. But it was all good fun anyway.

With the sinking of the sun the mosquitoes were on the wing in millions, and in astonishingly dense formations. Inoculation by the malaria-carrying mosquito resulted in an attack of fever in ten days, so we were told; but as an offset to this dark outlook it was reputed that there was only one malarial mosquito in twenty. Hourly I counted the odds of twenty to one on me diminish as I was repeatedly bitten! Once under the mosquito nets we were free from the pest, but spent a restless and miserable night. A 2 a.m. large drops of rain caused everybody to sit bolt upright to watch a heavy, black cloud pass slowly across the moon, but nothing came of the threatened visitation. On the first streak of dawn we were all glad to be up and active.

Once again we began to feel the baneful effect of scanty and unsuitable food – in fact, were almost starving, suffering long periods of abstinence that greatly lowered vitality. In vain we searched the whole place for fresh fruit, which we expected to find; but to our surprise there was none of it. With great relief I managed to obtain two tins of apples, after much effort and pains; the contents of one tin I consumed at once, unable to resist the luscious fruit and its juices. The other I shared with Len Jones and the junior partner in the firm of "Messrs Clap and Trap", who happened to be with us. (The officers suffered the same inconvenience as the men in this respect.) He at first gallantly said "No," and then, "Damn it, Campbell, it cannot be resisted!"

My over-indulgence had a risk of which I was well aware, but could not resist. The immediate effect, however, was stimulating, like alcohol, and, to my surprise, had a similar result.

After this I felt ready for anything. With the thrilling prospect of taking a Ford up the line I fell in with the volunteers and hurried off to obtain my kit. In high spirits I carried the whole lot (when I could just as well have employed a native) a quarter of a mile in the heat of the midday sun, only to find when I reached the parking ground that I was not required after all. I retuned to camp with a shaken opinion of the person who put me to all this trouble for nothing.

Just as we thought we should be spending another night in Mingoya, a sudden call at 4 p.m. transformed inaction into hurry and scurry, and, packing up, the whole company left at once in a dozen Ford lorries for up country.

These lorries, or cars as we called them, were built to carry light loads in the open, box-like space behind the driver's seat. They were comfortably sprung on pneumatic tyres, and the driver was protected in front by a windscreen, with partitions at the back and sides, and strong, waterproof canopy overhead. The handling of them was as easy as driving an ordinary touring car, and as comfortable, consequently we never called them lorries but always referred to them as cars.

We travelled along the open road, which was merely a fairly broad, sandy track where the trees had been cut away, but as yet not badly traffic-torn, with little inconvenience, the situation reminiscent of a joy-ride at the end of a hot summer's day in England. But in place of shady country lanes were the sandy track, tree stumps and rocks, and the doubtful prospect. The little Ford railway (on which the famous little cars travelled with flanged wheels on iron rails, hastily built to convey goods and passengers to a point ten miles inland from Mingoya) kept us company for a while, running alongside the track. Then we lost it and passed into tracts of country that took us up hill and down dale, swinging round corners at a dangerous angle, rolling, heaving, and bumping on treacherous paths, passing through long avenues lit in fitful shadows by the waning sun; thence down into the valleys of swamp and mud, corduroyed but rickety enough to engulf us at any moment, then up again into the hilltops covered with dense forest and bush. In burnt-out native hamlets and devastated plantations (bare of humanity) was visible evidence of the war's far-reaching effects.

On into the night with the aid of the moon the convoy slowly wormed its lonely way. Little now could be seen of the country-side which later became fogged with shadow and mist, until, with no knowledge of our whereabouts or destination, we began to question how much farther this gnomish ride was going to take us.

At last, an hour before midnight, we halted at a native camp all silent in sleep. In the welcome light of the blazing camp fire the native guard, closely wrapped up against the cold with only the whites of his eyes showing, watched us as we silently parked our cars and turned in. Some slept in the cars; others took the ground under the light of the moon, with the cheerful crackle of the fire in their ears.

Chapter 4

I woke with a start, knocking my mosquito net over and wondering where I was. Not yet dawn, I got up in the half-darkness, carefully rolled up my sleeping kit, and waited, shivering and miserable, for daylight.

And what a transformation accompanies the birth of day in the African tropics! With immutable regularity the great red orb rises daily, majestically to sweep the whole sky in a rapid extravaganza of brilliant colours – superbly rich, supremely variegated, bewildering to normal imagination. Thus, in an instant, the cold, gloomy drabness of the doomed night is turned into an early paradise, only too short in the sacred beauty of its transformation . . .

So it was to me as I stood and watched . . . The cooks – always the first members of the camp to be up and doing – had already prepared breakfast; sleepy forms arose, blinked, took up their beds and walked – to the cook-house, breakfast always the first consideration; and lucky were those who got a good one! On this occasion we were indeed fortunate, for the unusual aroma of cooking bacon was in the air.

After this acceptable preliminary to the day, volunteers were called to take six Ford cars farther up country – in most of these instances the duties necessitated the services of volunteers only.

It was really a relief to take charge of a car and get away from that low-lying, muggy spot, fouled as it had been by the recent presence of black troops, and smelling as it did of rank and dying vegetation.

Depression vanished with movement through the fresh morning air, the breeze coming to one's brow and nostrils as a tonic. The sun, already beginning to assert itself, warmed one's body with its life-giving heat, lifting us to light-heartedness.

The six Fords looked comical one behind the other by the manner of their slow pace and the laboured way in which they lurched and rolled, due entirely to the road surface. (It suddenly occurred to me how reduced we had become in numbers: from twelve hundred on the *Port Lincoln* to the ludicrous spectacle of six rough and jumpy men in six equally rough and jumpy Fords, travelling to where we knew not where.)

Progress was slow owing to a good deal of low gear work. Whenever any attempt at speed was made, so bad were the bumps that we were thrown clean out of our seats to bump heads on the canopy above. There was no compromise; it was either bottom gear or bumps and crashes, which made us despair for both ourselves and our machines.

As the vast extent of the country became apparent, everywhere was primeval forest, stretching as far as the eye could see. From our high elevation the impression was that of a vast inland sea, so wide and unbroken was the expanse of tree-tops.

Arriving at a depot where we were due to report ourselves, we left almost immediately, for which we were glad, as the place was a collection of dirty old shacks, accumulated rubble and swearing, bad-tempered personnel. We left in single file, augmented by more Ford cars, the whole company climbing the hill at full speed in bottom gear (to traverse the deep, loose surface successfully). Posted scouts warned us of bad places where an error in driving or a display of ignorance would result in a header to the valley below.

It seemed a strange thing to drive on through this sameness of bush and forest land without seeing a living thing; at Mingoya and the two depots we knew of there had been crowds of people full of the greatest activity – indeed, in the latter respect, as if life itself depended on the haste of every moment. Perhaps it did. However, this may be, the human element was swallowed up in the immensity of the forest...

Night came, and I found myself alone. The cars in front had long disappeared, and there was no glimmer of the lamps behind me. Coming to a ravine of which I had been warned, but had as a fact forgotten, the car took a sudden downward leap, when realising the situation, I contrived, by a frantic effort, with bottom gear slammed in and brakes full on, to keep a straight course, rising to the surface on the other side with a roaring engine and a sense of relief. It was too dark to see the depth of my fall, but the sensation was as if I had suddenly been thrown on to my face one moment, and gradually forced on to my back the next. The result was a succession of thrilling heart-beats, followed by a feeling of satisfaction with its successful negotiation as I went on into the mysterious darkness.

For hours I travelled alone, occasionally venturing the top gear. The feeble gleam from my oil lamps intensified the darkness, for the moon was of little assistance behind the thick and lofty trees whose vague shadows confused my sense of location.

Feeling at last that I was indeed completely lost – probably having overshot my destination or taken a wrong turning – I pulled up. In the eerie stillness of the surrounding jungle, dark and foreboding in its depth and silence, with rifle in hand, I went to investigate an alternative road which I had just seen, with misgivings. This proved, as I suspected, to be merely a native footpath. I listened intently for audible evidence of my companions, and then looked in the far distance for the friendly reflection of motor lights. There was nothing to be heard in the sombre silence that seemed to envelop me like a cloak, and nothing to see but the pale reflection of the moon's light above the trees. Clearly, there was no object in staying there; the situation was too trying, the loneliness too oppressive. So I started my engine again, for its friendly hum was soothing to jangled nerves. I was determined now not to stop again until I had reached some definite location.

It was midnight when I saw the black outline of a *banda* in a clearing off the edge of the road, and rightly or wrongly, I decided to stop. To my call a European, dressed only in pyjamas, came out and spoke to me in welcome English. He would listen to no apologies for disturbing him, but invited me inside and to a stiff glass of rum – it was the stiffest glass I had ever had, for the tumbler was nearly full. He assured me that I was quite all right, my destination being only a mile or two further on, and – I was to help myself to more rum if I wanted it. Had I been there a few days ago I would have been speaking to Germans, not to him, for it was their headquarters. Their one big gun (taken from the *Königsberg* when they were obliged to abandon that vessel in the Rufiji creek)[27] lay blown up outside, evidence of an effective and hasty departure. Until recently they had had command of the whole like, the place where we were being called Massasi. He thought the Germans would not be likely to return. He himself was a member of the Road Corps, who employed natives in the task of making the forest tracks passable for motor transport. Our camp would be somewhere on the top of the hill. Returning my thanks, I had to give all the latest news about England over another stiff glass of rum.

I was about to take my leave, convinced by now that I had found the finest fellow in the world, when, looking for any possible signs of the rest of the convoy, I saw their lights in the distance, bobbing about like the will-o'-the-wisps among the trees and gullies. They were not long in arriving, the men dead tired.

After such liberal hospitality it was all I could do to steer a straight course to arrive, in fine form, in the clearing on the top of the hill, where, stretched out on the driving seat, I fell

[27] SMS *Königsberg* sank HMS *Pegasus* in Zanzibar Harbour on 20 September 1914 before retreating into the Rufigi Delta. The ship was eventually scuttled on 11 July 1915, her guns being salvaged and converted for land use.

fast asleep.

Awakened by the sergeant shaking me and crying "Come on, turn to!" I wondered what could be the matter, for it was still dark.

"Come on, Merry and Bright!" he shouted again, returning and shaking me roughly. "Turn to!"

The others had already started up, and in the stillness of the night the engines roared and spluttered. The sergeant, selecting my car, led the convoy down the long hill to the *boma* in the valley (*boma* = Swahili for "a fortified place"!). Here we passed through to the dark, silent courtyard within, where barefooted natives quickly relieved us of the whole of the precious provisions we had brought.

We returned to the camp at the top of the hill to obtain whatever sleep was possible before daylight brought further activities. Then we were off again, the sergeant sticking to my car and ragging me playfully on my immobility of the last few hours. All day long we dashed about between camps, the hospital and the *boma*.

The *boma* was one of the very few to be met with between the coast and the great lakes. The doors and windows were heavily barred, the wall by which it was almost surrounded battlemented and very high, and its general appearance had the formidable aspect of a fort. In striking contrast, was the peaceful outlook of lines of graceful palms, patches of land under cultivation, winding walks – pleasantly inviting among the shrubs and rocks – and a mission house where local natives had assimilated knowledge of the strange, new religion, Christianity. The little chapel was now a hospital for fever cases, of which there was a deplorable number, and for patients both native and European who had suffered wounds in action. We spent a good deal of time conveying sick to the hospital, and in bringing away convalescent cases for down the line. Before sundown, a return was made to our own camp where an hour's relief was obtained.

Massasi – this lonely outpost of the white man's incursion

Road Corps Boys.   South African Supervisors in the Road Corps.

into Africa's wild tracts – was a healthy spot compared to the low-lying, humid levels of the coastal belt, being 2000 feet above sea-level and 125 miles from the coast. On two sides of the camping ground precipitous rocks dominated the district, while from the high road in two opposite directions, east and west, stretched a limitless expanse of forest trees, which, from this elevated position, confirmed the earlier impression of a rolling sea, with great lumps of rock in the middle distance rearing their bare heads to the blazing sun, like lonely islands, uninhabited and desolate. Of activity beyond that confined to ourselves there was little evidence. A few natives lazily attended to the improving of the so-called roads, but beyond that there was a great stillness, and over everything hung an atmosphere of lassitude and great heat.

This then was to be our headquarters for two months, though at the time we had no certain evidence of this, neither had we any idea of the strenuous times before us.

In the evening the convoy loaded up and stood by, ready for a journey. Before leaving, a convoy of Ford cars arrived from up country whose members were as bedraggled and unkempt a lot as could well be imagined: tired, dirty, unshaven, and covered in dust. To my surprise they proved to be old comrades of Salisbury Plain – more surprised to see me than I them, for, in the same company and on the same draft, I was left behind in hospital when they came out here. Now, a happy reunion took place and all news was exchanged. It appeared they had been in the country eight weeks, starved to death, worked day and night, stricken down with fever, recovering and going down again. Lieutenant Williams[28] and several members of his convoy had been ambushed and killed – a cruel death at the hands of black troops, who burnt their cars and were making a fiendish attempt to burn the bodies of their victims when they were intercepted, but got clear away. My friends did not know how long this sort of thing was going to continue, but they were all "fed up", observing that the sooner it was all over the better.

Shocked to hear of the tragic end of men I knew so intimately, and inquiring about the other, I learned with a sense of relief that my late officer, Lieutenant MF Ratcliff,[29] and my friend F Peach[30] (both of my own town) were safe, though the latter was in hospital.

After getting over my first surprise, I noticed how altered in appearance many of them were: one whom I had known as a portly, happy individual, with a round, fat face, was now so deplorably thin, sallow-complexioned, and hollow-eyed, that when he smiled at me from the dark depths of his long beard, I knew him only by his voice. I reflected on the possibility of my ever getting like that: providing their happy mien and cheery spirit remained with me, I had no misgiving. For dress they, like ourselves, wore open flannel shirts minus

---

[28] Second Lieutenant CE Williams, Army Service Corps, died 17 October 1917 (CWGC; WO 95/5378/5 631 Mechanical Tranposrsportt Company)

[29] Second Lieutenant Mortimer Frederick Ratcliff, Royal Army Service Corps (WO 372/16/152089)

[30] Likely Frederick Peach - Frederick C Peach, Army Service Corps M/333525 (WO 372/15/164503) OR Frederick J Peach, Army Service Corps M4/085199 (WO 372/15/164511) OR Frederick G Peach, Army Service Corps T4/142550 (WO 372/15/164508) OR Frederick E Peach, Army Service Corps T4/185895 (WO 372/15/164506)

sleeves (cut away), shorts or slacks (the latter for preference, because, although shorts were cool, trousers protected the bare knees from the unwelcome attention of mosquitoes), spine pads (in the form of flannel strips to protect the vital part of the back from the direct rays of the sun), the ordinary square-toed army boots (surprisingly comfortable with woollen socks, in fact, a substantial protection against the heat and ever-present sand), and pith helmet, serviceable if ungainly. No man ventured into the open, even for one moment, without his sun helmet, if he valued his health, whether the sun was shining or not. It was told how a sportsman, out riding one day, lost his helmet, and in the short time it took him to recover it, got a bad attack of sunstroke, an incident strikingly demonstrative of the necessity for great care. Incidentally, for the same reason that sleeves were cut from shirts, bonnets were removed from over the engines of motor vehicles, strips of canvas being substituted as sufficient protection from sun and possible rain. There was now no further time for talk, and, night descending, our convoy left camp and wended its way into the bush.

With little idea of our destination, we travelled all through the empty confines of the forest, slowly and tortuously, on a narrow, sandy track, between the never-ending trees; not a sound came from out the lonely depths surrounding us, and no sign of life was encountered.

At last, in the early hours, we reached our destination – a blackened-out wilderness; not a thing upstanding, only the gaunt, charred trunk of a tree standing alone in the midst of the ruin like an inanimate ghost. Recent habitations had been burnt to the ground; not a soul was to be seen in all that devastated area; gaping trenches yawned empty to the sky except for wooden stakes, cunningly hidden, sharpened points upward; little newly-made mounds of earth told their own story, and, from a carcass polluting the fresh morning air, vultures rose with heavy, flapping wing-beats, while a jackal, alarmed at our approach, slunk away into the bush.

While the convoy rested, the sergeant and I (we still drove together) went off to see if there was anybody left alive in such a place, the sergeant himself not very clear upon the point; but after a search we found an empty *banda* with officials ready to welcome us. Their great concern was for the provisions, and these we brought up at once.

It appeared that in the recent fighting that had taken place there the Germans had put up a stubborn resistance, ere they retired, as was their usual method, and where they were now was not known. So much we learned, and then, too tired for more detail, we breakfasted and turned in, sleeping soundly, the sun, hot as it was, comforting to bodies wearied by the all-night drive through the cold air of the forest.

An interruption to the serenity of the morning's peace was the passage, in a cloud of dust, of a company of two hundred British black troops, all showing by their excited voluble conversation and by the ambling character of their gait, tension and fatigue.

In due course, to the sergeant's cheery "Start up!" we left this dreary spot.

Considering we were passing through enemy country, we considered ourselves to be lucky in avoiding molestation. The gentle Germans had several subtle ways of intercepting motor traffic: by digging pits in the track covered lightly with a roof of twigs and dead litter; in concealing contact bombs in the deep ruts; by posting small scouting parties of Askari (native soldiers) in ambush; and by felling trees to obstruct the path – a less crafty method. It was not pleasant to reflect that we might, at any moment, be shot at from the blind bush, or be forced to a sudden and unpleasant halt.

Arriving back at Massasi, a complete and refreshing bath was indulged in, after which we were permitted to stay in camp all night. I slept on the driving seat of my car, having become used to the custom, and preferring it to running the risk of lying on the ground, or in a *banda*, and so courting the unwelcome attention of ground pests. I could not imagine any self-respecting snake or scorpion negotiating the slippery wheels of a Ford.

The next morning the convoy was on the road again, this time for down the line. Reaching Ndanda, we found the place not only spacious but comfortable. A great open space contained a large number of *bandas* and tents, a big display of stores of different kinds, the usual fleet of motor transport of one kind or another, and, in the centre, a giant baobab tree – one of those quaint-looking trees peculiar to East Africa with tremendous girth and a comical appearance of having been stuck in the ground upside down with the roots straggling in the empty air. At the base of this was the cook-house.

With the late part of the afternoon to ourselves, Len Jones and I went off to enjoy a bathe in the cool, tumbling waters of a mountain stream, whose inviting presence we had noted on arrival, descending in rushing cascades from a source in one of the high elevations almost surrounding this part of the district. It did not take long to strip and enter the splashing, swirling waters, wherein we buried our bodies in sheer joy and relief. But though it is said that where ignorance is bliss it is folly to be wise, it would have been better if we had been alive to the risks attendant on bathing under these conditions. The stream was strewn with rocks, and on one of these my friend had stretched himself, comforted by the little warmth that came soothingly to his naked body from the sun's dying rays; when suddenly he gave a yell, jumped up, and fled as if demented, up the bank and away. For a few moments I stood in the middle of the stream, nonplussed by his odd conduct, failing to discern any possible reason for his sudden alarm. When he returned, which he had to do in any case, pale of countenance and obviously affected by shock, he explained that a rock snake had crawled up his leg, a fact of which he was only at first half conscious as he had nearly fallen asleep. As he was free from any hurt we laughed over the incident (at least I did), but it brought a prompt end to the bathing. We hurriedly dressed and departed. In the excitement, however, we had reached camp before discovering that we had left behind some of our discarded clothing. Jones was not in the mind to return with me and recover it, so I went back alone. But I might have saved myself the trouble. Although the natives we encountered were unobtrusive enough to all outward appearance, they, nevertheless, were very much alive. When I had regained the spot our clothes had vanished!

As if nerves had not been tried enough, it so happened that, as I reached the outskirts of the camp on my return, I encountered a black mamba, five or six feet in length, which crossed my path and disappeared under the flap of the nearest tent. It was a near shave as I had failed to see the black, writhing thing in the darkness – the sun had gone down – and sprang back only just in time to avoid treading on it. It astonished me that the creature would have allowed me to tread on it, an apparent indifference probably to be accounted for by the fact that neither the hearing nor the sight of a snake is acute. It is generally admitted that the black mamba is one of the most dangerous of Africa's deadly snakes and reputed to be extremely vicious, even to the point of chasing a man and biting him on the leg. I heard of a cyclist who swerved to miss one having this experience, and, but for the fact that he was wearing leggings at the time, would have sustained a fatal wound.

To my cry of alarm many figures came running out with hurricane lamps, and a very cautious search was made for evidence of the intruder; but the tent in question was so heavily littered with stores that a satisfactory ending was hardly to be expected, and, after a while, the undertaking was abandoned, leaving the men uneasy with the negative result.

The incidents of the day were sufficiently convincing to strengthen my resolution never to sleep on any form of bed but that of the driving seat of my faithful Ford . . .

In one of the wild, midnight excursions in which we broke new ground, we came to a fork in the road which was an ingenious excuse for a heated discussion as to which was the right way. Of course, in view of the fact that the men were all dead beat – there was very little rest at this time, day and night – the discussion was all a sham. In all assumed seriousness it was decided that the matter must be slept upon. Thereafter was the strange spectacle of a long line of Fords (there were thirty vehicles) standing alone in the depths of the African forest, as still and silent under the pale light of the waning moon as the gaunt and sentinel-like forest trees by which they were surrounded. The respite was ended by the sergeant becoming uneasy and waking up to call upon everybody to be "up and doing". Lamps were lighted, as the moon had sunk, and engines started up, the roar and splutter they made putting new life into us as the journey was resumed. A large body of natives, all fully armed with bows and arrows, and spears, passed us in the darkness, giving cause for much speculation as to their identity and errand, and, at one place, delay took place while a tree fallen across the track was removed. But nothing came of these incidents, and, although imagination suggested all sorts of unpleasant possibilities, we reached our destination without further mishap. It proved to be merely a dump.

On these excursions, winding about in the blind forest, it was impossible to retain one's sense of locality or direction, and to all intents and purposes, away from camp, we became completely lost. Only the sergeant in charge had any idea of direction – at this time we had no commissioned officer with us – and he had to work by rule of thumb. We carried provisions with much haste and dumped them in far-away and isolated places, and that was all we were sure about.

On one of these journeys we met prisoners of war under escort on their way down to the coast. The Europeans looked hard and fit, though stooping somewhat as if wearied, yet marching with the steady, unhurried gait of men accustomed to the daily trek in the broiling heat of the midday sun, their scanty clothing ragged and their faces bearded, But even through this disguise there were distinguishing characteristics that revealed their identity. The native members of this hapless crowd, with light, jaunty air, so unlike their white fellow-captives, skipped along unconcernedly, indulging in wild leaps accompanied by yells, born either of pleasure or derision, we could not quite tell which. A peculiar feature were the native women who had faithfully followed their dusky lords and masters from fight to fight, serving them in state of virtual slavery, and now content enough to follow to the end.

A journey up country from Massasi to find No 2 Column, in order to supply them with provisions and ammunition, led us into higher elevations, with a distinct chillness in the atmosphere. Mountains of granite rock – like most of these African rocks characteristically distorted into quaint and fantastic shapes – rose high above the surrounding open country, majestic and noble in the solitude of vast, untrodden preserves. We found the troops stretched out all over the ground, in a state of complete exhaustion. Of the enemy, for whom they had apparently been searching, there was no sign. There was little occasion for discussion and less time for anything but to relieve the cars of their loads, after which we took charge of some sick and returned at once with them to Massasi.

In this way, motor transport continued to be hard pressed, with little time for rest in the twenty-four hours of every day. We did not mind this so much, hard as the work was, but we did miss the opportunity for keeping ourselves clean, and the strain of continuously driving with no appreciable break was beginning to tell upon us. We would have welcomed a break to speak with the members of other convoys we occasionally met on the road, but there was only time for shouts of greeting as the convoys passed each other.

The question of suitable and nourishing food was a serious one; one would have thought that in a country like this fruit and vegetables could have been obtained in plenty; in fact, the country we had traversed was practically uninhabited; we saw no village and no cultivation – only the trees, the sand, and the rocks; and in the depots it was famine.

The provisions we carried were, strangely enough, denied to us, each bag, box or drum being sealed and checked. But in any case, of rice, which formed the bulk of it, we were heartily sick, as we had to live on it. There was an inexhaustible quantity of pea-nuts – monkey-nuts – for the natives, but, acceptable as these would have been to us, they also came under the general ban.

Beyond Massasi, water was not to be obtained except at very occasional water-holes, and these were nearly empty owing to the long summer drought. We always found the water of an uninviting milky colour, while beetles, frogs, and other unpleasant-looking insects regarded it as their common bath. In consequence of having to drink this water, I began to suffer from abdominal pains in spite of the fact that I always took the precaution to boil every drop I used.

Ford Light Railway.

Chapter 5

I had exchanged my car for a comparatively new one, and the sergeant had been taken off the convoy and put to the "repairs and breakdowns." I was glad of this because with my new car he would probably have excelled himself as a speed fiend. Considering we were in danger enough, there was no need to add to the risks by driving along these treacherous roads in a wild and reckless fashion. He and I always led the convoy by the very fact that no one could catch him up and no one else would drive with him. I would sometimes venture to suggest, when the eccentric gyrations of the car permitted, that we drove with a little more caution.

"Caution be damned," he would say, laughing like a great big school-boy. "There's a war on!"

A sudden skid, crab fashion, for fifteen or twenty feet into the bush at a blind corner resulted in a general slackening up of speed; but he slid back, so to speak, into his bad habits again. Still he was a jolly fellow, and but for this fault I was extremely sorry to lose his cheery companionship.

However, to my surprise, like the cat, he came back, all smiles and assurances, as he took charge of my new car.

Straight away we led the convoy for fifty reckless miles. I chipped my companion for his "indifferent" driving, but he only grinned and, having broken down my objections, drove like the deuce.

"Very well," I said, "drive on, MacDuff, and hanged be he who cries, 'Hold! Enough!'"

What wild rides there were! Of course, the sergeant was really a first-class driver, otherwise I am certain we would have been smashed up. Tracts of treacherous loose sand through which we had to drive needed bottom gear and a good, strong grip of the steering-wheel – even the sergeant could not take these at speed but had to apply all the skill of which he was capable.

Overtaken by darkness we decided to stay for the night at a point ten miles from our destination. Here we could just discern the dark outlines of a native *boma* and evidence of native life in the bush in the form of a fitful glare from a camp fire. We were glad of this, for we were now in a part of the country notorious for lions. I paid a visit to the *boma*, but was glad to get away again as, after some difficulty in getting in, I was coldly received by swarthy natives, who, however, sullenly acceded to my request for fresh viands.

We spent an uncanny night in spite of the protecting presence of huge fires. We heard nothing of lions though this was no proof that they were not about – the roar of the lion is not synchronous with his search for food any more that is the mew of the cat with the stalking of a bird. But long, blood-curdling screams rent the still night air, and spasmodically vivid flashes of sheet lightning lit up the darkness for moments together, and, noiseless, intensified the silence.

Stirred into a state of cheerfulness by the brilliance of the sun's rising, the whole company departed, Len Jones and I volunteering to remain behind and prepare breakfast on their return. Light-heartedly we set to work, with the delectable aroma of burning wood in the air as the cooking progressed. It proved a great success when the boys rolled up for the little surprise we had prepared for them.

After breakfast one of our men fell sick – not from what he had eaten – the Lord save us! – but from the baneful influence of the climate. He collapsed suddenly and helplessly as men were wont to do when stricken down by fever. I took charge of him and his car. The journey to Massasi was a weary one, and slow, made necessary by the state of my suffering companion, who was now groaning and writhing in his agony. Tyre trouble followed, so that I was obliged to conclude the remainder of the journey on two flat rims. The breakdown car had long since disappeared, after the convoy, but in any case would have been of no use to me, having completely run out of spare tyres – twenty-eight in twenty-four hours.

I left my sick friend in good hands in the hospital at Massasi, glad to regain my own camp – but not for long: I was called out again with the rest of the company.

The night was again pitch dark, made worse, if possible, by the feeble lights of the Fords – when we could get the lights to function at all. This was one objection we had to the Ford lighting; if the night was dark we had to race the engines or come down to bottom gear to get light sufficient to enable us to see where we were going. Anyway, away we went, groping through the dark until, at last, without the slightest idea of where we were, or what would be next required of us, we came to a halt at 2 a.m. Now we were quite spent, and in preparation for a moment like this, I suppose, a liberal supply of rum was forthcoming. We were then directed to turn in.

We awoke to find ourselves on the edge of a spacious camp of which there was not the slightest evidence when we drove up in the dark. Now, in broad daylight, there was the greatest noise and activity, from native and Indian troops everywhere to be seen, comprising infantry, machine gun sections, mountain batteries, and a host of carriers – native porters. Such a babble and mixture of tongues I never did hear; there were, I believe, at this time native soldiers from districts as far apart as the Gold Coast, Nigeria, and Uganda; there were Indians, Swahilis, and all sorts; they were all jabbering together excitedly, conscious of the one fact that they were done, and undone at the same time, for Von Lettow had escaped the mesh they had so carefully attempted to draw around him, and had retired across the Rovuma River. This was the latest news.

To the advantage of the enemy had been the fresh,

undisturbed country through which they had retired, living on it, and leaving it destitute of anything of value to the luckless pursuing troops. It was no doubt to their credit to be able to do this successfully for, with all the advantages, their difficulties and privations must have been very great. Still, the circumstances were sufficiently advantageous to account considerably for their escape. Their retiring tactics also brought a good deal of confusion and doubt – confusion as to what they were doing and doubt as to their whereabouts. In the thick bush, opposing forces quickly got out of touch and became completely lost. In following the enemy up, lines of communication were drawn out to almost breaking point; the maintenance of transport service became more difficult, supplies shorter and shorter, until, at last, troops found themselves practically cut off from their base and in a state of exhaustion, as we now saw them.

The native soldiers elicited our sympathy by showing us the ragged state of their clothing, all in tatters, and their bootless feet, swathed in bandages. They earnestly declared that they were in a state of starvation, living on one half cupful of rice per day for each man!

Askari, or Native Soldiers.

"No good, sar," said one stalwart, native soldier to me, anxiously; "all time walk, walk, walk; no catch him Germans. He gone thick bush; no see! My country, sar, Gold Coast, not ver' good – but this country, sar, Godam, ver' bad, soon all dead! Why

English forsake us? Where new boots – new clothes? Where food? Plenty in London! London ver' rich!" (the personal reference embarrassing and not without pathos). "We are British soldiers!" he continued, pulling himself up with sudden pride. "We fight for you! You plenty boots, clothes, food got! Why we no boots, no clothes, no food got?"

The most subtle efforts to explain the true situation to these simple people failed. We were flatly accused of indifference, and no amount of assurance made the slightest impression. In an hour we were on the road again, leaving behind this motley crew of disgruntled and disappointed followers of a white man's cause, a cause they did not understand but which they felt most keenly at heart.

For passenger I carried a slightly wounded European officer of one of these native regiments, a young man typical of the breed thrust out into the wide world of adventure from the public schools and playing fields of old England. He proved to be good company, singing and chatting brightly the whole of the morning until the usual extreme heat of midday silenced him. We stopped by mutual desire. The rest of the convoy had straggled and we were alone. Now it was that, for the first time I realised the vast solitude of the African bush at midday; the great silence that followed the cessation of the car's noisy progress, as we smoked a cigarette and listened in vain for evidence of the approach of any other member of the company, was awesome, in the vast extent of its loneliness. To all appearance, the world stood still. From a breathless air the sun struck down without mercy, and the heat scintillated before our eyes in the form of dancing, shimmering waves of light. It was only after a while that one became conscious of a strange droning in the air – prolonged and unbroken like the sound of a distant sawmill. It was not a subconscious head noise as one might at first suspect, but the hum of myriads of winged insects in the air, on the trees, among the grasses and the weeds, and in the closer confines of the thick bush – yet the tiny creatures were so translucent and elusive as to be invisible to the eye, even in its flight.

We were glad to resume our journey, if only for the comforting draught that came to us through our open windscreen. In striking contrast to the extremely summer-like conditions we had just experienced was the sudden reminder of the imminence of the rains, which revealed itself in the form of a black cloud that burst over our heads, and in twenty minutes transformed the low-lying parts of the country into tracts of flood water, through which we floundered, axle deep, to reach Massasi safely in due course.

Bidding farewell to my agreeable companion, I returned immediately to my own camp.

There was no moment so delectable as that when we could enjoy a refreshing bath after an arduous day's journey. Stropped for the full enjoyment of this, I considered the empty middle of the camp ground just suitable in the darkness for the purpose. But I had reckoned without the ubiquitous motor car; an Overland with a belated party of officers swung in from the open road and stopped with their glaring headlights full upon me. As the lights were not switched off I had to endure an extremely public exposure, thanks to the thoughtless officers in question. However, I consoled myself with the happy reflection that I was at least conforming to the usual custom of the country. In this way I felt I had turned a broad mind, not to say a broad back, on to the situation.

The next morning augured ill. Not a movement was in the convoy although it was broad daylight. Waking, I thought this strange, and hastened to the sergeant. To my surprise I found that usually alert young man fast asleep. With misgivings I shook him, and shook him again, and had finally to be rough with him before he opened his eyes. He lay without movement, showing no concern for the daylight that nearly blinded him, looking up with that vacant, listless glare that told one only too well its own fateful tale. The curse of the country had got this fine, healthy body in its merciless grip, while unconscious lips mumbled unintelligible words. So this put an end to the activities of our one-time happy and good-natured sergeant, and the convoy knew him no more. I did get one final glimpse of him some time later on his way down to the coast. He bade me goodbye with a wan smile, at the same time slyly handing me a tin of milk, knowing full well the value of such a gift, humble as it was; he would have made it more if he had the power – so his eyes said.

A feeling of pessimism followed an increase of the number of sick cases on the line. Men were falling daily to the baneful influence of the deadly climate, the very indifferent feeding, and from exhaustion. To add to the general feeling of depression, which reacted on our health, was the visible evidence of the pestilential nature of the country witnessed in poor natives lying by the roadside and if asleep, but, as a fact, dead, with clouds of black, buzzing flies hovering over them. A lonely horse would sometimes be seen standing alone in the shade of the forest, bitten by the dreaded tsetse fly – a vicious little insect not unlike the common bluebottle that sometimes attacked us also, darting straight at our necks and arms with a sharp "z-z-zip," and stinging like a red-hot needle. Thus the animal would stand, head drooping to the ground, tongue out, rocking at the knees, wasted of body, hollow-eyed, and fatally sick – waiting for the inevitable end. Perched on the branches of trees close by were the vultures – also waiting passively for the collapse that would herald that end. Such sights as these were horrible, requiring a great effort of will to throw off the feeling of revulsion. The burial of natives in due course was not an inconvenience, but the more bulky carcasses of cattle and horses were a different proposition. Some were burned or buried – either being a long job – others left to pollute the already stifling atmosphere. In passing and repassing a carcass unburied, one could, if sufficiently interested, note the manner of its gradual disappearance. For days the vultures would live on the carcass, resting and eating, tearing sullenly at the flesh, and rising only on being disturbed. Probably, in the dead of the night, a hyena or other prowling animal would join in the feast. Scavenger beetles would account for the dung, shaping it into little round balls which they rolled away to their underground burrows. My first encounter with the scavenger beetle was intensely interesting. One day, standing at the foot of a short rise, I was surprised to see several objects like cricket balls rolling at my feet. They seemed to have arrived of their own accord, but instantly with the thought following an equal number of beetles of abnormal size. On gaining the balls they gave them a hefty push, and away they went again with the beetles after them; if it was up hill, they held the balls with their legs, thrusting them along in the desired direction, inch by inch . . . After all this, and the ants in battalions had done their work, what remained of the carcass would be a bare skeleton, bleaching white in the sun, scattered and half hidden in the long grass.

There was again more talk of lions. They were calling to one another nightly from the hills around Ndanda. They boldly dashed in and seized the cattle as they were driven along the road. They caused consternation among the natives, who were obliged to camp in the open, carrying some away – poor beggars – in the night. Being often under the necessity of camping out ourselves, we kept roaring fires and a sharp lookout. Yet, even so, when opportunity to indulge in one's natural taste for a bit of fun arose, it was not easily supressed, but contrariwise aroused by hidden menace. One night when camped near natives I slipped out, and returned in dusky disguise. Our camp was, of course, taboo to wandering natives, and to see one rummaging about the camp's effects called for stern comment.

"He's got a bit of a damned cheek!" declared one of our fellows, uneasily.

"Aye, I don't like the look of him!" volunteered another

man. "You never know what these blighters are up to!"

"What the devil's he muttering about?" asked a third. "What on earth can he want?"

But the dusky stranger, supposed to be totally ignorant of the nature of these ill-favoured remarks, continued to wander about until, at last, a sensation was caused when he was distinctly heard to mention the word *simba* (lion). The next moment he had gone. After the natural excitement born of this incident had subsided, he returned.

"*Ah, no good, no good!*" he was heard to mutter in the Swahili tongue, "*I go, I go!*" But this was a contradiction, for to the consternation of all he moved even nearer, until at last he collided violently with several incensed members of the company . . . Only a hasty disclosure of the intruder's real identity prevented a riot. In the amusing discussion that followed I am not so sure that the laugh was only on my side. They declared that as it was I who had represented myself to be a native the deception was easy!

The next morning the breakdown of my car, an old crock I happened to be driving, was not unexpected, so I found myself tearing back to Massasi with bottom gear out of action and brakes gone. I had to keep going – down hill because I had no choice, up hill because I dare not stop. This reckless pace broke the front springs; still I had to go on. A compulsory stop, or failure to take a hill on top gear, had possibilities upon which I did not care to dwell as I was alone. I had completed the journey before I realised it; but it had left me suffering from reaction and strain. With the car in dock, and no other available, I was allowed twenty-four hours excused duty.

In my old sailing-ship days there were men whose work had nothing to do with the actual sailing of the ship, and they were called "The Idlers". My friend Corporal Bell[31] might have come under that category, for I never saw him doing

---

[31] Possibly Philip Bell, 9505 Belfield's Scouts, 288 East African Mounted Rifles and 1648 East African Transport Corps (WO 372/2/87402)

anything in the camp but preserve snakes in glass bottles.

So, two in the same mind, off we went together, visiting a near-by camp, where Bell introduced me to his friend Corporal Robinson,[32] who held sway over a company of natives. Like Bell he was a South African, boasting some years of service in the country and looking the part. We found him installed in a luxurious *banda* of his own, lavishly fitted out with furniture and effects – plenty of the latter – with a comfortable divan to lie upon and with servants promptly responding to his beck and call. In fact, he had all the state and dignity of a potentate, and Bell agreed with me at once that we should call him henceforth "The Rajah".

Back to the Rajah we went in the evening, thirsting, so to speak, for information. Bell had invited me to stay the night with him in his *banda*, a somewhat dingy place at the foot of the rocks at the back of our camp. I did not welcome the prospect, and viewed with suspicion the heap of rubble that lay on the floor. However, in a weak moment I consented. Unhappy resolution! I had no sooner prepared to turn in, my bed being of necessity on the floor, than a tarantula, as big as a hermit crab, and as black as death, darted out from the rubble and disappeared into the folds of my blanket. Bell had earnestly assured me that no pests were to be feared, and he now eyed me from his bed – conveniently raised two feet above the ground – with a ridiculously sympathetic leer. Determined not to sleep here under any circumstances, I hastily dressed. Bell then graciously assisted me in cautiously lifting the blanket, but the intruder was gone in a moment, and, before we realised it, was making circles round our feet with a rapidity of movement that baffled us, and then, drawn again as if by some irresistible impulse, he disappeared once more into my bed. This time we made sure of him, and in spite of Bell's loud injunctions not to maim him – with a view to bottling – he was swiftly despatched.

It was, therefore, with this battered specimen we marched

---

[32] Corporal Robinson - unable to trace

down to see Corporal Robinson. It was still only nine o'clock. We found him reclining on his divan, sipping whisky, to a bottle of which we were invited. We explained that our visit was prompted by a desire to learn what we could of the poisonous nature and otherwise of African insects and reptiles, and the tarantula in particular. We had grave misgivings on the subject that we wished clearing up, and we felt, therefore, that we could not do better than to appeal to one like himself who had undoubted knowledge on these matters.

Taking the pipe out of his mouth and fondling it thoughtfully for a few moments, he agreed that it was a subject deserving of the closest attention. Some people thought these things flew at you on sight. Nothing of the sort! Such an insect as the one under review would do no possible harm to anyone providing it did not actually settle on you, a rule that applied to all insects and reptiles abounding in these parts. We agreed. Poisonous and non-poisonous kinds could be distinguished at once, as soon as one was able to tell one from the other, but, of course, that took time, and one could not expect to learn all these things in a country like this in five minutes! Again, we agreed, and helped ourselves to more whisky. Should a sleeper awake, he resumed, finding a snake crawling across his bare chest, what should he do? We didn't know. It was quite easy: he should remain perfectly still and allow the creature to crawl off again! He had known a case where a millipede had crawled on to a man's bare knee, and if he had remained perfectly still all would have been well, but he foolishly clutched at the slimy creature and tore it from him. In so doing he took away several inches of his skin on the little animal's numerous legs. Leave these creatures alone, he declared, and they would leave you alone. To emphasise his argument he pointed with a stick to an insect about five or six inches long, which had escaped our notice and was now to be seen hanging, head downward, from the roof after the manner of an inverted aeroplane.

"That fellow's been there for days and won't hurt anyone," he declared lightly; but seeing that we were not convinced, and that we moved uneasily, he added quickly: "Of course, if you don't like it, we'll remove it."

Giving us no change to express an opinion one way or the other, he aimed at it with his stick, missed it, jumped up and chased it round and around the *banda*, much to our discomfort. Amid a great noise of droning from the cumbersome creature's long wings he finally dealt it a crashing blow that brought it shivering to the ground, where, after a few spasmodic shudders, it expired. We hardly thought this conduct in keeping with his expressed opinion, but we let that pass.

"That's how you want to treat 'em," he shouted. And with, "Here's another!" off he went again, chasing round the *banda*, with insects' wings and legs flying in all directions. Bell, with the spirit of the naturalist, carefully collected the "bag", which he placed, with the tarantula, in a box. We were relieved when these alarms and excursions ceased, and thankful when more whisky was forthcoming.

We left the Rajah in the early hours, foolishly lingering to collect some more insects off the ground with the aid of the lamps we carried, among them being a horned beetle of rather formidable proportions, all of which we added to what we now called "our menagerie".

I slept in Bell's *banda* after all, turning in fully dressed, even to my boots, cap, and overcoat, but with the collar turned up. Bell called my attention to the fearful din that was taking place in our menagerie, but I was too tired to listen to him . . .

The next morning, perhaps not unnaturally, I jumped straight out of bed, stood bolt upright, and *shook myself!* The base of the rocks at the back of this *banda* was a veritable breeding-place for the greatest variety of Africa's choicest vermin that I had ever seen – I inspected the place afterwards and had every evidence of the fact. I therefore abandoned any intention of ever sleeping in Bell's *banda* again, and firmly refused all subsequent invitations.

After breakfast Bell and I proceeded to inspect our menagerie by daylight, with a result much to our amazement. There was nothing to be seen – that is to say, nothing but the horned beetle with distended sides in a state of stupor. It had devoured the rest of the unlucky inmates, including the tarantula, and nothing was left but legs and wings.

We made this an excuse for another visit to the Rajah, and the subsequent interview was both interesting and entertaining, for our host was, after all, a most genial fellow. Thus was our thirst for information, and accompanying incidentals satisfied, and a clumsy attempt to obtain a souvenir collection of East African insects brought to an end.

Rejoining the convoy, I was on the road again. About this time a notice was issued to members of the motor transport acknowledging their useful work. Reference was made to "untiring exertions, long distances, large numbers to feed, bad roads, abnormal work, and heavy strain."

We were now travelling up and down the line like a tabulated train service. The whole country for mile after mile, and as far as the eye could see, was parched and arid, the trees scraggy and bare, the sand deep and dry, water-holes shallow and dirty, and all over hung a great, shrivelling heat. This was the type of country we traversed in order to reach the Rovuma River.

In due course, after a series of protracted journeys, we found ourselves on the banks of the Rovuma itself. Its broad, silent waters barred any further progress for the automobile. Just before sundown a plunge into the cook, running water was beyond resistance. But in the full enjoyment of my bathe, and in turning a bend, I found a stranger – the sergeant of one of the native corps – sitting on the bank, with a gun across his knees. I waded up to him and ventured to ask what it was he was expecting to have a shot at.

"Crocodiles!" he answered laconically.

"Oh, thanks!" I returned, beating a hasty retreat.

I had not forgotten the folly at the mountain stream at Ndanda.

Abandoned Transport.

A Halt for the Midday Meal.

Chapter 6

The Rovuma River is a broad and noble waterway, forming a natural boundary between Tanganyika Territory, country that was German East Africa to the north, and what is still Portuguese East Africa to the south. With its source near the great Lake Nyasa, it travels slowly, majestically, for three hundred and fifty miles, through the heat and scrub of Africa's vast wilderness to the Indian Ocean.

Livingstone ascended this river when he went into the heart of Africa, never to return, and the mind dwelt upon the exploits of that bold pioneer as one gazed across the half mile of water and sand which separated us from the dark and mysterious banks on the opposite side.

The Germans had forded the river, which is shallow at this part, with all their baggage and long line of followers, including the indispensable women.

According to rumour, they were having it all their own way on the other side, a garrison stationed there having been overwhelmed, valuable stores, arms and ammunition falling into the hands of the invaders, who, no doubt, were well pleased with their initial conflict with the timid Portuguese. They then disappeared southward into the bush.

We now travelled regularly between Massasi and the Rovuma River, taking a day to journey up to the river, and a day to return, a total distance of over a hundred miles. Our convoy was known as the Ford No 3 Triangle convoy and consisted of thirty cars, each one displaying the distinguishing symbol in the form of a miniature triangle in front of the radiator. There was a little friendly rivalry between us and the only other Ford convoy, as we passed and repassed each other.

Up at dawn, breakfast over, loaded up, and ready for the road, it was usually with high spirits that we faced the coming events of the day. As already stated, Massasi was a comparatively healthy spot, high up and dry, and free from the mosquito pest – at least during this period of the year. There was every encouragement to feel well. The view from the top of the hill was strikingly impressive, for we could see to the far horizon the nature of the country we had to pass through: one great carpet of forest with a pleasing relief in the evidence of the huge bare rocks that stood out boldly above the surrounding levels. After leaving Massasi and dropping down the hill to the meadows below, there was a level stretch of hard surface for five miles along which we used to race in the early mornings before the sun had attained its power, enjoying to the full the refreshing morning air. As we travelled to and from the river we came to know the road very well, becoming familiar with the acute beds and dips and other hazards. But there was one place we never did get used to: squeezing between the trees, zig-zag fashion, for miles, through heavy, loose sand. There was no great chance of the two convoys meeting in the middle of this. But one day it did happen. And in the confusion, before we finally cleared each other, a great deal of energy was expended together with a picturesque flow of bad language containing words some of us had never heard before.

During these all-day runs the cars began to straggle out more and more, some racing on ahead, and others content enough to come along steadily behind. The break-down car, as usual, brought up the rear. I contrived to strike the happy medium and consequently escaped the dust. It was also more pleasurable to be alone and thus commune with oneself. Considering "there was a war on," as our late sergeant used to say, we enjoyed a good deal of liberty and were left pretty well to ourselves. The suspension for the time of military discipline was all to the good, for it placed responsibility on individual effort, which was better.

Although it was a fact that, up to the present, we had seen very little of big game on the road, it was due entirely to the unusual noise of motors. Abandoned cars were to be seen here and there. Although inert, they were useful sometimes for providing spare parts for otherwise serviceable cars. If any passing vehicle required anything the other car could provide, it was taken. This resulted in time in some of the poor derelicts presenting a skeletonised appearance. It was round these cars that we would find that other hands besides human had been, for, apart from the monkeys' imprints, nuts, bolts, and screws were scattered all over the place.

The first intimation I had that animals were getting less shy now of approaching motor cars was when I ran into a large pack of thirty or forty baboons. Although excited, they had no intention of getting out of my way, but ran to and fro in front of my car. It was very interesting to study these creatures in their wild state. Some of the more bold came right up to me with artful side glances as they stood up, pawed the air with their empty hands, and looked at me and then at my running engine. Smaller, or young members of the group – and probably the females – kept up an incessant chattering in the background. I thought they were becoming too inquisitive, and so, with a noisy racing of my engine, I scattered them and went on. But only to have another surprise in the form of an ape, of man-size, blocking my way on a track too narrow to hold the two of us. I was far too near to him – about ten paces – to be comfortable, as I had come upon him suddenly. while I allowed my engine to tick over slowly, I enjoyed to the full the magnificent picture the savage creature had made amid his wild and natural surroundings. He stood to his full height ravenously eating something he held in his hands, watching anxiously a spot in the bush from whence he had probably just emerged. He stopped eating to subject me to one keen glance, after which my presence was ignored. Suddenly, with a startled gesture he sprang back, turned, and ran upright – like a man – into the bush for twenty paces. Here he continued to eat and still watched for evidence of some expected interruption. As I went on I looked into the direction from whence he seemed to expect this interruption but saw nothing. It so happened at this moment that I met two more cars coming from the opposite direction, and in their own interest I drew the drivers' attention to the unusual spectacle of the man-ape. I never expected them to molest the animal; but not only did they do this, they dismounted from their cars for the purpose, running towards it and firing their rifles at the same time. Screaming with rage that awakened the echoes of the silent forest, the infuriated beast dropped what it was eating, and came for them open-mouthed . . . the reason they were not torn to pieces lay in the fact that they ran faster than they had ever run in their lives before, regaining their cars safely and dashing off at full speed . . . For novices to take pot shots at an animal in this manner was a foolish thing to do (although under slightly different circumstances a friend and I were guilty of almost the same folly later). The danger was considerably increased in their instance if they knew as little about fire-arms as some of our men who had never fired off a rifle in their lives. (Our company training in England included no actual firing practice.) . . .

Snakes crossed the paths in large numbers, and sport was enjoyed running over them. And it was surprising to note how quickly a snake would recover from the shock of the wheels passing over its body, to dart with amazing rapidity into the bush. So general had this practice become, and so familiar were the boys with this sport, that it resulted in a story going the rounds of an MT driver picking up a snake with his wheels, whereupon the reptile *bit him in the back of the neck!* This was an African story with, most likely, an American flavour – some of our drivers hailed from the latter country.

Black ants also would be seen crossing the track in a thick, black line – an army of tens of thousands on trek. To run over them was unavoidable. A car passing through their ranks would leave behind two black patches of seething animation. With remarkable celerity, the dead and injured would be seized and carried forward – pulled along if necessary. But, in any case, from a state of confusion and chaos, order and system were restored, and in a surprisingly short time ranks would be re-formed, leaving no trace of the recent catastrophe as the march was resumed. In watching them one day I was attacked by a party of them from the rear, their menacing presence only becoming apparent to me when I felt numerous little pin-pricks on my legs. When I turned round, they were coming up in massed formation. As these little creatures were nearly the size of earwigs their attentions could not be accepted lightly, and so I beat a hasty retreat.

At a spot near the Rovuma River, crossing a native footpath, ants had built a covered archway like a tunnel, and in this way were passing over, unseen, except for a part of the archway that had been inadvertently broken. The exposed portion disclosed the moving multitude within, three and four deep, hurrying forward in one long, unbroken line, scrambling over each other in their haste – some made double speed by running along the backs of those running below. Little ones sat pensively on the backs of older ones, content to be carried along in this way. But all were imbued with the one idea: to get there – wherever that was – with the greatest speed. I broke a little more of the archway; a hurried investigation immediately ensued; those temporarily knocked out were helped on to their legs; the injured were seized and dragged along unceremoniously. From behind, the on-coming host had not the patience to wait a while – probably they had no option – but came blundering on, temporarily blocking the passage. Feverish activity was necessary to clear this, but it was done, and once again the march was resumed in perfect running order. The archway was guarded by soldier-ants flanking both sides of it in three lines of extended formation. With ceaseless action, as if sensing danger, and when I came near they were thrust upward in defiance to me. Barefooted natives, passing at the time, paused in their stride to steady their head-loads, the better to look where they were treading.

At the commencement of the rainy season, another species of ant – the flying ant – came out in hordes from their breading places below ground. They flew about in great clouds that darkened the sky. Their aerial evolutions only lasted a short half-hour or so, then they fell to the ground, shed their wings, and walked about the earth rejoicing – at least the females rejoiced, for, really, this was the nuptial flight, when, after pairing, the males all died.

The wings usually became detached of their own accord, but if there was any doubt about it, the insects assisted one another in pulling them off – falling over sometimes in the effort. So numerous were flying ants' wings in one part that we stood ankle-deep in them.

Natives looked upon these ants as a great delicacy, and devoured them with relish. They adopted the extraordinary expedient of artfully tapping on the ground in imitation of rain as an inducement for them to come out.

The edible qualities of the flying-ant appealed to other greedy mouths. One day a fat bull-frog was seen squatting over a little opening in the ground, gobbling up flying-ants as fast as they emerged. They were being literally swallowed alive. They came out of the ground in two and threes at a time. And they all met the same fate. He had a tremendous feed, for the company was unlimited and there was only one "managing director." To us hungry fellows looking on it was the most gratifying sight we had seen for some time.

In the vicinity of Massasi, chameleons, those quaint, slow-moving, lizard-like creatures, were to be seen on many parts of the road, and in the trees. They won favour in the hearts of everybody for their extreme tameness, allowing themselves to be picked up and petted, like a kitten.

In size they were as big, but a little longer, than one's hand;

in movement so slow and hesitating as to be almost painful to watch, giving forth the impression of slow-moving photography. Their round, staring eyes worked about as if on swivels, and had the peculiarity of independent movement. When they were not staring at you with a sad and sympathetic expression, one eye would be looking ahead, and the other taking a sly peep behind. In habit, their feet, like little gloved hands, gripped the slender boughs of a tree, and there they would wait, in patience, for the near approach of a succulent fly. If the fly proved to be beyond reach, and was likely to remain so, a cautious approach would be made in their typically slow manner. The fly they would seize, swiftly and unerringly, but shooting out a string-like tongue, nearly as long as their own bodies at the end of which the insect was instantly imprisoned in a glutinous pouch – thus coming to a sticky end so to speak. The actual operation began by taking careful aim, as a sportsman sights his gun, the subsequent "shooting" and withdrawal of tongue and insect into the mouth being so quick as to escape the eye. I never saw an object missed once the "gun" was "fired."

To test the veracity of the general belief that these little animals can change colour to suite their surroundings, we picked one up from the sandy floor where he was russet brown and placed him on a green object. To our surprise a change gradually took place from one colour to the other. Several experiments of this kind gave the same result. It was not surprising when we put one on a tree among thick branches we lost him. Finally, when we tenderly lifted him on to one of the Ford cars and he turned to the familiar slate-gray we then felt that we had indeed a true and sympathetic little friend.

By the very fact that these quaint little animals were indistinguishable on the road and that they were incapable of getting out of the way many met an untimely end by being run over. Unlike the snakes, they were killed instantly.

On our journeys to the Rovuma River we would sometimes

be puzzled by the appearance of trees on the roadside lying full length with their branches lopped off, smouldering at one end, after the manner of alighted cigarette cast aside, and, in a similar manner, leaving a white ash behind. They would smoulder thus for weeks, and in some cases must have been doing so for a much longer period, for trees that had been twenty feet long were now mere streaks of dust. We were under the impression that this was the native way of keeping in touch with fire, but as many of these trees were encountered in out-of-the-way places, where there was no sign of native life, we had to look elsewhere for an explanation. It was said that passing natives on espying a bees' nest in a tree set fire to that tree at the base, so smoking out the bees and felling the tree when it had burnt through. In this way they obtained the coveted honey. If this were the case, it seemed to us a wasteful method. But trees were plentiful and stings, even for natives, painful.

Gangs of natives would sometimes be seen felling huge trees and carrying them bodily to span gullies, but this work was, we thought, rather belated and unnecessary, and new roads that were being cut to avoid bad places were made as if to act permanently, which seemed obviously useless. It will be many years yet before that part of the country will see life of any kind beyond that of the prowling wild beast.

On the hospitable banks of the Rovuma River itself was the dump – the *banda* in which were stored all the provisions we had brought. Farther along the banks were camped native troops and followers, but we saw little of them owing to the dense nature of the bush, which restricted the view to a few hundred yards only. Some of the troops had gone back through the bush. There was no intention to follow the Germans over the river, and only a small garrison remained behind to guard that part of the district. It was for the purpose of stocking this garrison with the necessary supplies to last them throughout the rainy season that we were here. The rainy season would continue for about three months, during which the garrison would be cut off from the outside world. There were already ominous signs of the rains in the form of heavy black clouds that rolled themselves along from the distant horizon, to pass, however, without breaking. Once the rains had started the present dry ravines would be transformed into roaring torrents if tumbling water, the black cotton soil into tracts of grease, mud, and water, and whole stretches of low-lying country, meadows, and valleys would be submerged under flood water. In these circumstances motors – or even porters on foot – would be helpless. So Christmas time came and found us busily employed carrying supplies to the Rovuma.

One night, camped on the banks of the river, the reeking atmosphere humid and foreboding, the thick foliage and trees heavy with moisture, we heard that four natives had been carried away by lions. Among the unfortunate victims was an Askari whose cap and rifle only were found. It said something for the cunning of these brutes when a man whose duty it was to be on his guard, rifle ready and eyes open, could be thus swiftly and silently surprised. With the night pitchy dark, rain began to fall, each drop a spoonful it splashed heavily upon the hollow canopy above my head. I tried to get what sleep was possible, cramped as usual on the driving-seat of my car. Low rumblings of the storm coming from the far distance increased to loud peals of thunder that rolled heavily across the sky. Spasmodic flashes of lightning momentarily turned night into day, and occasionally the air was rent with the mournful, soul-stirring cry of what we thought to be a human being in agony, but which, probably, was a hyrax defying sleep with its long-drawn-out moans. A number of tethered donkeys brayed long into the night. All these noises, and the hot, humid atmosphere, made attempts to sleep a torture, and I was glad when daylight brought activity.

If remaining awake all night makes one more hungry in the morning I cannot say, but I did enjoy, with relish, a breakfast of curry and rice, particularly the curry. On my return to Massasi I had with me an Indian commissioned officer who proved interesting company. In his quaintly-spoken English, peculiar to Orientals of education, he expressed anxious concern for the welfare of England and her allied interests. He was a really British patriot at heart, a quality met more in the abstract than in the concrete, a refreshing reminder that we still had people fighting for us who had faith and confidence in British administration and justice. "Of course, the Indian people would much prefer to rule their own country," he declared, but every intelligent Indian knew perfectly well that this was impossible, as the people were not capable of it. Until that time came they must be ruled by a greater nation. If we lost this war India would be ruled by Germany, and although it mattered little to them which country it would be, as both were equally capable, they much preferred the British as they knew them, and did not know the Germans.

During the return journey to the Rovuma River an incident happened on the road that might have had a fatal

"On the inhospitable banks of the Rovuma River itself was the dump. . . ."

termination. It chanced that I had with me, as passenger, a young fellow who claimed big game-shooting experience in Africa, and he impressed me with the matter-of-fact account of his adventures. Although there was always the possibility of meeting something exciting on the road, most of the journeys were uneventful, so it was a remarkable coincidence that, just as my friend was absorbed in his discourse we ran into a pack of fifteen or twenty wild dogs. They were spread all over the road, and appealing quickly to my experienced friend, I followed his instructions and pulled up in the middle of them, allowing my engine to stop, which was not my intention. We both jumped out, rifles in hand, but instead of the animals fleeing, as I expected them to do, they not only stood their ground, but began to close in upon us with menacing growls, and a snapping of their jaws. Some were snarling, baring their white fangs; others emitted a succession of sharp barks; and all had their ears erected and thrust forward as if waiting a signal for a concerted attack. With tense nerves and faculties strained I waited on my friend, who, however, seemed at a loss. We could have actually touched the nearer dogs with a sweep of our rifles. In this dilemma we both did the same thing: fired over their heads. The animals, with a surprised leap, fled into the bush and stood staring at us, but only ten yards away. We fired again, and they retreated even farther, but stopped once more, as if uncertain to quit. At the sight of this I tried a shot in earnest and had the satisfaction, such as it was, of seeing my animal spring into the air, but whether seriously hit or not I never knew, for the next moment they all disappeared.

Though conscious of having escaped from a perilous situation, the conviction forced itself upon me that we had not come out of the episode with credit. I ventured to say so as we resumed our journey, and my companion's subsequent remarks confirmed my suspicion that he knew less about the intricacies of hunting wild animals that he laid claim to, otherwise he would never have advised stopping and interfering with these animals. People of experience confirmed these views afterwards. These dogs (by the way, very much like Alsatian wolf-hounds) are notorious hunters of big game, giving chase in packs of fifteen to thirty, and unlike many wild animals are fearless in the presence of man. On the Lindi line it was reported that an Indian had been trapped by these dogs and torn to pieces, the only thing left whole being his turban. Our escape was considered lucky, and we were congratulated.

On the return journey I saw a driver in front of me obviously in trouble; he was turning his car this way and that in frantic efforts to turn round. This he eventually did and I steadied my car for him to come up, which he did, meeting me end on.

"Lions!" he shouted excitedly.

"Where?" I asked, now equally excited.

"There!" he declared, pointing back, "dozens of 'em!"

"*Dozens of lions?*"

"Yes; they burst out of the bush in front of me and crossed the road – running like mad!"

Convulsed with laughter, I realised he had seen our erstwhile friends, the wild dogs. I explained this to him and he seemed pacified, but begged of me to continue the journey with him. We saw no more of them. As a matter of fact, these dogs are very rarely seen in Africa, some hunters having been in the country for years without coming across them.

With the prospect of running into larger game, transport men kept a sharp look-out. Some excitement was caused when news was brought into camp of a herd of elephants having been seen. The prospect of suddenly running into the midst of such big game on the open road was a little more than exciting. At one place where I had an involuntary stop for an hour, I measured the footprints of an elephant; the impressions, which were near a waterhole, were ten inches deep, twenty-four inches from toe to heel, and eight feet in stride.

Sometimes the fleeting glimpse of some shadowy form hurrying away through the bush would give cause for speculation and excitement, and frequently an animal dashing across the track provoked such remarks as:
"Good Gawd! Did y'r see that?"
"No; what was it?"
"The devil! I don't know!"

By way of sport, and also to add to our scanty larder, we sometimes got a shot at guinea-fowl feeding on the track, or perched up in the trees; but they were very difficult to get near to, and more difficult still to hit – with a rifle bullet. Feathers flew in plenty, but that tantalising stage was about as near as we usually got. When one was brought down there was much rejoicing, and a tasty bit for supper. We once gave chase after an animal recognised as a wild pig and succeeded in killing it, but we were disappointed as the flesh proved as tough as leather.

One really successful "bag" was an inanimate (50 lb) box of dates, which happened to lie exposed in a most tempting position in the rear of a car whose driver had his back turned, his mind reflecting on the sins of the world, the flesh, and his own pals in particular. The hungry boys seized the "game" and carried it swiftly into the dark recesses of the forest, where it was formally "despatched" with a tomahawk (still in my possession). It was a bad dip in the road that gave the favourable opportunity, a place where the cars, once safely through, had to wait for the remainder. One of the drivers, a Dutchman, ignorantly entered the ravine at speed on top gear, with the result that he swung round at the bottom, burst all his tyres, and reclined on his side in a cloud of dust. The delay thus caused gave us time to carry out our dark designs. Everyone had a grand feast, even the NCOs took their share – strangely silent, as we knew they would be.

When we finally arrived at our destination there was the very deuce to pay. Everybody had bland, innocent faces, and the driver's excuse that the box must have "jolted" out on the road had to suffice.

But a treat like this only happened once, and the absence of fats, milk, and sugar was sorely trying. Rice, mealie, quince jam, and bully day after day was nauseating and telling its own tale on the health of the men. A story going the rounds about this time, the truth of which I cannot vouch for, related to a party of transport men, very hungry as usual, who waylaid a poor native cattle-driver and persuaded him to part with one of his bullocks for a tin of bully. But the man, uneasy, asked or the usual chit. This was given to him and read as follows:

> "Mr *Hapana yama* (no meat) starving
> to death, does hereby *kamata* (seize) one
> bullock for one brother in tin."

The native, now perfectly satisfied, bowed gravely, and took his departure. What became of the bullock is not recorded.

Bully beef was looked upon as a great delicacy by the natives. At our midday halting-place on the way to the river, crowds of lynx-eyed darkies prowled around in an endless circle, waiting for the exciting moment when the leavings of a tin of bully was on offer. Instantly a perfect pandemonium would break out; the lucky recipient would become the centre of a struggling mass of black humanity, the scene resembling a football scrimmage. The poor man not only invariably lost the better part of his prize but would be half killed into the bargain.

I obtained possession of a musical instrument at this place (still prized among my curios) by the offer of a few tins of the precious bully beef. Elaborately carved and hollowed out of one piece of wood, it has seven metal keys, not unlike tuning forks, and when played upon (by the thumbs) gives out a dulcimer-toned effect. These little instruments made the sweetest music of the wilds, like sounds one would expect to hear from the ringing of a miniature set of church bells – if I may so express it – with changes included – a delightful

Banda Building.

The Artistic Result.

effect. In the quiet tropic evenings one would often be charmed to hear their sweet notes float along on the night air from the surrounding bush, and, if lucky enough, would be able to catch a glimpse of the bare-footed, unsophisticated beggar – whom we in England would call a savage – passing through the near-by clearing, thumbs busily at work, a little song on pouting lips, his head raised to greet with passionate eyes the vanguards of a million stars.

Charms of magic to frighten away devils and other evil spirits dangled from the arms and chests of most of these innocent children of the wilderness. They were generally little packets of script wrapped in many layers of parchment and encased in leather securely sealed. But the knife sometimes revealed, not script, but the head of a lizard, or chameleon, or a monkey's paw. In my first clumsy attempt to come into possession of one of these curious things, I walked up to a native who was covered with them, a man who held himself aloof from his fellows with an air of superior rank.

My purpose not being at first clear to him, he let me approach him and his precious packets before he realised what I was about to do. With a cry of horror which startled me, he sprang back, the palms of his hands thrust out before him as if to ward me off. With a vehemence that nearly stifled him, he let out a succession of expletives that sounded like crackers going off – and then bolted. Fortunately I was impervious to what he had to say as I did not understand a word. One of our own natives volunteered the information that he was a "big chief man" with particularly big chief charms, and that these charms were very wonderful, protecting him from the bow and arrow of the "bad" man, but with the supreme power of assuring him the death of the bad man on the first pull of his own bow-string. The trouble was that I had touched one of his magic charms and probably now the magic had all gone. I was not pleased with the inference, but I let that pass. I quite believed in the man's sincerity, but had no idea that he had himself had such beliefs until I ventured to acquire his own little charm, when he gave one yell and fled. This was the only occasion on which I tried to obtain charms from a living native. I did, later, obtain a few specimens, but they were from the bodies of dead men (who tell no tales). I offered one to a native but he said "*Hapana!* (No). if that's the best it's done for him, it's no use to me!"

Christmas Day found us on the road, travelling to the river. We felt that a good dinner was in store for us that day. But no! it was mealie and jam for breakfast, mealie and jam for lunch, and mealie and jam for the evening (Christmas) dinner.

The boys were silent as they sat round the camp fire on the

dismal banks of the Rovuma that night. Perhaps their thoughts were in the same direction as mine . . . I felt a little joy in the reflection that I had contrived to get a wireless from Massasi. Would it have arrived yet? Maybe . . . Anyway, it was a cheering thought.[33]

The darkness crept down and around us, the bright fire throwing into sharp relief the sad, serious faces of the men who would not talk . . . They seemed to be waiting for something . . . At last there were raucous cries of *"Rum up!"* It had the electrifying effect of sending everybody, helter-skelter, to the rum tub. The liquid was really a poor substitute for the real thing, but it seemed to be enjoyed all the same. There was no limit to the quantity this Christmas night! I applied for my share and they filled my cup . . . It was hot and burnt the throat, and turned one's inside into a boiling cauldron . . . but who cared? Nobody, not just now . . . Why, things could be much worse . . . In fact, things were quite good! We were not hungry – not now! The rum was good after all – it was only the first taste of it that seemed to burn . . . And pipes were going, and no one suffered, or wanted for anything . . . Indeed, the situation was quite a romantic one . . . Somebody began to sing; talk became general; laughter was loud and long – now . . .

Sometimes I felt that the sounds of revelry were mocked by the empty, dark void. The silence – that deep, awe-inspiring, mysterious silence – hung like a pall over the broad waters of the floating river, clung to the thickly-wooded banks, and haunted the dark recesses of the surrounding jungle. Those laughing faces were not real; the noises that rose into the air and startled one, died. Only the great river was real, wending its lonely way, swiftly and silently, through the night . . .

It was late; the pungent smell of decaying vegetation was more pronounced now the fire had died down, and the mists were thickening round the banks. Some of the boys had turned in for the night, asleep in their cars or in the near-by

---

[33] CCW: The message arrived within forty-eight hours

shack, but those who were left were still singing, half in fantasy:-

> Fifteen men on the dead man's chest
> Yo-ho-ho, and a bottle of rum!
> Drink and the devil had done for the rest –
> Yo-ho-ho and a bottle of rum!

At last, jumbling his speech badly, the last man turned in, and all was still . . .

The welcome sun rose in the form of a ball of fire, as it always does in this tropic land, chasing away the early drab greys that gave place to sweeping stretches of crimson and gold, which, in their turn, faded and disappeared, to flood the new-born day with white light.

An early start was made on this particular morning; the roll call was two hours late. An NCO came up to me after breakfast with the information that I was to remain behind to drive our OC, Lieutenant Parker,[34] back to Massasi after the convoy had left. This was not to the liking of the NCO – but more of that anon.

The convoy left, and a little later we followed on. We were both suffering from recovery, but the fresh morning breeze, which we caught as we rushed along, cooled fevered brows, and brought the smiles back again.

I was not at all surprised when my officer directed me to pull up at Wells Camp – a rather delightful place of two or three artistic *bandas* and an equal number of rather exclusive officers. The latter now appeared, greeted the OC effusively, and they all disappeared within.

I was left perforce to kick my heels in the sun, but I was not sure whether that last grimace from the OC, as they went off, was a wink or a nod.

But something happened – I knew it would.

A native servant arrived with my lunch. This consisted of a delicious repast of guinea-fowl rissoles, cold toast, and hot

---
[34] Lieutenant Parker - unable to trace

coffee with milk and sugar, delivered in the correct attitude of stiff formality. With a delightful feeling that all hope was not dead, I made amends for the wretched Christmas dinner the night before!

The sun was high in the heavens when I became uneasy at the time. Nothing had disturbed the peace of that typical African morning except a solitary Ford motorist who, approaching at speed amid a jangle of loose parts and a wobbling of wheels as if the whole machine were going to fall to pieces, burst a tyre with a loud report just as he got near to where I stood watching his eccentric approach. I helped him to put it to rights by stuffing it with dry grasses, after which all was well, and away he went with a noisy resumption of jangles and jolts. What a game it all was! In his hurry this ardent and enthusiastic member of MT's failed to see any humour in the situation – perhaps naturally, from his standpoint.

I had only to remind the OC of the late hour for him to come out at once, bidding farewell to his friends. (I ventured a few words of thanks which they smilingly acknowledged.)

Going onto Massasi my companion and I chatted the whole of the way. So engrossing was his conversation about wild animals and hunting, of which he had had an extensive experience, that we both failed to notice the sun's ominous drop to the horizon. A mighty spurt had to be made to get into before dark – with just five minutes to spare.

Another interesting passenger I had from the Rovuma River was a European officer of Askari, who predicted the return of Von Lettow in twelve months' time. His surmise was fully justified, the Germans recrossing the river at the end of the time stated . . .

On New Year's Eve a concert was held in the camp of our cheerful friend the Rajah – a break away from the daily routine, a wonderful stimulant for jaded nerves. The open-air stage was complete with lighting, scenery and curtain. Men and officers floated in from the camps round about, being accommodated on seats made from petrol tins. With the open roof a canopy of velvet studded with stars, an enjoyable al fresco entertainment was received by an appreciative audience with rounds of applause. My "Merry and Bright" contribution was considerably enhanced by the eccentric behaviour of our long-legged pianist, who had to make the best of the accompaniment on a small, wheezy harmonium – "captured" from the German mission close by. The last item (at midnight) was, appropriately enough, a "ghost" scene, the fearsome apparition, clothed in white, evoking the customary groaning and moaning from affrighted victims. This abrupt transformation to the "supernatural", however, had an entirely unexpected result, ending in terrific uproar. Yells and screams from a hundred and fifty savage throats put consternation into all hearts – until the true situation turned alarm into roars of laughter. It was only the large number of natives who always looked on from the background on these occasions, and who, at this moment, seeing the ghost appear, fled in a terrified panic. The fall of the curtain was the signal for a vigorous striking of iron bars on suspended hoops of iron. With this noisy clamour ringing through the air, loud bursts of cheering, hearty handshakes, and good wishes exchanged all round, the New Year was ushered in.

My officer had already thanked me for my contribution to the evening's entertainment in a very practical manner – the brand was White Horse – and now introduced me to the Post Commandant himself, who, seeing me uneasy, at once begged that no question of rank should be allowed to stand between us, as he too (hand on my shoulder) was "one of the lads of the village" – or words to that effect.

At the end, it was arranged (much to my satisfaction) that a shooting excursion should be undertaken on the morrow and that I should have my car ready at 6 a.m.

Chapter 7

The early hours of the first day of the New Year were spent in vain waiting for Lieutenant Parker and the Commandant to go shooting, as arranged the night before. The OC was two hours late in arriving, and the Post Commandant never turned up at all!

The convoy had by this time, of course, gone up to the river, so Lieutenant Parker told me to take the rest of the day off, which I was glad to do, for it gave me the opportunity to oil and grease the car thoroughly all round, attend to my own toilet, and put personal effects in order.

In camp the day was not without at least one exciting incident. This time it was a stand-up fight with bare fists between two natives. Our cook's assistant was a coal-black giant of enormous proportions, ugly of feature, arrogant, and ignorant of manner. His opponent was a Swahili of small stature, a gentle, inoffensive man who had won his way to all hearts by his kind, ingratiating ways. It was strange that these two men of such opposite temperaments should meet thus. But possibly because the little fellow was highly sensitive to the general insolent attitude of the big fellow he threw down the gauntlet for the rest.

Sudden sounds of heavy snorting and of hefty blows struck in the heat of anger, the scuffling of feet and the noisy clatter of pots and pans scattered in all directions, brought everybody running to the cook-house. A wide ring was hastily formed; although in the open, it had to be wide as the fight was taking place amid tables and benches. The combatants in fierce earnestness swung terrific blows to the face; being unguarded, as they knew nothing about boxing, they fought like wild beasts. As the struggle progressed it was to our gratification that we noticed the little fellow, the nimbler of the two, gradually wearing down his burly opponent who lost his head and exhausted himself dealing wild blows to empty air. Time after time the big fellow stopped such terrific blows with his face that one eye was seeing nothing – the other red murder. He was a horrible sight, his face distorted with pain, his attitude repulsive as he turned suddenly to the onlookers for commiseration. But he got none. It was then that he worked his way round, his diabolical intention covered by theatrical shrieks and yells, till he had reached a bench upon which lay a bayonet. This he suddenly seized, and with a fierce cry charged at the little fellow with the weapon at his side. But he reckoned without the latter's quick perception and our quick intervention. It took six men to hold him, and ten minutes for them to make him understand that the fight was over.

He was turned out of the camp, but he hung about the outskirts for many days, and for hours on end could be seen, a dangerous and repulsive character, watching over the boundary fence the movements of those within.

The natives were, to us a curious lot. Many were recruited from widely different parts of the country, with the result that different tribes, or classes, got mixed up and fought amongst themselves. Members of opposite factions when meeting had a playful way of showing contempt for one another by clicking their fingers under one another's noses. Whenever actual contact took place, then hasty blows were quickly exchanged. The carrying of weapons was rightly forbidden by the authorities, but nevertheless the quarrels were animating and usually ended up in a free fight with sticks, pieces of old iron, or anything else they could lay their hands on.

The medley of natives varied considerably in personal appearance. Teeth sharpened to a point, V-shaped, were the distinguishing characteristics of one tribe who were reputed to be cannibalistic; but whether there was any truth in it was doubtful in the absence of convincing proof. Many of the other natives, however, would not associate with these men under any circumstances, and would frequently point to them in disgust and say: "Him bad man! He eat fellow man!" Members of another tribe had the front teeth of the lower jaw missing, having been extracted in early life, a curious custom resulting from a serious epidemic of lock-jaw that once nearly devastated the whole tribe. The methods of dressing the hair and the various styles adopted were other peculiar features. There were top-knots, screw-buns, balls of fluff, and corkscrew-like erections – the last a most comical sight on the heads of grown-up men. Some were bald-headed, having the whole of the head shaved, a painful operation performed with cold water and an old knife or a piece of broken glass. Others affected a compromise, with one side of the head bald, the other side growing a profusion of woolly locks. Indeed, there was no limit to grotesque personal ornament. Many had their features completely spoilt – in fact disfigured – with tribal marks; designs cut into the face with a knife, made to fester, to heal up afterwards with an appearance of proud flesh. And yet I caught one of these fellows pencilling his eyelashes!

Apart from those of unattractive appearance were others free from embellishment of any kind. They lived a more simple and natural life. Their skins were clear and their features regular. They took a pride in keeping their bare limbs polished like mahogany; they kept themselves clean and their hair was allowed to assume natural growth. Dressed scantily but with neat modesty, they cultivated a manner that might do great credit to many in not so low a phase of life as that in which these simple creatures existed. Their unspoilt innocence and their frank, open countenances never failed to appeal. One had only to show a feeling of kindly sentiment towards these people to be rewarded with broad smiles, and a display of pleasing, happy mannerisms. They appeared shy, and would squirm about with embarrassment until a smile, broader than the rest, forced apart unwilling lips, to reveal a regular set of perfect, white teeth. Arm in arm, or hand in hand, they would walk along unconscious of prying eyes, laughing and talking together, sometimes staying awhile to gaze innocently into each other's eyes and exchange pleasantries like children – indeed they were little else.

Of women, the few we saw ran away, hiding their faces. Any attempt at photography resulted in a wild scream and a speedy disappearance of the subject. There was an exception at a water-hole where a woman had arrived to replenish her pitcher. She seemed to have no fear of the little magic box, probably knowing nothing at all about it, or of the superstition connected with it that was the evil eye, as believed in by her more "enlightened" neighbours. It might interest some of my lady readers to know that the dress she wore was made entirely from the bark of a tree, beaten out to a fine texture. Higher up the country they were not even so particular as this, content to go without any clothes at all.

All manual labour was done by the natives. Paths were cut through the virgin forest, trees felled and carried away, the banks and gullies smoothed out for the passage of transport, camps made, *bandas* and workshops built. Quite a little army made of natives was employed on nothing else but keeping the camps round about in a clean and hygienic condition. Motor transport was loaded up and unloaded by natives, and at the point where motors could go no further natives carried supplies to the troops.

The motor car itself was a source of never-ending wonder to the native. Those who had never seen a motor before ran pell-mell into the bush, screaming and hiding away. None ever got used to those self-moving vehicles, but would crouch on the ground of their approach, trembling all over, and looking with bulging eyes at the wheels as they revolved. Even the natives employed in camp and used to the cars were never quite easy in their minds, the magic of the automobile being incomprehensible to them.

Blazing fires lit up with a weird glare the surrounding forest land, telling of the camp of our own natives in the valley to the south, beyond the outskirts of Massasi. At night-time the incessant hum of the community of a thousand souls rose like the murmur of a restless sea. With the advent of the new moon the excuse for the monthly *ngoma* was eagerly seized upon. With the first appearance of the new moon's silver streak in the sky, the resounding boom of a beaten drum, feint and spasmodic at first, echoes through the empty forest shades and floated up to the heights of Massasi from the valley below. Soon the drumming was augmented by the beat of another, and still another – from the far distance came the faint echo of other drums in reply – weird, barbaric soul-calls of the Wild, pregnant with mysterious romances of past ages of dark superstition and holy – or unholy – custom . . . the call of the pent-up souls of men – and women – seeking self-expression. For a while the sounds ceased, only to start again almost at once, now continuous and rhythmical, louder and louder, frenzied and wild, calling to the stars with the shrieks of the women and the chanting of the men, resounding deep and hollow-toned through the depths of the forest, exciting the senses of men and women and sending them dancing into the circle of dark figures that moved slowly round the great fire. As the night advanced, it grew into a wild orgy of joyful abandon, when the chant was loud and long, the dance frenzied, and the *pombe* good.

On – on through the night it lasted, the singing and dancing becoming hysterical between the hours of midnight and 2 a.m. Towards dawn the noises died down, and at daybreak all was silent and still.

The rainy season hastened our efforts to get the requisite amount of supplies up to the lonely garrison on the Rovuma River before heavier rains put an end to activities.

It was when returning to the river on one of these

excursions that I came into the possession of a curio which I still possess and value above all others. A native chief, or headman, appeared on the scene as if attracted out of curiosity by the traffic. He was exceptionally tall, dressed in a robe of white linen, wore army putties (flopping round his legs, of course, like two pieces of old sacking), sandals on his feet, a fine collection of medals across his chest (really silver coins), and a crown of egret feathers on his head – surely an incongruous combination. With an exaggerated display of self-importance he held in his outstretched right hand a staff, five feet long, the top part of which was carved into the shape of a human head and shoulders. Like many of these native carvings, the face displayed an expression of marked severity, with elongated features, almond-shaped slits for eyes, and thin, protruding lips – of the kind which at first sight (to Europeans) excites curiosity, and then amusement.

He stood for a moment with the stick thrust out before him, the top almost level with his shoulder, gripping the image by the back of the neck, its wooden face and dead eyes ahead. It required a good deal of tactful energy to break through the natural reserve of this dignified personage, but five tins of bully beef, three packets of cigarettes, half a dozen silver coins, and a packet of safety-pins were strongly persuasive arguments. I became owner of the stick, and cutting off the stem, I stuck the grotesque and surly little image before my windscreen, with an inscription painted on a sheet of canvas below it, reading as follows:-

MY MOTTO
"ALWAYS MERRY AND BRIGHT"

The display of the model with its contradictory inscription was the means of bringing much fun to the front whenever it appeared. Officers' grave countenances relaxed into broad grins as they raised their hats in acknowledgement of the happy inspiration. White troops were tremendously bucked with the idea and greeted its appearance with vociferous cheers. And members of my own company were elated with the distinction it conferred on our convoy.

On the road the natives viewed its sudden advent with unmixed alarm, crying "Allah! Allah!" pointing excitedly at the image, and making a puffing noise with their lips.

At one place where I had left my car unattended I returned to find a crowd of frenzied natives all dancing madly in front of it. They had worked themselves into a state of uncontrolled excitement, emitting prolonged shrieks, sharp, ear-splitting, yells, shouting and jeering as they mocked at the image, put their tongues out at it, and pointed. Yet never once did any one of them attempt to approach it, but touched chin with knees in the ecstasy of their dancing. Where all these natives had come from baffled me, for when I had arrived there was not a soul to be seen. However, I was glad to get on board and drive away as quickly as possible, the natives scattering and fleeing in all directions.

Little children came to know the car with the strange wooden 'god', and would leave their play to greet me. On one occasion I could not resist the temptation to make a grimace at them in imitation of the exaggerated expression on the face of the little wooden god. Instantly all the little coons fell on their bare backs in the hot sand, kicked chubby toes in the air, and held their sides in a convulsion of laughter.

Unfortunately the idea of the mascot did not appeal to at least one – the NCO who had been annoyed at my having been selected to drive the OC from Rovuma. Although he could not interfere with this, or with the other duties given to me by numerous officers, he probably thought it would discountenance me if he reduced my efficiency by forcing me into accepting old cars for new.

The convoy would be standing easy, awaiting instructions, when a commissioned officer of troops from up the line would approach and address me: "I want you to take this convoy to ___" "Certainly, sir," I would say, "I'll inform the NCO in charge." (The flimsy bits of ribbon denoting NCO rank were indistinguishable through wear and tear – and dirt.) The NCO would now reveal himself with alacrity. "I want you to take this convoy to ___," the officer would say to him, "but I am going to ride with this man," indicating me, and pointing to the image. Then briefly: "We'll take the lead!"

The NCO's protest as to "who was the flicking NCO of this blinking convoy?" fell on deaf ears of unconcerned men used only to obeying orders . . .

I showed no resentment when he took my first car from me, soon making the second as good as the first. This car, in its turn, he now ordered me to give up on the morrow. I made such a forcible protestation against this unprecedented conduct that I fully expected "to be shot at dawn." I was. I was shot out of my car. He could not, however, make any objection to my demand to see the OC before I would obey any further orders.

This was a change in the situation from which it was going to be difficult for him to escape with assured success, so, in his dilemma, with an object in view that was not quite apparent, he ordered an open touring car to be driven up, and instructed me to drive it to Ndanda, but for what purpose he made the mistake of failing to explain. Still I refused to move. He therefore ordered someone else to take charge of the car, and turning to me ordered me angrily to "get in" and "get out." This, I felt, was a definite instruction, somewhat to my liking, as the impossibility of ever doing any further good in this convoy was obvious.

Jumping in with the whole of my kit and telling the driver to drive like blazes, we swung out of the camp in a cloud of dust, the boys, who had been watching all this unseen, bold enough now to come into the open and raise a hearty cheer over the head of the enemy.

The driver (not a member of our convoy) proved to be a typical Scot, with a typical sense of dry Scottish humour, and, as I suspected, was thoroughly enjoying the situation.

"Ah, weel," he said at last, "Ah've mah ain affairs to look after when Ah get t' Ndanda, and" (slyly) "Ah've nae instrooctions aboot mah passenger!"

So I left him at Ndanda, unloading my kit and taking up my quarters in an empty *banda*. Here the realisation of complete isolation forced itself upon me . . . I had to assume some sort of standing, and, after reflection, considered myself justified in adopting that of a free lance – an extraordinary situation.

Still, this position I knew quite well could not continue indefinitely, and must be turned to my advantage if possible. I had roamed similarly about the camp for the most part of the afternoon, becoming rather at a loss to know what to do, when whom should I see but Lieutenant Grosse[35] himself of "Messrs Clap and Trap" of happy memory. I dashed up to him and asked if he had a vacancy for one who was weak, but willing.

"Good gracious, Campbell, what the devil are you doing here?" he asked incredulously. But I told him it was really serious, explained the situation, and begged of him to see me through. This he did, right promptly. There was no question as to the vulnerability of the position I had taken up. He called up the sergeant and I was put on the strength, the OC himself finding me a brand new car. My new sergeant paid me the compliment of inviting me to become his driver, but I was not in the mind to be anyone's driver, being thoroughly fed up and wishing to be alone.

All the same, within forty-eight hours I led Lieutenant Grosse's Ford No 1 Disc Convoy into Massasi, the surly little image well to the front, the light-hearted inscription to be seen of all men. I received curt instructions to return to my own convoy, but an appeal to my new officer had the desired effect. I never went back . . . Thus ended an incident which, as a breach of military regulation, was probably unique.

While the roads had been improved by widening and flattening, tracts of flooded country in the low-lying districts

---

[35] Lieutenant Grosse - unable to trace

defied all the ingenuity of the Road Corps to make passage for motor transport anything but a hazardous task. Sometime the whole front wheel of a car would disappear into a mud-hole. If lucky enough to have natives near they would be called upon for assistance. These dusky fellows would seize the car (so long as it was inert and helpless) and place it bodily on an even keel, laughing and throwing jibes at it the while. But as soon as the engine was started away they would go like the wind, real mischievous sprites and imps, floundering through mud and water with loud yells.

What the Fords could stand in the trying circumstances of bad roads and rough usage was really amazing. Their light build and simple construction enabled them to penetrate to places inaccessible to all other cars. It was only possible because they were asked to do the almost impossible that many fell by the roadside. Incompetency among drivers also caused accidents that put cars into dock or left them stranded in the open forest. And sometimes these incidents led to amusing situations, as witness a man who ran off the road and crashed full force into a tree. When I came up to him he was calmly frying himself a dainty over a slow fire as if he had no cares in the whole wide world. His only comment in relation to the smash was, briefly, to curse the authorities for expecting him to drive a Ford, when never before in his life had he driven anything else but a gang of niggers.

Natives were bad drivers. I only saw one on the road and he, singularly, came to grief before our very eyes. Tearing towards us at full speed, he had not the slightest idea of how to steady up on approaching our rather big convoy. He bumped and jumped all over the road, missed the head of the convoy by a hair's breadth, drove right off at a tangent, knocked a native clean off his feet, much to that worthy's astonishment, and then, careering off into the bush, carried another unfortunate creature, also a native, much surprised, fifty yards through the thorn-bushes, the victim hanging on to the radiator like grim death. He was none the worse for this adventure except that his clothing was torn to shreds and he was scratched from head to foot with "wait-a-bit" thorns. I never recall this incident without visualising the terrified look on this man's face as, clinging desperately to the radiator of the now stationary car, he resisted all efforts to extricate him.

These incidents, and such-like, were brought about from the desperate necessity for employing new drivers to fill the places of those too ill to continue. But it was bad policy, and was courting disaster to employ any other but experienced men on such roads, their very attitude as they went flying by, with clenched teeth and eyes bulging, proclaiming the ignorance that would lead to the inevitable crash. Sometimes even a competent driver would be caught off his guard or, too weak from illness to prevent it, would have the steering-wheel wrenched right out of his hands. In the loose sand this would result in what was known as wheel-lock, the front wheels flattening themselves out on the ground. There were many made derelict in this way. Wear and tear added to the number. From these various causes motor transport was severely depleted.

Excitement prevailed one day when we learned we were about to enter a district as yet unknown to us. For mile on mile we travelled north-west into flat, bare country, scanty trees here and there. A deep valley ahead thrilled us with the possibility of becoming bogged as we crawled through the marshes below; thence over the next hill, across more sparse country, the convoy straggling out as usual. The track became fainter, and then obscure, and finally fizzled out altogether. For a while we proceeded by guesswork, keeping an eye on the sun for direction. Then we picked the track up again where it entered a thick wood, giving us the worse driving of the day as we ploughed through deep undergrowth and tried to keep all four wheels on a path three feet wide. In the midst of this we met a party of natives, two dozen strong. Upon seeing us approaching they fled with great cries, hiding themselves behind trees, from which safe vantage points they peeped at the noisy, spluttering cavalcade as it lurched its way out of sight.

We had to rely on more "dead-reckoning" as we climbed over bare, rocky ground into mountainous country. At last, reaching a great split in the rock, we passed through, and descended the other side, arriving at our destination, a dump above the Lemasuli River, at 4 p.m., exhausted and hungry.

After unloading, we parked in a clearing under the trees, preparations being made for a night's camp. No sooner was a fire lit than a storm-cloud burst and put it out. The rain turned the track into a raging torrent that thundered its way down to the river below. In an hour it was calm again, the water ran itself off, the air turned close and humid, heavy moisture hung on the trees and dripped upon the canopies over our heads, echoing hollow and loud in the tense silence. We had neither lamps nor oil, and night coming on we sat alone in the shelter of our respective cars in the dark, feeling anything but comfortable, the atmosphere full of a strange foreboding. Forlornly we watched the fitful flashes of sheet-lightening revealing for vibrating moments the dark shadows in the dense bush around us, and particularly a white object that stood out, strangely enough, within full view; the skull of an elephant, its empty eye sockets staring into the night, as if crying in its very immobility – "Fate, fate, fate!" Thus we waited for sleep, and the early hours of a new day to bring fresh hope and good cheer.

Three times we made this journey to the Lemasuli River, heavy storms of rain adding considerably to the difficulties of the road. The possibility of getting cut off during these visitations was a real one for, although the water drained quickly after a shower, the rains might now easily become a permanent deluge from which there would be no escape. Provisions were, however, badly needed in this quarter, and we carried on, although it was generally admitted we should tempt providence once too often and, indeed, during the last journey, disaster all but overtook us.

A part of the track that threatened most risk of our becoming bogged was in a valley of black cotton soil which the recent wet weather had turned into a slippery bed of thick grease. In this morass some of the cars stuck. I declined to face the ordeal and went round through the bush, forcing a passage by pressing the tall reeds and slender trees down under the weight of the car, the rest of the convoy following suit. We then helped to extricate the bogged cars with the aid of twenty-foot creepers torn down from the adjacent trees – a novel but effective plan. One car was abandoned.

Most of my friends who had accompanied me into this country were now down and out – many of them fever cases in hospital on the coast – leaving me among new-comers. Feeling the lengthy strain myself of continual hardship and privation, I longed for the time to come when this work would be finished and the line evacuated. Of this, there were already signs.

Returning one evening to Ndanda, I had my most serious attack of abdominal pains and dysentery. Thankful indeed to arrive safely, but too late to obtain any relief, I was in great misery until past midnight. There was scant regard for my plight from anyone, beyond the remark from fellow-sufferers: "That poor devil's got it bad!" the cheerful equivalent to saying *"There's no hope; he's done for!"*

Too weak to stand, but with a set determination to survive, I crawled to where I thought I had left my car, but got off the track. My agony was increased by an over-zealous native sentry who desired to leave nothing to chance but finish me off there and then . . . Reaching the haven of my car, I rolled in, longing for the dawn. Unfortunately for me, operations at the cookhouse did not commence until 5 a.m. I found this out by several fruitless and painful journeys to that Mecca under the giant baobab tree long before the appointed hour. At 5 a.m. precisely I was there begging for hot milk to save my life! Tins of the precious fluid were of greater value than gold, and to my pleading the white cook listened in sceptical doubt, but, fortunately, my plight of the night before had been witnessed by his assistant, a fellow-sufferer, who confirmed my story and himself handed me half a pint of hot milk. I considered that gift one straight from Heaven!

How wonderful it is that a man's dying vitality can respond so promptly to the right treatment. I required no more after this, but was on the road again, ready for anything. I remember my load distinctly. It was the last I took up the line: twelve drums of cooking oil that smelt abominably, and copiously leaked all the time.

On arrival at Massasi I found everybody on the tip-toes of excitement, packing up for the final journey down the line. Derelicts had been rounded up, and convoys called in. it was probably the unusual excitement and bustle that accounted for the fire that broke out in the evening, several *bandas* being involved and the flames seen as far away as Ndanda, thirty miles off. Like demons dancing all round the edge of Inferno, the darkies in their hundreds yelled and screamed, taking a huge delight in pitting their combined strength and numbers against the all-devouring flames. They tore down as yet unaffected *bandas* by the roof; they hauled away the walls piecemeal; they uprooted poles and protective fencing, carrying them bodily away, the while bamboo framings burst with the spasmodic crackle of rifle-fire.

Strange to relate, a fire took place the following night at Ndanda, when, in our turn, we watched the flames from Massasi. It was due to a native trying to light a fire with petrol. He certainly lit it all right, and stood, trembling in every limb, while the whole show went up into the air.

The ignorant use of petrol by another native resulted seriously for him. He held a tin vessel full of petrol over an open fire and allowed the contents to dribble. Instantly the flames shot up, and in his sudden alarm he shook the whole contents over the lower part of his body. For several moments he danced and shrieked in terror until he was taken way. To our astonishment his dusky friends then gave a pantomimic display of the poor fellow's antics, complete with yells, which, native-like, was drawn out for a callously long period.

The native sense of humour is a gift exclusive to such simple folk; they are not constrained by the dictates of "manners"; their minds are not cloaked by the false veneer of convention. Following the natural feeling to laugh or cry, they do so whenever the occasion should arise, with unrestrained frankness.

I saw one of our fellows deliberately knock a native's hat off. True, it was one of the old-fashioned topper kind, several sizes too small, and perkily balanced in a temptingly exposed position on the top of the man's woolly head. But, all the same, conspicuous as the sight was, the wearer was obviously ignorant of the fact as he gravely conversed with his fellow companions in passing. The hat went flying through space, and the native, mystified by its sudden disappearance, turned to ascertain the cause of this strange phenomenon. When he realised that a white man had seen fun in an act so barren he laughed the louder of the two. It prompted a thought as to whose sense of humour was the better.

At last orders were received for our convoy to make direct for the coast. It was with extreme relief we turned our cars for the last time down the line. There was a good deal of traffic on the road. At one place delay was caused by a stampede of donkeys attacked by a swarm of wild bees. Drivers of the donkeys ran away – small blame to them! – but it resulted in a perfect hullabaloo. Two of the animals lay dead, and litter and baggage strewed the road for nearly a mile. Although we waited an hour, further progress was still impossible, and so the journey was resumed by making a detour of several miles through the bush.

During a further halt a dozen women in customary single file marched by, each with a pillbox-like ornament inserted in the upper lip. This was our first meeting with the *pelele*, or lip plug. The women's unhappy appearance was made worse by extreme old age, their faces, and almost completely naked bodies, covered with designs carved into the skin with the knife. The *pelele* cannot be discarded once it had been adopted, because of the abnormal extent to which the upper lip is stretched. When the *pelele* is withdrawn, the lip, now an unnatural and ugly ring of flesh, hangs down to rest on the chin. The custom of wearing such a hideous ornament originated with the desire to discourage the amorous attentions of the male members of a more powerful neighbouring tribe. In our presence these women were very ill at ease as they hurried by, giving one the impression that they were ashamed of their own existence. It was when brought face to face with ignorance in this form that one was shocked.

Another strange sight was that of an albino woman standing alone on the edge of the track. She had the broad, big features of the negro race, but her skin was milky white, and her eyes were pink!

Long before reaching our destination, the convoy had straggled out . . . Alone and exhausted, I arrived at last at Mingoya, the place where we first landed after sailing up the creek.

Transport Difficulties.

Chapter 8

The last five miles into Mingoya had to be taken through deep, loose sand. Weak and ill as I undoubtedly was, it required all my strength to prevent the wheels from doubling up beneath me. I was glad at last to reach our reporting depot. The pace had a forlorn and deserted appearance. There was not a soul to welcome us, the *bandas* were empty, and there was no sign of food.

We turned our attention to the canteen, our only hope. Prominently displayed on the tightly closed and locked door was the following notice:

CANDLES, SALT, TOBACCO, PENCILS,
TIN-OPENERS, and KEATING'S POWDER
*only in stock; if any of these are required
apply at the back door.*

". . . . a woman had arrived to replenish her pitcher."

Children—a happy side of native life.

Cheerful reading for hungry men! Desperately we applied at the back door – not for any of these luxuries but in the hope of obtaining food. We banged at the door to empty echoes, reminding us somewhat of the Christmas comforts sent to us up the line – "comforts" of unnecessary fancy shirts and scented soaps, but never a dressing for the inner man!

Darkness fell quickly, compelling me to return to my faithful Ford, hungry as usual to a comfortless couch.

Mingoya simply swarmed with mosquitoes that came up in their millions from the surrounding marshes, and it was to escape from the attentions of these pests that I turned in earlier than usual.

My naturally cramped position on the driving-seat made it impossible for me to erect the mosquito net effectively. Utterly tired out I fell into a troubled sleep, and in my restlessness the glass stopper of my ammonia bottle beneath my pillow came out. Awakened by the fumes, before they asphyxiated me, I promptly replaced the stopper. Then it was that I discovered that my leg had been in contact with the mosquito net and that I had no fewer than forty bites thereon. Troublesome pests that I would exclude I found, after all my trouble, to be inside, not outside the net, and that they were struggling to get out, not in, after a great feast. What with the pain of the bites, the smell of leaking petrol, the fumes from the spilt ammonia, the incessant hum of the myriads of insects, the oppressive heat, and cramp from the sustained effort to keep away from the sides of my net, my complete wretchedness can be imagined.

At dawn all these vindictive mosquitoes took their departure, leaving me free, but free only to get up.

We had all spent a night of similar misery. Eventually I found chubby-faced, happy little Mercer walking about and looking like a very well-done sausage. As a result of these mosquito bites we fully expected to be attacked by fever in ten days, and sure enough we got it.

For the last time I started up my Ford, driving it into a very wide clearing reserved for the purpose of parking, and here I carefully dismantled my mascot, tucking him away in my kit-bag with a smile and a blessing.

Properly equipped sleeping accommodation was now found for us in tents. But the mischief was done. no sooner had we settled down in our new quarters than the rains descended and the winds blew and drove us out again. After this, we dug deep trenches round the tents.

Orders were now given for sparking-plugs to be removed from all the Fords, an indication that the cars were to be left standing (the one and only road to Lindi being locked by the rains). The plugs were accordingly removed and wooden pegs put in their places, the wisdom of the latter course doubted. But orders were orders and had to be obeyed. As soon as the work was completed, the rains descended again and the winds blew. To our astonishment we were then told to remove all the wooden pegs and replace the sparking-plugs! The wooden pegs had, of course, swollen with the rain, and, having been driven in tightly (for presumably the cars could not be moved for two or three months, the period of the rains), the utmost difficulty was experienced getting the pegs out again. To make matters worse, water and sand had found their way into the engines despite the effort to make the pegs waterproof, and with all our efforts we could only get a small percentage of the cars to start at all, and that took two days. One man would sit at the wheel of a car, with the top gear engaged, while we all pushed the clogged thing round and round the playground – as the boys called the parking place. One car had to be cranked up by hand, the yellow mixture of water and sand shooting out through the plug holes in spasmodic spurts. The men began to chant –

> See the little Fordies all in a row!
> A man at the engine turns a little handle;
> Puff! Puff! And away they go!

But they didn't go, and there they were left.

Still more orders. Orders were always disturbing unless the reason for them was clear. This time it was an order to move all the tents from – just here, and place them – just there. We could see no early justification for this, but what we could see were the heavy black clouds rolling up from the horizon. We had no notice of the striking of the tents, and the consequence was that all our belongings soon lay exposed to the on-coming storm. And once more the rains descended and the winds blew. It was so severe that some of the bedding and kit-bags lay in two feet of water. Men looked on at this hopeless muddle, dejected and miserable. A sergeant, ill almost to death, stood in the open, indifferent to the rain, and soaked through. He turned deaf ears to my entreaty to him to take shelter, saying that he had given everything he had, and they could now have his body.

Then came still another order, the most incomprehensible of the lot. We had been occupied re-erecting the tents, and drying our things as well as we could. It was the following morning when a small company of about a dozen of us were told off to join a gang of natives and help them unload material arriving from up the line. It was an unprecedented position. Never before had Europeans been put to such a task with natives, and we strongly protested. But to no avail. A European overseer forced us, with threats and bad language, to the work, with savage imbecility spying upon us from the corners of *bandas*. Apart from the terrific heat, we were not in a fit state to do this work, and, indeed, did little or nothing. One of the natives, elated with the equalling of the ranks, in loud protest against our immobility began to abuse us, but a quick blow from someone's fist settled any further argument in that direction. We waited for no dismissal at noon, but took French leave, never going back, and never being required to. I am perfectly certain the sun's power caused many of the extraordinary vacillations that trebled the difficulties of our unenviable experiences in this dark land.

Distressed and depressed beyond measure, we felt that

death and ugliness lurked everywhere. It was in the air we breathed, the water we drank, the sun that warmed our bodies; it crawled on the ground, dripped heavily from the rain-sodden trees, hung suspended in the humid, reeking atmosphere. Every living thing went in fear of its life, or tuned upon another in self-preservation. Human life itself was an embodiment of ignorance and suspicion. It permeated our very souls, turned bright thoughts into dark, and made one long for the fate that he feared. At Mingoya the natives were being buried, six at a time, in common pits. The notes of a bugle sounding the Last Post punctuated beating hearts, as some of our own fellows were put to their rest.

No wonder the place was Avernus-like, and men behaved unnaturally! The food we ate to keep us alive could only be described as *swill*, if a truthful definition is desired. The camp cooks served it out to us with a surly disregard for our bitter complaints, declaring they lived on it themselves. But investigation revealed the fact that these men, while pretending to subsist on this stuff, regaled themselves, in secret, with feeds the like of which we had never seen since we first landed in the country. On charging them with the deception, they showed sullen silence. On pressing our point, they used choice army expressions that closed the subject forever.

Had it not been for my fat friend Mercer, who knew sufficient about Mingoya to be able to return from mysterious nightly excursions laden with fruit in the form of delicious mangoes, I should have quickly followed the rest of my companions in collapsing daily. Another delicacy for which my friend was responsible was a slice of bacon which we cooked in secret, by night, over the combined heat of two candles . . .

At last, one morning after the break of dawn, we mustered six men, two NCOs and no officers left, out of our original company of one hundred and twenty-five of all ranks, landed at Lindi ten weeks before. The ominous remarks of the one I had designated the optimist returned to my mind as I fell out of the ranks, helped by kindly hands to the hospital...

Away from the strife and familiar odour of camp life, I lay in peace under the double roof of a spacious marquee in the hospital grounds, free from the heat that day after day sapped one's vitality; the sun that seared one's brain with a virulence that stunned; away from the signs of disease, the evidence of dirt, and the pest of flies – the pugnacious flies that entered the mouth, sucked the very juices from one's eyes, nose and ears, with a voracity that allowed them to be killed in the act! The tent was heavenly, sun-proof, fly-proof, delightfully cool, and quiet with a soothing peace.

All the day – my natal day – I lay on an easy bed, waited on by a kindly doctor and a considerate orderly. In the evening I talked with fellow patients and the orderly on homely things under the glow of swinging lamps.

On Sunday, Mercer with a friend visited me. His kindly red face reddened more when I playfully chided him on grumbling because I had disturbed his sleep. "Thought I was *snoring*, didn't you, old boy!" I said. He turned his head away to conceal a smile and a slight twitching of the lips. But we soon had the whole company laughing again. This time the story was of a Scot somewhere up the Lindi line who was trying to teach his "boy" to say, after him, "Och, bonny Scotland! If ye could only see how ah'm sufferin' for ye noo!" The native's sorry efforts to repeat this lingo so upset the loyal Scot that he threw a boot at him which caught him fairly on a tender spot. "Och, bonny Scotland!" roared the injured one, "bonny Scotland *hapana mzura*! (no good!)"

In a day or two I was passed well enough to go down to Lindi. But it was a poor band of wearied humanity that made its way slowly to the creek. Boarding a boat, we duly arrived at the little settlement at the mouth of the river – I with no actual recollection of the journey. We all bestirred ourselves on arrival, however, enjoying the luxury of a cold bath, lingering over the refreshing, soothing influence. In a hospital tent in the grounds of the old Arab fort we found sweet solace lying abed in the cool evening, half conscious, but blissfully aware of the great peace that had come to us; the while a vision in white flittered by – a gentle hospital nurse – the first white woman we had seen since leaving Cape Town.

My last night in Lindi was peacefully romantic. There was nothing to do but watch the lights bobbing about among the huts and between the trees, the reflection from lights on small craft in the river, and more lights seen in the dark recesses of the thickly wooded hills across the water, suggesting mysterious and lonely habitations of natives. Fireflies made circles of magic light beneath the trees. High in the sky was the new moon. For several nights the warning of the *ngoma* drums had been heard, and now came the sounds of revelry, the frenzied beating of the drums, the high-pitched chanting of many voices:

Typical Field Hospital in the Coastal belt.

>Come, fill the pombe-bowl with wine,
>For now is dance and singing time.
>Watch the maid with sparkling eye!
>Nay, fear not the lion's cry
>While the camp-fires burn up high!
>*Mzuri sana! Mzuri sana!*

It was a typically Eastern night! Under the black, velvety sky of a million stars, imagination carried one to where dusky throngs were wriggling their bare bodies in the fitful glare of fires, excited faces turned upward, elated; laughing eyes rolling round, pearly teeth grinning white between thick, parted lips. As I turned in, the sounds of the all-night festivity followed me into flights of fancy – to Durban, where we were bound on the morrow.

Next morning, soon after daybreak, we were afloat, sailing out to a large, two-funnel steamer we could see patiently waiting for our arrival some miles out in deep water. To our surprise she turned out to be one of the giant Cunarders. An Atlantic liner out in this god-forsaken spot! – the *Caronia*.[36] Her passengers – mainly war units and civilians from India and intermediate ports – with undisguised curiosity watched us come aboard, fascinated by our woe-begone and motley appearance, palpable evidence of hard adventure in Africa's mysterious confines. Our presence at once gave rise to a great deal of animated discussion. No sooner was the last man on board than the great ship swung round and headed for the open sea.

How glorious to feel once more the life-giving ocean breeze cooling one's fevered brow, blowing strongly through one's scanty clothing, and bringing new life to men half dead! How delightful to taste the salt in the thin wisps of fine spray that occasionally rose to kiss tenderly the hot lips of those who courted the caress! What joy to stand barefooted on the open deck and feel the heave of the ship responding to the swell of

[36] RMS *Corinia* – built for Cunard 1904, armed merchant cruiser until 1916 when converted to a troopship. Returned to Cunard service 1919.

the ocean! – and with nothing to do all day but dream of the past, and hope good things for the future. That night I thought I could hear the call of the *ngoma* drums – so much does Fancy trick one . . .

As I had received no mail since leaving England, it was interesting to learn from Alex de Bussy, who had been stationed at Lindi, that there was an accumulation of mail there. The neglect to distribute it earlier was remedied at Durban, where every man received what mail was due to him. The distribution was not equitable, for where some received as many as twenty letters, others got none at all. The latter thereupon were permitted to read the letters of the more fortunate, which they did, with mixed feelings . . .

On the voyage to Durban every man was ordered a bottle of stout a day by the doctor, an order that was carried out with a due regard for what was right and proper! But some managed, by the exercise of a little ingenuity, to augment the benefits to be derived from the assimilation of such agreeable medicine. It was the only time within the knowledge of many that the teetotaler's lack of taste was appreciated.

On arrival at Durban the great ship broke her mooring ropes, which snapped like string, and she had to be coaxed by the gentle nosing of several tugs from the outside before she consented to come alongside the landing-stage. Her massive presence naturally created a good deal of interest, and many people were on the quay to welcome us. We disembarked at once.

Durban – a name with which to conjure magic thoughts to all who know her charms, as she is known in all the four corners of the world. "Know Durban? *Rather!*" is generally the accepted term of acknowledgement. Those who have enjoyed the warm hospitality of the garden city of South Africa know how blessed the town is with a fascinating climate and a beauty all its own. Every morning the semi-tropical sun rises in rich splendour over the distant edge of the sea, and beams generously upon the coastal town all day long; the whole of the broad, open streets, the harbour, the sweeping bay on whose sparkling surface flicker the white wings of boats belonging to the local yachting club, is flooded in a light of transcendent brilliance; the whole of Berea, the residential quarter, spread out amid the dense mantle of green trees on the steep slopes of the hill behind the town, is caressed by the sun's exhilarating, benevolent embrace. Its charm is appealing, alluring, seductive.

We enjoyed our experiences of Durban. As men from the Old Country, we were given hospitality without the asking.

Socially, music predominated. Most of our evenings were spent at the Hut, West Street, where Mrs Vincent, the vivacious leader of an orchestra of sixteen lady performers, held sway.

Through the influence of this charming lady, the more musically inclined were invited to a greater number of social functions than we could possibly attend.

During the day the daughters of prominent city men sat with smiling faces at the wheels of their automobiles, ready to take the boys a run round the country.

In fact, everything was done that was possible to add to the enjoyment and comfort of those who were looked upon as guests of the city. To all the willing lady-helpers, to all the residents of the town itself, we were grateful for the sacrifice made on our behalf, and for the many unforgettable kindnesses we received. It even went so far that a stranger in the street, from whom we had made a casual inquiry, emptied his pockets of all the money he had, and startled us by inviting us to take the lot! Truly, as one of our fellows said, "East Africa was 'ell, and Durban was 'eaven!"

Among the wonderful variety of cosmopolitan life in Durban's thoroughfares was the rickshaw boy. There were many of him! Dark, swarthy Zulus they were, adorned in ostrich feathers, bullocks' horns sweeping from the forehead, clothed in leopards' skins, beads and cowrie shells dangling from their bare arms and open necks. Big-limbed and not without artistry, they smeared their skins in coloured pigment, their arms and legs grotesque in white, elliptic designs. They solicited custom by blowing lustily on a horn, or bellowing with the mouth. Frequently they sprang into the air, completing the illusion that they were wild animals. But they were ready to be "tamed" for a small consideration. Through these gymnastic gyrations and daily service they were abnormally developed, especially in the calves. These boys would run for miles, their action really graceful as they took long, easy strides, and, if down-hill, would, with dexterity, balance themselves between the shafts of their light, two-wheeled vehicles for moments together. But let the novice passenger beware at the psychological moment of these balancings! Should he lean forward, or should he lean back, over goes the whole show, and the volcanic language would flow in two different tongues.

Now for the other side of the picture.

When we landed at Durban we were sent to the wooden huts at Congella Camp on the outskirts of the town. Very soon we realised conditions there to be so bad as to cause us to ponder deeply. To err is human, and lapses of sound judgment may be excused at times, but the state of affairs as we found them at Congella Camp, and as they afterwards developed, baffled our common and unenlightened intelligence. On leaving England, the evidence of trouble taken, money expended, and ingenuity exercised to enable the successful collecting and shipping of a large body of men for service to foreign parts, was all too obvious to the meanest understanding. But, strange to say, during the voyage we were so badly off for food (as already recorded in an earlier chapter) that nearly everybody suffered from skin eruptions as well as hunger. The vital question of food supply seemed to be of little account – a serious drawback this to troops who had to face arduous duties. When they arrived at their destination they weren't fit to face a looking-glass. It was the same when we got up-country: nearly starved to death when there was plenty of food in South Africa that could easily have been brought up the coast to us. I will not have it that the supposed difficulties ever existed. When, at last, men collapsed and were carried into hospital, nothing was too good for us. One might just as well deny food to a growing infant, and then coax it back to life again with liberal doses of soothing syrup. As useless hospital patients we had a Cunard liner to bring us down to Durban, the doctor prescribing – as he should know – first-class treatment in food and liquid. This put us in the best of good spirits.

But what happened when we arrived at Congella Camp? We were paraded and informed by a commissioned officer that this was a rest camp and from that moment we were to consider ourselves on holiday. Where would be no drills; no work beyond light, personal duties. And we were to have every day off from two o'clock till ten. "I hope you men will appreciate this," he concluded, "and hurry up and get well again for duty in about two months' time." This was bracing news which we cheered to the echo.

Then in stalked the two official humbugs, "Messrs Confuse and Confound!" While we had no reason to complain of the food, which was excellent and plentiful in camp (seeing that there was also a plethora of it in town), to our great surprise we were put on drill and physical jerks every morning, a flat contradiction to what had been promised. As for Congella being a "rest camp", this was a misnomer. It was so "restful" that we had to sit on the floor, as there were no benches, no tables, and no beds. In fact, we simply lived in empty huts – very simply. Then the duties of guard were foisted upon us. At first it was only a small guard, which made a question of protest difficult as it would savour of pettiness. In time, the drill and physical jerks developed into doubling at full speed round the parade ground, when we felt like a lot of old cripples pretending to be young again. The guard also, by now, had extended to bring every man into it. Then, one fine day, all afternoon leave was stopped. That did it! There was no question of the men having taken advantage of this privilege. No reason was vouchsafed the men for this autocratic action, so, without any further parley, the men all went on strike. So strong was the feeling of hostility that an open riot was feared, especially when stones began to hurtle through the air, over and above the men's booing and yelling.

The men's grievance against authority was that there had been distinct breaches of good faith.

A return at least to the afternoons off was demanded, and at last, under pressure, reluctantly conceded.

There were some NCOs who were "old army stiffs" amongst this little band of city men, used to dealing only with "regulars", and unable to discern the difference between such and the present company. Certainly they were unable to realise that these men, although Tommies, were capable of interpreting an officer's spoken words.

We entered this camp three hundred strong. Within a few weeks we were reduced to an active contingent of sixty only. Naturally, the guard was so depleted that those of us who were left were in the unhappy position of having to do a twenty-four hours guard every other day! And this was a rest camp! Can it be wondered at that some of the more outspoken ones consigned their "superior officers" to a sphere of lurid light?

The men held a meeting and decided that, on the following morning, when the sergeant called "Fall out the sick!" we should *all* fall out. Well, this was done, with the exception of an insignificant few who failed us at the last moment. When the sergeant – this particular one secretly sympathetic – saw ninety per cent of his men fall out, he survived the shock by hiding his face behind his hand, grimly remarking, "That's buckled up the guard all right!"

We were all marched off to the medical officer. Indifferent at first, he soon became interested in the tale of woe that was imparted to him by chosen spokesmen. By his surprised look we could tell that he had only a vague idea of the true state of affairs in this camp. He came outside, had a look at all the men standing there, spoke to the NCO in charge, and then, returning to his hut, with one sweep of the pen drafted every man into hospital or, as an alternative, "excused duty" . . .

I was amongst those drafted into hospital – on Ocean Beach where the very waves dashed almost to the doors – and when I walked through the wards I was greeted with chirpy cries of "Hello! Here's Merry and Bright at last!"

We were treated capitally in this hospital. The great object of our being there was to get our strength back, and now that we had every opportunity and encouragement we were all gradually getting better. Some of the men developed into very bad fever cases and were treated elsewhere. These were the exception.

There were Dutchmen there, a hardy, rough lot. They were against us in the Boer War but on our side today, and fine fellows most of them were. They liked to be called South Africans, especially the younger men, who were blessed with robust health and good looks. But some were not very particular in their manners, and if they wanted to expectorate through the window – well they did. One continued to do so, though rebuked by the nurse; therefore, as a punishment, she took away the flowers that decorated his table; and, unconscious of any offence, he was much surprised, brusquely suggesting a volcanic destination for the flowers and the nurse with them. Upon this, she made some pretence of tidying up and whispered as she left the offender, "*You are pretty enough without flowers!*" the next morning he woke to find himself buried under a collection of blooms from all parts of the ward and the perplexed nurse looking down upon him in anger. She thought he had collected them himself and would not accept his denial. The boys had had their revenge!

During convalescence some of us were privileged to be invited to a cricket match. Generous-hearted motorists whirled us out into the sunshine, for miles along the winding, leafy lanes to the rendezvous. During the match we were entertained by the ladies, who in their turn demanded an account of our thrilling East African experiences, the while they handed round the tea and cakes . . .

That night, when we had all turned in, some wag shouted: *"Fall in 'The Guard!'"* We all fell asleep.

A privileged twenty patients were sent up from hospital to complete convalescence at Caister House,[37] the property of Senator the Hon Walter Greenacre, lent to visiting troops from East Africa. Off we went, in a waggon that seemed entirely of iron, with no springs – at least I didn't notice any, all my attention being absorbed in seeing that I was not chucked out! Up the long, winding hill we clattered, the team of mules urged on by our picturesque driver, who handled the reins and wielded the long whip in the manner born to the Kaffir. A turn to the right and an entry through the wide open gates brought us to the house which, to all intents and purposes, was to be, to us, a private residential hotel.

I cannot speak too highly of the warm hearts that prompted the idea of lending the house, and of extending to us the generous and kind hospitality we all enjoyed while staying in this beautiful home. We had nothing to do but stroll in the gardens, play games on the lawn or tennis courts, walk into town and be back at a reasonable hour, and for food we were supplied with as much of most excellent quality as we required, under the direction of a kindly matron and a staff of genial, warm-hearted sisters. Medical attention was from a visiting doctor every morning. Truly, at this time, every glorious summer day was a long daydream.

It was my pleasure and privilege to be taken round the extensive four acres of gardens by the custodian, Mr Moore,

---

[37] Caister Lodge, 264 Musgrave Road, Durban, a two storied house (now an upmarket retirement house), significant as an example of developed Tudor Revival. The original building on this site was erected c1890 by Sir Benjamin Greenacre, prominent entrepreneur. (Independent on Sunday
https://www.iol.co.za/ios/behindthenews/greenacres-durbans-harrods-38541657)

inspecting the orange, lime, lemon, grape, fig, and other trees almost too numerous to mention, the red-flame trees, Dutchman's Pipe, creepers, roses and acacias. We walked through the well-stocked greenhouses to see a selection of rare tropical plants from all parts of the world, and we visited the tiny banana plantation. Mr Moore was naturally proud of his trust, and boasted, with truth I believe, that it was the finest horticultural collection in South Africa.

Naturally, we were keenly appreciative of all these many kindnesses. I should like to record the names of those who were more directly responsible for our welfare: they were Matron Roberts, and Sisters Percy, Francis, Power, Jacobs, and Wheeldin.[38]

When Sister Jacobs left for a holiday to Jo'burg we boys quietly subscribed a present, and saw her off at the station. I was late, and in my anxiety to be included in the final handshaking, the boys joined in assisting me to reach Sister's hand – the carriage window being high above the platform – so heartily as to push me clean through the window. I got good-bye in all right, and dashing from the carriage – it was a corridor train and I had a long way to go before I could get out just as the train started off – I came face to face with Lieutenant Grosse of Messrs Clap and Trap. "Hello, Campbell; merry and bright as usual!" he said.

After three weeks at Caister House I found myself back at the "rest" camp, peeling potatoes as a special favour to allow me to get off free in the evenings – a false representation during the day, my natural self at night – a sort of Jekyll and Hyde existence. But it deserved its purpose, enabling me to enjoy a good deal of liberty, even to midnight and sometimes later.

Guard duty was resumed as men petered back in some strength. The real effectiveness of the guard was apparently of no consequence, for it is a fact that there were men

---

[38] Records are in South Africa.

standing guard over a prison close by with fully loaded rifles who had never fired a shot in their lives. "They couldn't hit a blooming gasometer," one man forcibly declared, "not if they fired at it point-blank! It would be any odds on a convict escaping if he only had the sentry to contend with!"

I could not, neither did I wish to, escape my share of guard duty. My station was at the Point – a quiet, deserted spot near the harbour mouth, where opportunity for rest and writing and reading in the guard room was welcome. The members of the guard relieved one another during the night, the one in charge allowed to sleep till morning, when, to his assumed surprise, he was wakened to enjoy a refreshing cup of tea. Some pretence of annoyance for not being called every regulation two hours had to be indulged. But the active members of the guard had advanced views concerning "folks in authority": "Let sleeping dogs lie!" was their comment. On this occasion I happened to be the sleeping dog.

One sunny day a singular incident happened in the vicinity of the Point. From the direction of the dock gates a runaway team of mules attached to a waggon tore down the fairway, driverless, with harness loose and chain rattling amid the thunder of hoofs. At full speed they missed one massive standard in the middle of the road, but ran full tilt into the next, the pole dividing the team, the mules, thus held up, swinging together with terrific force, and with a loud crash. One lay dead. The remainder, on their backs, entangled in harness and mixed up, kicked and struggled. A horse in a trap (unattended) bolted after the runaways at full speed, and landed in the midst of them with another resounding crash. The sight of the heaped-up wreckage round the standard was heightened in sensational character by the frantic struggling of those animals now on their feet and trying to get away. Several succeeded in this, and careering madly, fared very badly, one at least being killed instantly against some packing cases. With the others now out of action from wounds and exhaustion, the incident ended.

Before we left Durban, De Bussy, Bunn,[39] Shaw[40] and I made many excursions, which included a visit to the races. A whole half-day was spent in the native market, where one could buy anything from a tooth-comb to a lion's skin. Or, if one had sufficient faith, one could buy bottles of a concentrated mixture of reptiles' heads and tails, sworn medicinal remedies for any ailment, from a touch of toothache to painful spasms supposed to be endured by those unfortunate ones possessed with devils. The people who traded in these markets were a curious mixture of all sorts, and all nationalities, from the Eastern ports, South Africa, inland countries, India and from Arabia. Over all hung the pungent, heavy smell of the East, so overpowering as to drive us out long before curiosity was satisfied.

One fine morning, in the middle of April, we were asked on parade if we considered ourselves well enough to resume duty.

Those of us who were really well (and had a conscience) said "yes," for, after all, we had had a wonderful time.

The next day a large number of us embarked on the *Ingoma* and, once more, found ourselves steaming up the far-flung East African coast.

---

[39] Staff Sergeant Charles W Bunn, Army Service Corps M2/078813 (WO 372/3/170308)
[40] Shaw - unable to trace

Chapter 9

When General Von Lettow-Vorbeck crossed the Rovuma River he was conscious of the fact that the coming of the rainy season, and the hopelessly long-drawn-out lines of communication, would make it impossible for us to follow him into the remote regions of Portugal's wild and forest-covered colony. He could gain no decisive victory against our troops, and his object was now to keep as many of the British forces as possible away from the principal seat of war – Europe – by engaging them in a hopeless and futile chase after him and his hardy little band of followers as they retreated into the dense bush. That he was determined to do this, and to hold the field at all costs, in the face of great privation and difficulty stood very much to his credit.

The situation as it was then is better understood when it is realised how successfully warfare in the bush can be prolonged by a determined enemy resourceful enough to maintain himself, and clever enough to take full advantage of the bush to cover his hide-and-seek policy. Tens of thousands of square miles of forest, a good deal of it tangled and impenetrable, and little of it permitting a wider range of sight than twenty to a hundred yards, wild tracts of barren scrub and great mountain ranges, effectively hid Von Lettow from view. With his main force in the background, scouts and small mobile fighting parties roamed about and kept him informed of the movements of his enemy. Past experience had shown that when opposing forces met, Von Lettow would fight so long as he held the advantage, but did not hesitate to retreat as soon as this policy was deemed prudent. If the advantage were not entirely in his favour, rearguard actions kept off the enemy until he had got clear – not a difficult operation in the bush. These, then, were his tactics until he saw a favourable opportunity for taking the offensive, when he struck, and struck hard, with his entire force, retiring immediately no further achievement could be gained. Detachments of British troops, in their following-up efforts to locate the enemy, often fell victims to ambush, as helpless to avoid disaster as the lonely stranger groping his way down

Port Amelia—from the Harbour.

The Harbour—from Port Amelia.

an unknown and dark lane to the waiting miscreant.

It is very clear that Von Lettow anticipated this war when he landed in East Africa in January 1914. He made every preparation to meet it. He spied in British territory, made himself familiar with the frontier boundaries, and travelled right through German East. When on a journey of inspection to Lindi, he fell down a rocky hole and got water on the knee, which put him out of action for some time. Unfortunately, he recovered!

When the Great War broke out there was a popular feeling in East Africa that no fighting would take place there because of the native element which would be drawn in. It was unthinkable that European-trained blacks might be pitted against whites, no matter about nationality. But the popular opinion was a fallacy and this hideous form of warfare commenced. The Germans were the first to start, and they invaded British East Africa. For the first twelve months they did very well, having it practically all their own way. But when, at last, the apathetic British began to make war,[41] they drove the enemy completely out of German East Africa in two years – a creditable performance.

Towards the end of this time – which was about the date the *Port Lincoln* arrived[42] – the Germans were on the Lindi line fighting against our troops, who were half dead for want of food and worn out by long, forced marches. The Germans themselves were, by comparison, well fed and fresh: well fed because they lived on the country, fresh because they were in the position of a waiting force. They also possessed that undeniably valuable quality, the will to win. Of that there was no doubt, and it reflected itself in the determined, and sometimes desperate, manner of their fighting. It was equally certain they were determined to continue the struggle at all costs. It was a matter of knowledge that the British forces wished to end the campaign because of the

---

[41] The big push started in February/March 1916 following the arrival of a contingent from South Africa under the command of Jan Smuts.

[42] October/November 1917

protracted killing and maiming of white men by their own trained black troops, one against the other, which had a sickening effect on the minds of all decent-thinking men, and this was undoubtedly a strong motive for our sending over a flag of truce to the Germans with the object of bringing it to an end.[43] The suggestion, too, was that as the fate of these colonies could only be determined on the battlefields of Europe, it was futile to continue. However, the German commander must have thought otherwise, for our overtures were rejected.

The fighting on the Lindi line resulted in some of the hottest engagements of the campaign, with a loss of over a thousand on the British side, the Germans having decidedly the best of it. Here was cut to pieces all that was left of that staunch little band of Legion of Frontiersmen – the 25th Batt. Royal Fusiliers.[44]

Captain Tafel with two thousand troops, European and Askari, was farther up country, making efforts at joining up with his confrère, Von Lettow, but got lost in the bush, and, being pressed by our troops, was forced, like Von Lettow, on to the Rovuma River. Even here desperate efforts were made to get in touch with his brother commander, but the silent bush revealed nothing, and day by day there was no response to his call. Thereupon, thinking all was lost, and further effort futile, he surrendered.[45]

Von Lettow's company was not averse to throwing up the sponge after the Lindi line engagements and viewed the crossing of the Rovuma River with ill-favour. But the commander's wonderful forcefulness and magnetic personality over-ruled. It must not be thought, however, that loyalty alone was responsible for keeping the black troops together. It was the plan of the German to place his native

---

[43] 30 September 1916, see Anne Samson, *Britain, South Africa and the East Africa camaoign 1914-1918: The Union comes of age* (2006/2020) for details.

[44] For more on this unit, see www.25throyalfusiliers.co.uk and https://frontiersmenhistorian.info

[45] 28 November 1917

soldier on a higher social scale, far above that of any other native. It was forcibly instilled into the mundane minds of ordinary native folk that "a German Askari could do no wrong!" – so it was written. The German Askari therefore had become a bit of a martinet, and it was a good deal fear of humiliation of pride if he were beaten, and consequent liability to jibes from his menial friends on his inglorious return to the homelands, that forced him to continue the struggle. Von Lettow was courageous (and cunning) enough to allow these men all the latitude and wild freedom they desired. They had as many *bibi* (wives) as they wanted, and babies were born to become new members of this cavalcade, being carried about on the backs of their mammies. The native soldiers were taught and encouraged to assert their will on all and sundry, and they made full use of it. Thus was the spirit of "Germany over all" preserved. English civilian prisoners caught up country and in the hands of the Germans had been forced to do work that only the meanest native would do, and this was before the faces of jeering natives – a pretty German way of dealing an irrevocable blow to British prestige in the eyes of the native. Von Lettow subsequently denied responsibility for this, but nevertheless it was true, reflecting badly on the German system if not on Von Lettow himself.

Thus did the Germans cross the Rovuma River and enter Portuguese territory, imbued with the idea that they were invincible. A quick and determined attack on the weak Portuguese garrison stationed on the other side of the river resulted in a complete victory for the Germans, the Portuguese flying in panic and leaving behind a mass of stores, including valuable medical supplies, food in plenty, arms and ammunition, that completely refitted the whole German force. Thereafter, mightily pleased with the result of their first encounter with the new enemy, they retired into the interior and hid themselves away amid the broad confines of that elusive country, secure in their natural fastness against any possible outside interference for, at least, the period of the rainy season.

Our troops were then withdrawn from the Lindi line, leaving only a garrison on the river. Some of the regiments were disbanded and sent to their homes, others given a rest before being sent to Port Amelia, the new base for operations in Portuguese East Africa. The troops[46] from the Lake Nyasa, or inland district, after failing to get up in time from the westward (I think it was to these troops we hurried supplies to the Lemasuli River) remained inactive for a time, and then proceeded southward to take up a position of offence from the west, or inland side, of Portuguese territory. In this way, from all sides, it was hoped to round up the enemy when the dry season set in.

This, then, was the situation as we sailed up the East African coast on the muggy little steamer *Ingoma* . . .

On the 23rd we came upon a shallow coastline, so low and flat that it threw into sharp relief the palm-trees that fringed the water like a long line of immobile sentries standing guard over the land. The steamer's head was turned sharply in, and, entering the river's mouth, we came to anchor. We were rather fascinated by our surroundings. Deprived of the breeze we enjoyed whilst the ship perspired under the sweltering heat of the midday sun. Under the great void of empty space above, the flat stretches of shallow country lay insignificantly below, within easy reach of the greedy encircling waters, as if it only required one good-sized tidal wave to engulf the lot. But the waters, far from being turbulent, had the aspect of sheet glass, shimmering quietly under the heat and great stillness. On the almost submerged beach a frail jetty projected for a few yards. A few scattered buildings showed themselves along the water front, rather mean and unpretentious. In their midst, proudly displaying the Portuguese flag – but which hung like a limp rag to the flagstaff – was the government house. With no sign of life or

---

[46] CCW: General Northey's

movement, this was Beira, the capital of Portuguese East Africa. On a narrow strip of golden sand close by lay the old wreck of a sailing ship, its white skeleton ribs bleaching in the hot sun.

This was not our destination, and as night came on we were still lying idly there for no special purpose that we could see. A little distraction – in a double sense – was the arrival of a cloud of hippo-flies. We were soon conscious of their unwelcome presence, as bare arms and legs received vicious little nips from their sharp jaws, drawing red blood – and some red language. This unexpected attack was endured until we could stand it no longer, when everybody thought it was time to beat an ignominious retreat and quickly disappeared below. Here a heated discussion ensued on hippo-flies, their cause and effect, punctuated by condemnatory remarks and a good deal of bad language.

The next day found us still there, wondering what we could be waiting for. More heat, and from the horizon cumuli rolled their white, woolly shapes, tier upon tier into the heavens, curled up and went to sleep. At midday the heat was again terrific, the air, humid and still, over the glassy, shimmering waters. Just as we began to think we had taken root, an order suddenly sprang out, the anchor was hoisted, and we steamed out to sea.

A breeze once more. The land behind soon disappeared and the great, white wool-packs that had been with us all the morning gradually receded and lost their shape astern. In long, undulating sweeps the graceful flying-fish sped through the air and broke into ripples the still surface of the sea. Overhead, the fierce sun beat down, while the *Ingoma* steadily thrashed her lonely way onward. The troops on board were content to laze the hours away, with little to do and no inclination to do that. A motley crew, they were composed of all sorts, from the English patriot to the honest Boer farmer now in with the common cause. For my part, as I lay out on deck, taking a critical survey of the situation, I suddenly thought of Gilbert's words: "A policeman's lot is not a happy one!" wondering what that great philosopher would have thought of *this* life . . .

The moon was up, flooding sea and land with its pale light, as the *Ingoma* moved slowly into Port Amelia harbour, dropping anchor before the twinkling lights of the little settlement; from other ships, close by, came the murmur of voices. After watching a while, we all turned in. Port Amelia, established on the south side of the harbour, was revealed to us in clear daylight next morning. Scanty and mean little buildings and habitations were scattered along the harbour front; indeed, they were mere mud and wattle structures, with corrugated iron roofs, relieved, however, by a plentiful application of colour-wash. Rising from the low level of the town, the land swept up to a high bluff, which dominated the bay and ended in perpendicular cliffs at the edge of it. The bay itself, eight miles across, and almost completely landlocked, is reputed to be one of the finest natural harbours in the world.

It was with a feeling that strange adventure lay before us that we prepared to go ashore. We were off at once, a hundred and fifty strong. The *Ingoma*'s draught would not permit her to go farther in, so we had to rely on a large number of dhows to carry us successfully from ship to shore. We left amid a succession of clicks from cameras as they were levelled at us by the passengers, a hearty cheer speeding us on our way. Many of the boats went helplessly astray as they made a bee-line for the landing-stage, the respective crews bungling their sails, and steering badly. The result was that many of us had to wade ashore, philosophically taking our wetting all in good part.

Once ashore, we collected ourselves and our gear, and away we went, marching to the top of the hill, where we lingered a while to recover breath. Port Amelia, with its ramshackle little buildings, appeared small and insignificant at our feet. In the harbour the tiny *Ingoma* could now be seen slowly making for the open sea. Close at hand was the governor's house, and the police barracks standing out boldly on the high eminence. These prominent buildings were plainly square-built, thick-walled, and white-washed. Venetian blinds protected the open windows from the sun's glare. On the very edge of the bluff an array of old muzzle-loaders gaped vacantly across the water.

Another tramp of ten minutes over the hard sun-baked surface of the hill-top, with a long left-handed sweep towards the coast again, brought us to where the motor transport tented camp was pitched – with a splendid view of the ocean.

Bunn, Shaw, Thompson and I had a tent to ourselves which we promptly made our home. It was Saturday and we felt like taking a holiday, and, especially as no one came near us, we took it. Hearing that Harris was in camp I made a search for him. At first I failed to dig him out. Eventually I risked inquiry from an eccentric-looking little man who stared at me through a huge pair of tinted goggles. I asked him if he could tell me where Harris, the pianist, was (a man's accomplishments, or otherwise, were always mentioned in tracing elusive members). A thin, wheezy voice sorrowfully replied: "Oh yes! I *should* know!" and it was Harris himself! His laugh was as hearty as my surprise was complete. He had altered somewhat since I bade farewell to him at Dar-es-Salaam, and the wearing of goggles disguised him. Glad to meet once more, we marched off, arm in arm, to compare notes and exchange all the news in the YMCA *banda*. He had been in Dar-es-Salaam the whole of the time, felt the heat very much, and was glad to be drafted to Port Amelia, where it was not so hot. The question of a concert in the evening, as desired by the OC, was the next consideration, after all our talk was over. This was carried out in the evening with the usual success that always attended these functions. There were officers from the camp and from the ships in the harbour, sisters and nurses from the hospital, and three hundred men, all with happy, smiling faces. One turn followed another in rapid sequence on the little stage with its miniature appointments and effective lighting, assisted by a tiny orchestra of three – Harris at the piano, Mounce[47] on the violin, and Green[48] joining in lustily on his cornet.

While preparations were being made to leave Port Amelia for up country, a great deal of doubt existed as to the location of the Germans, what they were doing, and what they were likely to do. A fast-moving German patrol had penetrated to the coast and looted the little town of Lurio, at the mouth of the river of that name, and had disappeared again into the bush (the bush is very thick all round these parts) before the astonished inhabitants had realised that they had been favoured by a visit from the enemy. Port Amelia itself was a bit too strong for a small patrol, but quite worthy of attention from Von Lettow himself; so, perfectly aware of the danger, an SOS was sent out. In such haste were British troops sent to strengthen the port that the ship ran ashore, and twenty-four precious hours of inactivity had to be endured before getting off again. More hurry less speed. They arrived, however, in sufficiently good time to cause Von Lettow to change his mind. He never turned up.

The Germans had the extraordinary advantage of the friendship of the natives of the country, who, oppressed and heavily taxed by their Portuguese overlords were only too glad of the opportunity to welcome the Germans as their deliverers and friends. The natives looked upon the British as enemies because they were on the side of their Portuguese masters. The Portuguese themselves hated the very sight of us because it was through us that their peace had been disturbed, the country invaded, the natives upset, and their property threatened. "Besides," as one Portuguese official said with grave suspicion, "the Germans may come and go,

---

[47] Either Stephen J Mounce, Army Service Corps DM2/179533
(WO 372/14/125695) OR Thomas A Mounce, Army Service Corps M/314894
*WO 372/14 125697)

[48] Green - unable to trace

but the English have a way of *coming* and *staying!*" The Germans fostered this belief for all they were worth. Thus we were literally surrounded by enemies.

Small bodies of troops were now arriving fairly regularly, to leave again immediately by sailing across the bay to a little place called Bandari, the starting point for the journey up country. There was an alternative land route which led round the head of the bay, but so bad was the road that the journey across the water was preferred, notwithstanding natural drawbacks, for the landing was of the worst possible kind, with long, shallow stretches of water and mud to negotiate first.

Many of our own transport drivers had now gone, following the troops across the bay, and the camp was nearly empty. Unlike the usual jovial way of the men when they marched off with a song and a laugh, all units for up country left in silence. A sharp order, and merely the steady tramp of their feet could be heard. Apart from the ordinary risk of campaigning, the district they were bound for had an evil reputation in Port Amelia, especially for blackwater. Detained in camp on local transport work, my duties carried me on a Ford up and down the hill, ceaselessly, from dawn till dark, and on again into the night by the aid of the moon. In the little settlement the shops were closed and the suspicious occupants out of sight, but hunger and an ungovernable craving for fruit if I could get it drove me to enter the dark portals of a store that had its doors half open. But my visit was received with hostility, and I was not at all comfortable when angry voices left me at last, alone in the darkness.

One afternoon during the week I came unexpectedly face to face with the commander-in-chief himself, General Van Deventer.[49] His presence in Port Amelia was not generally known, so it was with a good deal of surprise that I saw this well-built, rather massive man suddenly emerge from a

---

[49] Jakob Louis van Deventer (1874-1922), South African General

wooden hut and stand talking a while, surrounded by a staff of officers. The striking personality of this South African soldier and diplomat was apparent. Of middle age, he affected a dark moustache and a goatee, and seemed shy of manner as he repeatedly tapped his leg with a cane, and changed his weight from one leg the other. As he looked up he was smiling, and altogether there seemed a quiet air of confidence as he and his staff moved away.

The concert party from HMS *Talbot*[50] came ashore at the week-end and gave an excellent entertainment in the YMCA *banda*. In my effort not to fall below their high standard I appeared in full Highland costume (home-made). The effect was disastrous. One of two Jocks at the back of the hall was heard to remark, "Well, if yon's a Scot, I'll eat ma hat!"

On Sunday, volunteers were called to take six Ford ambulance cars up the link, and as the adventure appealed to us, we fell in on Monday at 6 a.m. and took charge.

Away we went: Corporal Robinson (not the Rajah of blessed memory), Corporal Bunn, Thompson, two or three others and myself. We got on the road of bad reputation, passed through a village where the natives all fled, and then began to realise what a bad road really was.

The wheels sank deep in the loose, dry sand. Speed on bottom gear and concentrated energy were required to keep the cars straight, with the addition of skilled driving to prevent the front wheels from locking, or the cars from coming to a dead stop, when of course, it would be difficult to get a start again. As we neared the head of the bay, the road led sharply to the right and dropped down the steep sides of high cliffs – really a continuation of the escarpment from Port Amelia. So reckless did the prospect of descending these cliffs seem that we felt we could only shut off everything, jam the cars into bottom gear, put the brakes full on, grip hard and trust to luck. I have still the impression of a thrilling

---

[50] HMS *Talbot*, light cruiser operating in East Africa May 1916-Nov 1918, ;ogs at https://www.naval-history.net/OWShips-WW1-05-HMS_Talbot.htm

The open Portuguese Road.

"... a broken back axle put an effective end to the day's work."

arrival at the bottom, sliding sideways like a crab and finishing up in a cloud of dust. The others got down in the same way, and the next moment we were careering away across the valley, but not for long. First one stopped, and then another, for minor repairs and changing of tyres. Then, in the middle of the vale, the most serious accident of all, a broken back axle, put an effective end to the day's work. We had travelled eighteen miles in eight hours.[51] From another car abandoned by the roadside we endeavoured to effect repairs, but it was a formidable job and approaching darkness put an end to operations. Taking bearings, we found ourselves on low, marshy land that had been baked hard by the sun, almost surrounded by scraggy scrub and high grasses. A water-hole with the imprint of numerous animals still fresh was close by – too close, we thought, to be pleasant. Beyond that, and consistent with the usual state of nature in these wild and desolate spots, there was no sight of life and all was still – a grim aspect.

Our native boy, whom we had brought with us, soon had a fire roaring merrily and busied himself cooking the evening meal. Profiting from past experience, I had the foresight to bring from Durban a small consignment of oatmeal, syrup, milk, sugar, tea, cocoa, Yorkshire relish and curry, and these things now began to come in useful. From the outset I had a medicine chest which only required to be replenished at Durban.

We packed the cars end to end, and, after enjoying an excellent supper, were content enough to sit around the fire, pipes alight, and wait for someone to tell the first tale.

"Well, I know of one of our fellows," commenced Thompson, "who was taken by a lion, and they buried his remains in an empty petrol tin the next morning!"

"Yes, that's very subtle and to the point, no doubt, but can we have something a little more interesting and less tragic?" asked another.

"Well, how about this one?" suggested a third. "A company of MT men went into the bush to shoot a guinea-fowl. Led by a particularly zealous sergeant who insisted on the strictest silence, the party came in sight of their quarry, and, of course, proceeded to approach with the utmost caution. Within easy shooting distance of the birds, the men waited

---

[51] 18 miles = 28.96km. Walking at an "easy pace" (20 minutes per mile or 12.5 minutes per kilometre) it would take 6 hours.

expectantly for their leader to give the signal to fire, instead of which the sergeant began slowly to retire, even with greater caution than before, directing his men to do likewise. At a loss to account for this remarkable reversal of tactics, and when a safe line of retreat had been gained, they listened, with mixed emotions, to the sergeant's explanation that he had come into full view of a lion, lioness, and four half-grown cubs!"

Another story told of a man who strolled away from the camp in the cool of the evening, but went further afield than he intended. Suddenly a full-grown lion – a huge beast, so it was explained – broke cover, and proceeding to cross the road, stopped dead in his tracks when he saw the stranger, and fixed him with his eyes. There these two stood, each watching for the other's next move.

"Good gracious!" we exclaimed, "what happened?"

"The lion walked off, the man went into hospital, his hair had turned snow-white, and for weeks he lay in bed *ab-so-lute-ly helpless!*"

We all laughed at this, which was followed by another lion story.

A party of MT men were stranded in the bush. They had parked their cars, end to end, and after supper had turned in. They were kept awake by the roar of lions (we turned uneasily to look at the shadowy forms of our own cars as we moved up a little closer to the fire), admittedly nervous as they crouched, rifles handy, within their cars. The roaring came ever nearer. Suddenly the noise ceased, and was followed by a snuffling as first one lion, and then another, came around, until there must have been a dozen of the huge beasts grunting and snarling as they passed and repassed one another in a set determination to break through.

"Well," we all asked breathlessly, "what did they do?"

"Why, nothing," returned our narrator dryly, "they all went off!"

Another episode concerned a luckless MT man who,

suffering from dysentery, left his Ford on the track to rest himself awhile in the quietude of the bush. He saw nothing around; but as be bobbed down, a lion bobbed up, whereupon the poor man bolted, his desire for solitude abandoned. Dishevelled and confounded, he tore off in his car, reaching camp in record time.

Needless to say he also went into hospital...

All these stories were perfectly true, reminiscent of many incidents of a similar kind that took place in these wild parts, where so many men inexperienced in the habits of bush life had been inadvertently thrown together. It was seldom that encounters with lions ended tragically for the white man, for the lion was more familiar with the ubiquitous nigger. In any case, the end of the victim was usually a quick and gruesome affair. The lions – sneaking, prowling man-eaters – generally attacked their prey silently, approaching under cover of night, and with one swift bound seizing the unconscious victim by the head.

And so our talk this night went on. A song followed, and then, the mosquitoes becoming unbearable in spite of the fire, we turned in. But it was a night of torture. Thinking it best not to be entrammelled in the folds of mosquito nets, we lay uncovered all the hot, sweltering night, bitten badly. We might have contented ourselves all the same, for not a sound disturbed the oppressive silence of the long night. At dawn we were glad to rise to activity.

While our boy prepared an appetising breakfast we spent two fruitless hours trying to replace the broken axle with the whole one on the abandoned car. The task was beyond us.

Smiling grimly at the car we had to leave behind – one more relic on the road – we crossed the valley to a nullah, or dried-up river bed, a formidable obstruction, which, after inspection, we charged in the usual reckless manner, down the steep bank, through the heavy sand, the cars behaving like ploughing machines, and up the far side with roaring engines, on to firm land again. Leaving Bandari on the right, it was not long before all our bumps and jolts were forgotten as we gained the high road, relieved to find a hard, flat surface to travel upon. Before us was familiar African bush, an expansive plain covered thickly with scrub and trees, broken only by a great solitary rock that reared its massive head high above the surrounding level. It is doubtful if there are more striking contrasts of scenery in the whole world than are to be seen in such typical stretches of East Africa.

The remainder of our journey, as we travelled on and on for fifty miles, always though bush and numberless trees, was void of incident, and almost void of life. As we climbed a hill from the valley below, the air became laden with the scent of burning wood. To the left was another of those great lumps of solid rock – standing guard, so to speak, over the entrance to the camp – that the Germans tried to establish themselves, but it proved unscalable. Beyond the rock, and spread over the wide surface of a flat plateau, were the many smaller camps of the different units, from the important long *bandas* of the heavy lorry workshops, hospitals, telegraphs, and administration, to the humble camps of working natives with little sleeping places not unlike a collection of beehives, a native bending over a fire preparing the evening meal for the *bwana* who, from the relative comfort of his substantially built *banda* near by, would soon be yelling for his *chai* if it was not there to his beck and call. Armed sentries of native troops stood guard, overlooking the immensity of forest that surrounded this high elevation, staring with immobile aspect in the direction of blue, hazy mountains in the distance. Travelling on till we had nearly passed through the camp, we turned off to the right, and came to a stop in the grounds of the motor ambulance depot, a collection of *bandas*, tents, and a small, improvised workshop. Here we reported our arrival, unloaded our kit, and waited further orders. We were now naturally anxious to hear all the latest news.

Our Camp at Ankwabe.

"They were well fed, eating the food out of one common pot and scooping it up with their fingers."

Chapter 10

It appeared that the Germans were at Medo, a small Portuguese outpost fifty miles higher up the line. They were getting behind our troops and seriously interfering with the British transport that was following.

That it was risky work on the road was confirmed by the news on our arrival that one of our own ambulance men had been killed. The Germans declared later that they did not see the red cross and complained that members of the Corps carried rifles. It was true that wear and tear had slightly effaced the crosses, but they were still prominent enough to be seen from any reasonable distance. We had little confidence anyhow in the level mentality of black troops who were not particular what they shot at. And as for rifles, they were certainly on the cars, but were of little use to a man engrossed in driving, certainly of no use – and not permissible – for defence when covered by a rifle from the blind bush. In any case, we considered ourselves justified in carrying guns as some sort of protection against possible hostile natives and wild beasts . . .

Two of the workshop men, the designer and the blacksmith, made a unique monument for our fallen comrade, built up entirely from sections of an old Ford, and this, suitably inscribed, was erected over his grave by the road-side where he fell. The younger of the two who took on this self-appointed task – AJ Hall[52] – himself fell a victim to fever later and was buried on the line.

Thompson and I were now in the workshop, where all the old crocks – all Fords – were patched up and sent out on the

---

[52] Private Alfred J Hall, Royal Army Service Corps 648 MT Company DM2/154640, died 6 December 1918, died Influenza (WO 372/8/204261)

road again, fair to middling. Our other two companions, Bunn and Carrick,[53] with whom we shared a tent, were sent on the line, much to their disgust, and were away from dawn till dark. While they were on the familiar routine of exhaustion amid dust and dirt, our life in camp was one of comparative comfort. In the workshop we numbered about a dozen, with an equal number of native assistants. The latter were not the Swahili natives we were used to, but local men whose language we did not understand. We had to indicate to them in dumb show what we wanted them to do, and then hope for the best. Their best was usually to stand, looking helplessly on, with an expression like a philosophic monkey. We tried all expedients to improve their intellect but to no avail. Then we lost temper, raved and shouted, but that was worse, for they became quite incapable of anything at all, except to stand in front of us speechless, their naked bodies trembling with fright. Forced into accepting the inevitable and learning to be as patient as possible with these poor fellows, we in time got on much better, and came to understand each other fairly well.

These natives, and the natives employed in *banda* building and in keeping the camp clean, were recruited from villages near and far. The recruiting agent, a South African Sergeant Fineberg[54] by name, I knew

---

[53] Carrick - unable to trace

[54] Sergeant Samuel Fineberg, 185 2/3 South African Infantry Brigade, 5899 East African Labour Corps (WO 372/7/62957)

". . . they arrived fully armed."

very well. He told me stories of fleeing natives and empty villages, of his difficulties and trials when on this peculiar errand. Accompanied by a small party of Askari, his plan consisted of entering a village without ostentation and quietly endeavouring to win the confidence of the head-man or chief, which was not an easy job. His suggestion that the whole of the active male members of the village should be rounded up and handed over to him did not generally meet with the approval of the head-man. His work, therefore, was very difficult and full of pitfall. Suspicion and mistrust were general and the agent was glad, on occasion, to escape with a whole skin, if empty-handed. In some places the very opposite occurred, his appearance being the signal for all villagers to fall on their faces, grovel in the dust, and offer up prayer – whether for his own soul or for theirs was doubtful. They thereupon would bring him fowls, eggs, and milk. But when the question of business was introduced, then the difficulty would begin all over again. Sometimes he was successful, sometimes not. When rounded up and brought to the camp, the new blood arrived fully armed, with spears, bows and arrows. These they had to hand in to the camp authorities, according to conditions agreed upon, until such time as they received their discharge. It was a unique sight to watch these men, more or less in a savage state, passively delivering up their precious weapons ere, one by one, they passed into the camp. They were paid weekly in cloth for wages, with which they appeared immensely pleased, holding lengths of the gaudily-coloured print up to the sun to admire the effect with childish pride. They were well fed, eating the food out of one common pot and scooping it up with their fingers. By their half-starved appearance they looked as if they could do with it too, eating it ravenously. After a week or two in camp, these fellows began to show visible signs of good living.

We came to like our black workshop companions for their unaffected, innocent simplicity. I remember one day

147

watching my boy squirting grease through the bung-hole of the differential gear box. His face was a study. With the inside of a motor car a complete mystery to him, it must be understood that although the actual operation was carried out all right, after I had started him, he had not the remotest idea of the object. He simply squeezed on, slowly and steadily, and as grease squirmed and twisted its way into the little dark hole before him, so his face squirmed and twisted,

The Source of our Water Supply at Aniewabe.
(The Lions frequently came here to drink.)

his eyes glared, his mouth became wide opened, and his tongue hung out. As the operation came to an end, his eyes closed, his tongue disappeared, and his thick lips came to with a click. He then stood up and, deep in mental conflict, contemplated the greedy, gaping bung-hole in rapt abstraction.

But they were not the passive creatures that we took them to be – at least among their own kind. This was obvious from the scars that they bore on their heads, noticeable whenever they bent over their work. There was hardly one in the whole camp who did not show traces of having been well tapped on the head at one time or another. Even in our own camp confines they were fighting, one having to be taken to hospital, where four stiches were put in his head. When he came out they were soon at loggerheads again. They were continuously a source of interest, if only for their outrageously crude conduct.

Our labour in the workshop was really very trying, especially in the heat of the day – dismantling and assembling heavy parts of motor cars. I think the long break for lunch, between twelve and two, kept us from going mad, and five o'clock was a happy release for tea, the day's work ended. An appreciated diversion was that of going on the road with a reconditioned car to tear up and down for testing purposes. While the natives had no fear of stationary cars in camp, they were very frightened on the open road, a rattle or jolt or sound of the horn being sufficient to send them pell-mell into the bush, dropping whatever they were carrying. It may be recorded that I never met one of our fellows who ever sounded his horn with the mischievous intention of deliberately frightening the natives. They were frightened enough, in all conscience, some of them running away and never being seen again, probably returning to their own village.

At the end of each day we had a soft spot in our hearts for our less fortunate comrades, Bunn and Carrick, on the road.

One night Thompson and I specially prepared a tasty repast, which included sliced plantains and onions, done to a turn in bacon fat, and this unexpected feast was ready for our famished and dirty chums when they rolled into camp at sunset. But there was a moment of breathless anxiety when, rather cramped for room in the small bell tent we occupied, the rickety home-made table received a severe jolt from somebody that all but swept the supper to the ground. In the cool of the evening, within the homely light of an oil lamp, and with pipes aglow, the news of the day was exchanged. Bunn and Carrick had covered a hundred miles, they said, and this set off an argument between the two, as to who did the most work. The agile Charlie Bunn insisted that he did more during the day than the less active and easy-going Carrick, a puzzling statement to us as they always seemed to leave camp together and arrive back together – in fact Carrick's car was often the first one in, Bunn straggling in soon after. I ventured to say so.

"That's because I have to stay behind to look after him!" declared Bunn.

"You can't stop for me when you are too busy trying to catch me up!" retorted Carrick.

"I'll guarantee we are not on the road an hour to-morrow," said Bunn, ignoring Carrick's remark, "before my honourable friend calls for assistance. You should hear –"

"Half a moment, please," interjected Thompson, who was a bit of a philosopher, "neither of you would be any good if it were not for Campbell here and myself. We keep your jolly old cars running for you!"

"Well, I like that!" snorted Bunn, the rest of us laughing, "Thompson, of the *blowing-up* department" (Thompson was on repairs to punctured tyres) "taking credit to himself for something! Blowing up *balloons* would be more in his line, and would give an added interest to the contour of his features!"

Carrick had been busy cleaning the glass chimney of a

second lamp and was about to light it when Bunn stepped in, seized the glass, declared the work badly done, polished it himself, placed it in position, and lit the lamp with marked improvement. During this time, laughter prevented Thompson from making any reply. Dwelling firstly on the eccentricities of the lighting operation, he summed up sarcastically with a wave of the hand: "Bunn and Carrick as a combination are simply wonderful! . . . Individually, *no good at all!*"

And so the evening passed.

We came out of the workshop the next morning to wish Bunn and Carrick good-bye, for they were off, with full kit, and the tent as well, rolled up, for an unknown destination. After a few hurried words and a final hand-shake, they were off, almost before we realised it, leaving us looking down at the empty space where our tent had stood.

We had, perforce, to find new quarters and became accommodated in the long *banda* that housed most of the members of our little community. Straw beds, built on wooden frames two feet above the ground, were arranged down each side, the furniture consisting of a few empty wooden boxes. But we were quite comfortable here and became, if anything, more noisy than ever. When not singing, which was a source of great annoyance to our neighbours, there were heated arguments on politics, the war, its cause and effect, and on the exploitation of the native. In the last connection the system that brought about the training of the black man to shoot down the white was strenuously condemned. The philosophic Thompson declared that we had no moral right in the country at all, as it didn't belong to us but to the natives. "And the sooner we are out of it the better!" he concluded. "Hear, hear!" shouted everybody . . .

The latest news from up the line informed us that Von Lettow had retired into the bush. Evidence of the recent fighting showed itself in the arrival of some wounded at Ankwabe for down the line. I went on the road for a while, a welcome change from the workshop, carrying dusky patients as tenderly as the roads would permit, a nasty jolt at times being painfully unavoidable. I learned that there had been some desultory fighting at Medo[55], Von Lettow being content to rely on harassing tactics and gradual retirement. This was satisfactory so far as it went, but disappointing otherwise, as a decisive action had been hoped for.

High up on this hill our camp was healthy enough. We erected mosquito nets every night, though there was little need, if any, for them. But there were plenty of mosquitoes on the line, and also one or two tsetse-fly belts in one of which I happened to stop, unconscious of the fact until I received a needle-like prick on the hand, another on the neck, and as quickly as I brushed the hissing insects away they returned savagely. The only method of escape was to remount the car and dash away. The authorities looked upon the tsetse-fly as a real danger, having to treat several cases of sleeping sickness in the hospital, the first instance, so it was said, of white men contracting this disease (which, by the way, is not to be confused with sleepy sickness).[56] The apprehension led to an order for all "Auto" driers on this route (Bandari-Ankwabe) to be covered to the waist in mosquito netting, and a pretty sight they looked, perched up in the air (an unavoidably exposed position peculiar to these machines) as they drove off – like a procession of vaporous ghosts. No wonder the natives ran when they saw this caravan advancing!

One day, to our surprise, our friend Bunn turned up, but it was a different Bunn from the one we had known. He was ill, and on his way down to the hospital at Port Amelia. We tried to get from him what had happened, but he could do no more

---

[55] 12-24 April 1918; Medo Hill also known as Churimba or Chiriimba Hill.

[56] Sleepy sickness or Encephalytis Lethargica which is not the same as trypanosomiasis. Between 1915 and 1928 approximately 1 million people died of sleepy sickness but is relatively unknown because of the Spanish Flu which caused approximately 5 million deaths worldwide
(https://www.medlink.com/article/encephalitis_lethargica)

than stare at us with pale face and glaring eyes as he was helped into one of our own ambulances. He then departed without a word. It was a bad omen when cheery young fellows were laid out in this helpless and pitiable fashion. Malaria and the sun were the principal causes. Mean feeding and the drinking of water that had not boiled, or boiled long enough, had a good deal to do with it, but both food and water were nothing like so bad here as in German East.

In striking contrast to Bunn's unhappy state was the cheerful, "Hi, hi, Cammy!" from Shaw, as he greeted me from the tall seat of an "Auto," looking down with dirty but happy face, all smiles. I had not seen him since parting at Port Amelia. He immediately jumped down and we exchanged all the news. He was on the road from dawn to dark, he said, doing nothing else but constantly carrying supplies up the line. In reply to my inquiry as to how he liked the heavy "Auto" after the light Fords, he, like many more, complained of lack of protection from the sun, the stilted position of the driver over the front wheels, the consequent increase of jolting and bumping which wore one out, and the heavy work of driving and steering these ungainly machines. However, he was seemingly happy, evinced the greatest interest in my concerns, and then, feeling that time was pressing, mounted his seat, smiled down at me again with his sunburnt face, and dashed off – a typical example of the hardy transport driver.

Besides Shaw, I came into contact with Sergeant Townsend[57] (the one who had to hide his merriment behind the palm of his hand when we all fell out sick at Congella Camp), Sergeants Day and Double,[58] and many more of my old friends. Harris turned up with his ever-present companions – Mounce with his violin, which he carried about him in his kit-bag, and Green with his precious cornet, likewise carried about with great care, though it sustained

---

[57] Townsend - unable to trace
[58] Sergeants Day and Double - unable to trace

one hefty dent which its owner used to look at ruefully. The trio were immediately seized upon by the padre, a real good man to the boys, a hard worker, but helpless with fever – in fact we lost him soon after when he went into hospital. He fixed up a scratch concert in the "church institute" as it was called – a long, barn-like *banda*, open at one end, a raised platform at the other – empty except for a few old magazines and a prehistoric piano full of tiny notes, ants, and spiders. Captain Ash,[59] Lieutenant Dale,[60] and Sergeant Fober[61] were all excellent turns, and the concert was greatly enjoyed by a large and enthusiastic audience; but the sensation of the evening was when one of the troops, by profession a clog-dancer, out of sheer good spirits danced exuberantly right through the platform into four feet of space below. Fortunately, he did not hurt himself, and resumed his seat amid tumultuous applause.

We had not retired long that night before we were awakened by a pungent smell; a strange, muffled, hissing roar came to our ears, and explosions, like jumping-crackers going off, rent the still night air. We noticed a light getting brighter and brighter, and then realised, with a start, that the camp was on fire. We rushed out at once to find a *banda* in the camp, next to ours, well alight, the flames licking the topmost branches of adjacent trees, and throwing a lurid light around.

Nothing could be done. We simply had to leave it to burn itself out, watching that no sparks settled anywhere to start another fire. As these *bandas* were built entirely of dry grasses, bamboo, and wood prop supports, it would have been impossible to save the whole camp if once one got alight but for all the protecting spaces between, which were usually wide enough to prevent any serious danger in this respect. The possibility of having one's personal belongings

---

[59] Captain AL Ash, South African Army Service Corps (London Gazette 8 Nov 1917)
[60] Dale - unable to trace
[61] Fober - unable to trace

destroyed, including camera, photographs, and records, presented itself. On the Lindi line I lost valued photographic records through the abnormal heat, and risks were run when my kit-bag was several times submerged in water, but loss was avoided by the forethought of using waterproof bags.

With no news of Von Lettow, who seemed to have completely disappeared, the tension was relaxed in Ankwabe and on the line. A Sunday ramble, pleasant and idle enough for a hot day, led us through the bush, silent and empty except for the ever-present insect life that hummed around us. The thick scrub and forest trees presently gave place to cultivated spaces. We came upon a cluster of native homesteads where the inmates must have been very shy, as there was not one to be seen. Presently, however, an old darkie appeared and tried to warn us of something we could not understand. With his venerable appearance, kindly, wrinkled face, grey hair and slight stoop, he was a real "poor old Joe." As he spoke to us in slow and measured tone, we could not help seeing in him a striking likeness of the hero of our young days – Uncle Tom in *Uncle Tom's Cabin*. Proceeding farther, we were eventually turned back by dense undergrowth, reviving the doubts created by "Uncle Tom". On retracing our steps we surprised the women at the hamlet, who, on thinking we had gone, came freely into the open. They fled to their houses, like startled rabbits to their burrows. The primitive existence of these lonely inhabitants of the forest, tilling the soil for a bare sustenance, their frail homes protected from outside enemies only by a piece of equally frail bamboo partition, afraid to leave the smoky interior of their homes after dark, without book or occupation of mind, except to croon to the little ones and wait for the drowsy influence of sleep to capture them, was an absorbing subject for reflection.

At midnight a succession of rapid bugle calls woke up the whole camp, and brought everybody tumbling out to ascertain the cause. It was soon apparent. Quick as the alarm had been, a fire had taken a good hold, and in a few moments the whole middle part of a *banda*, a hundred and fifty feet long, where black troops were sleeping, was a raging furnace. Impressive as this sight was, the lurid spectacle was enhanced by the excited antics of the two hundred native occupants who came running out, and, without the loss of a moment, tore away the still unaffected parts of the *banda* to the ground, by sheer weight of numbers hauling whole pieces of roofing and the sides out of danger. The portion in the middle was left to burn itself out. The fire fighters were now homeless and stood in groups, volubly discussing the catastrophe.

The following day, Thompson, who had complained of feeling ill, was admitted into hospital suffering from an attack of fever. Davies,[62] our little Welsh friend, Berins[63] and I visited him later, taking a few little luxuries and comforting him. One could never tell if one's friend was going to recover or pass away.

Since the date of the complete disappearance of the elusive Von Lettow, troops had been slowly returning down the line, work had slackened off, Harris and his friends had gone back to Port Amelia, and I, for once, found myself inactive. A diversion for me was a trip down the line to the relief of a man stranded with a broken chassis frame. Curiously enough I found him to be a man of my own town, Hall[64] by name. He was obviously relieved to see me, not so much for his own sake as for that of his companion who was ill. I had, perforce, to take charge of the sick passenger and leave Hall to make the best of his lonely situation. Like the rest of the boys, he was prepared to put up with anything for the common good. One part of the road was so bad that, in an attempt to make it passable, a layer of straw had been placed upon it, but instead of this being a remedy, it was merely a

---

[62] Davies - unable to trace
[63] Berins - unable to trace
[64] Hall - unable to trace

delusion and a snare. Although aware of possible hidden danger, and in consequence of going dead slow, my front wheels dropped into it with a thud and the front spring snapped. With the fore part of the car banging itself to pieces, we were lucky indeed to reach the next encampment just as darkness had set in. I found an empty *banda* for my suffering companion, saw to his comfort, got his assurance with a smile that he was all right now until morning, then turned attention to my own requirements.

I gladly accepted a warm invitation to join a party of lorrymen who were parked there for the night: Sergeant Henderson, Corporal Bailey, Clipson,[65] and a young fellow from South Africa whom the rest called "Broncho." We were a merry crowd as we made ourselves comfortable in the cab of the lorry, which was just spacious enough to allow us all to get in. With "blinds down" and "curtains drawn," a bottle of White Horse – or was it two? (we had several callers who were invited to "come right in," which was impossible) – and with a box of cigars which had been nicely matured by the natural heat of the country, we were as cosy and happy as in any bachelor's den in Mayfair. The talk was long and varied, and as some of the men had been in the country a long time and knew the ropes, the subjects were wide and peculiar. This interesting flow of conversation lasted till midnight. Then one by one we slipped out into the darkness and were gone, leaving Broncho wedged between the steering wheel and the change-gear lever, still bravely endeavouring to carry on the conversation.

After an excellent night's rest I was up betimes, but being in a state of isolation and without rations, my kind friends of the night before helped me out of my difficulty. I was even fortunate to be able to procure a spare front spring from a breakdown car. This I was able to fit in good time, resuming my journey down to Bandari without further mishap, leaving

---

[65] Henderson, Bailey - unable to trace, Clipson - possibly Private Harold A Clipson, Army Service Corps M2/135832 (WO 372/4/170190)

my patient there in the hospital.

I returned in due course to Ankwabe. Here there was much talk of lions. They had been roaring all night, keeping everybody awake with the noise. They had been seen on the open road by our transport drivers. There was always a fascination about any subject connected with lions. Those reported seen on the road merely looked on on-coming motor traffic with indifference, contenting themselves with a fixed stare of curiosity which lasted so long as the vehicle was in sight. If there was any fear or fright, it was all one-sided. It is true that an Askari and a lion came face to face and the lion bolted; but it was probably due entirely to surprise. An extraordinary incident recorded was that of a lorry full of men, just before entering Ankwabe, sighting a lion by the roadside. He watched the approach of the ungainly vehicle with stately dignity, not deigning to take advantage of the bush as a safe retreat. Where one man of experience might hesitate before raising his rifle to a lion, it was not so with the twenty men in the lorry, who, as they drove close up, blazed away for all they were worth. Without the usual sporting chance, the lion dropped stone dead.

Another remarkable instance of close contact with a lion but a different story with a different ending, was that of a member of our company who had bogged his car late in the evening. He therefore decided to leave it where it was and walk back to the last encampment, which, he thought, was distant about four miles. Throwing his blanket over his rifle, and his rifle over his shoulder, off he went. He had not gone far, however, before his heart gave a jump. By the roadside a lion squatted, its paws stretched out, and its huge head turned towards him. It was too late, as he explained to me later, to turn back, and he found himself in the uncomfortable position of walking past that lion, with the creature's eyes following him. With a coolness and self-possession that he never realised was a personal gift, he walked on in this way, resisting the temptation to look back, until he had gained a bend in the road when, he declared, he never ran faster in his life! He arrived at the encampment, which proved to be eight miles rather than four, in the dark, and in a state of nervous exhaustion and collapse. Here he was quickly made welcome and congratulated on a very lucky escape, as the district was notorious for man-eaters, that had taken quite a number of natives during the past week.

At the Road Corps depot at Ankwabe, lions had walked right through the camp, my friend whom I was visiting showing me the spoor. Evidently they were not man-eaters or there would have been a very different tale to tell of the hundred or so men of the Road Corps who slept there in scanty enough shelter. I reflected on the thrilling possibility of a lion walking in at the open end of our *banda* and passing out at the other, as unconcerned as if the abode were an avenue of trees, an incident that really did occur at least in one instance.

The subject of lions was the topic of the evening on my return to Ankwabe, and, just as we had exhausted the long list of stories to be told, our nerves well on edge, a late-comer dashed in from off the road, all excitement.

"I've seen one!" he yelled, wiping the dirt and perspiration from his forehead; "I've seen a lion! For God's sake don't talk to me of seeing lions again! I was like some of you" – nodding to several of us – "dying to see one, but never again! It was in a dip in the road, and there he was, looking at me straight through the eyes! I felt I couldn't get away from him and swerved all over the road. I was frozen stiff! How I got past I don't know, but when I did, you couldn't see my car for dust!"

A wag, with no sense of shame, shouted "Walk up! Walk up! And see the show! Lions to the right of you, and lions to the left of you! Lions all around you! Why pay money to go to the Zoo when you can see lions out here for nothing? Walk up! Walk up!"

". . . the three chums were duly photographed."

"It was an impressive sight to see their big brothers . . . arrive loaded up with their broken bodies."

Chapter 11

One night an alarming accident occurred in camp that resulted in putting me out of action for the rest of our stay in Ankwabe.

It was our practice to make cocoa every evening on the open fire outside the cook-house, under the light of the stars and hanging lamps, and it was my turn to prepare this pleasant beverage for Thompson (who was well again) and myself – Berins and Davies not caring for it. As I thought of the humorous saying that a watched kettle never boils, and watched patiently nevertheless, all the ingredients ready, for the crucial moment when the cocoa should be added, I became conscious of a suspicious roaring at the back of me that prompted me to look round in some doubt. It was a spirit stove burning, not paraffin, but petrol, cooking porridge. The owner had thought, after charging it well with compressed air, that it could look after itself. It did – so effectively that it burst with a loud report. The whole wretched combination of boiling porridge, burning petrol, and bits of stove caught me full in the back. The several lamps hanging up, and the fire as well, were blown out, so, for a moment, everything was pitch dark and my mind turned a blank.

Then I realised that my legs – I was unfortunately dressed in shorts without putties – were on fire. I began to dance about like one demented, frantically rubbing one leg and then the other, until, probably helped by the wet porridge, the flames were subdued; but, feeling the heat on my back (really more porridge), I thought I was on fire there and called upon Thompson, who was the first to arrive, to, "Put me out, Thompson; put me out!" to which he kept saying, "You are out, Campbell; you are out!" and wondering, as he said afterwards, why I was sceptical about it!

Surrounded by good fellows – the explosion had brought everybody on to the scene – I was hurried off to the first-aid *banda*. Here, when a lamp was brought, I braced myself for the shock I expected, but, happily, although the skin was off my legs and some of the porridge had found its way into my right boot, I had in all other respects escaped serious injury. Some of the pieces of the stove and porringer were afterwards picked up beyond the boundary of the camp. I considered I was very lucky.

That night, in the *banda*, when all the boys were fast asleep, I lay awake, my legs swathed in oil bandages, moaning with pain and not daring to move. Now, if never before, could I hear all the mysterious night noises of the African forest. The yelp and cry of wild animals was sometimes a long way off, at other times quite close. Sometimes I distinguished the distant roar of the lion and the answering call of its mate. A sharp report, just one single crack like the sound of a rifle shot, reverberated into the far distance, and so empty and still was the air that I heard the echo, long after, rebound from the far distant mountains in the form of a faint, hollow bump.

I was glad of the dawn. After paying a visit to the hospital, I was permitted to return to my own *banda*, where I could find better rest and contentment with my friends.

Roughing it as we men were doing out here in this strange wilderness, enduring experiences the like of which had never existed in our wildest dreams, there was a strong inclination to drop into the use of course vulgarisms, and the fear of its becoming a habit forced upon us the feeling for conversation or discussion that would help to keep our minds elevated. These wrangles and arguments also acted as a grand stimulant.

"Are we civilised?" was the subject of the moment. What was the meaning of the word? There was no such thing as civilised warfare. The outbreak of war showed that the state of civilisation had collapsed, real civilisation only existing in our vain imaginings. Our civilisation was merely an effort to attain to the ideal state, and we were a long way off that yet. Had the natives, in their ignorance of the world and in their simplicity, a life nearer *real* happiness than we? Watch them, dancing, laughing, and singing in the sun, like little children! They didn't bother about convention, or clothes, or the passage of time. If their state of mind was a happier one than ours, then possibly they were more civilised than we were!

"And a damned sight more civilised than some of us!" interjected one man with enthusiasm, amid laughter.

Davies, our Welsh friend, who never had much to say, on being appealed to, contented himself by remarking in his quaint English: "Well, gentlemen, I listen; indeed to goodness go on; was all right – isn't it?"

"Ah, well; it will be a good thing when it is all over and we can return home again!" remarked one, at the close of the discussions.

"What?" retorted the philosophical Thompson. "Home? – All over! – Good gracious! What do you fellows want? *I'm* in no hurry! Why, I was never so well off in all my life! Think of it – no business worries; no bills; no rent; no income tax; all food provided free and cooked for you; special times to get up in the morning and special times to go to bed at night; the use of a motor car for nothing, with petrol and tyres free; if it goes wrong, bung it in the workshop and get another! And mark you (with emphasis) a Cook's Tour,[66] personally conducted, free of all expense! What more *do* you want? And, mind you, during all the time, *paid for*!"

A rumour reached camp that Von Lettow had been captured, but we were not convinced. He had been "captured" so many times before. Indeed we began seriously to fear that this elusive Scarlet Pimpernel would never be caught. Admiration for one who had so cleverly escaped the net that had

---

[66] Thomas Cook started tours in 1841, expanding to Africa in the 1880s. The company remained in the family until 1928.

been drawn around him was openly evinced by several members of our company, one man declaring that he would raise his hat to him if he saw him walking down the road. I made the admission that I would like to photograph him. What a third man said had better be left unrecorded. Some natives in the camp, following the lead given by a Swahili, gave voice to the following chant as an expression of their opinion –

Von Lettow, oh!
Von Lettow, oh!
Von Lettow, kwenda! (go away)
Ah!

Handling a disabled lorry, they all gave one big push on the last ejaculation.

An incident of the day demonstrated the inefficiency of the professional native driver. He was seen underneath an overturned Ford, the wheels still revolving in the air. First a dusky bare arm appeared from underneath, groping about in the dust, then a dark face, eyes bulging and teeth chattering, looked out on to an otherwise peaceful world. When the man was released, he stood up trembling in every limb, his knees knocking like castanets. Dazed and stupefied, it was obvious he had had the fright of his life!

With two more fires breaking out in two days, we began to think of the danger from this direction becoming serious. The first was a *banda* connected with the officers' quarters that suddenly burst into flames and was consumed within a few minutes. The second was a much more serious affair. The lorry workshop took fire after midnight. When we looked out, the whole show was going up into the air. Unable to resist the temptation of a close-up view, I hobbled off after the others, setting teeth against the pain that came to my legs through the effort, and arriving on the scene to be dumfounded by the magnitude, intensity, and heat of the blaze. But there was not the slightest panic; in fact it was rather wonderful to hear the roaring of the flames, the exploding of the bamboo, and the crisper noise of exploding cartridges, with not a word from the men who were putting every ounce of energy into helping to save all they could. I joined in the fight, and, entering a *banda*, helped to throw out everything of value. In the excitement we got cut off and were forced into a cul-de-sac. Our cries of alarm brought ready help from outside, and an opening was made in the wall through which we were able to escape. The next moment, where we had been working was a mass of flames. By this time many natives had arrived; they were swarming the roofs, around the sides, and all round the outskirts of the fire, with one object – to isolate the conflagration. In this they were successful. The whole of the workshop, however, with several lorries and material, and four large *bandas*, with kit and personal property, were destroyed. Several casualties resulted from the explosion of rounds of ammunition. As usual, the origin of the fire was a mystery.

I suffered acutely from reaction after my efforts at the fire, the pain in my legs at times almost unbearable. However, it was easier in a day or two, and once more I was able to hobble about the camp with the aid of my stick.

During these lonely and somewhat painful perambulations, I found much to interest and distract me from my woes. My enforced leisure enabled me to study the natives at work, loading, unloading, carrying, and cleansing the camp – the last very important and necessary. Some were building *bandas* under the supervision of a European overseer, so artistically and hygienically as to be something of a revelation. On the outskirts of the camp there were always strange sights, sounds, and happenings.

For the whole of the five weeks I was out of action there remains one vivid impression stamped indelibly on my mind: the terrific, scintillating heat, day after day, striking down from the cloudless sky, and beating up into one's face from the hard, dry sand, never for one moment relaxing its power from early morn to evening roll-call. Then came the sweetest hour of day, in the cool of the *bandas*, when exhausted vitality gained its soothing respite.

In attending hospital for daily dressings I necessarily came into frequent contact with the doctor, a kindly man whose work was made tolerable by a sense of humour. In exercising this quality, he assured me, with a shake of his head, that the war in East Africa would not be over until six months after the fighting in Europe was finished!

"Von Lettow, oh!
Von Lettow, kwenda! (go away)."

"We crossed the river the next morning ..."

He received the sick parade every morning, a sorry spectacle of stricken humanity. Some came for relief because they needed it, and others because they imagined they did.

Let me give you the picture.

Time: 7a.m.

SCENE: *Doctor's consulting-room* – a *banda* containing one home-made table, one ditto chair, one ditto hand-basin, medicine bottles and equipment, and one orderly (fed-up).

Crowd of sick men outside. Enter the doctor. Jones' name is called. Enter Jones.

The Doctor – "What's your trouble?"

Patient – "Fever, sir." (In goes the thermometer and the patient stands aside.)

"Smith!"

"Sir!"

"What's your trouble?"

"Cold sir."

"Let me see your tongue ... Had much fever? ... Bowels all right? Very well; ten grains of quinine."

"Johnson!"

"What's your trouble?"

"Touch of fever, sir." (apologetically).

"Oh!" (in goes thermometer).

"Next! ... What's your trouble?"

"Pains in the back, sir." (examination follows).

"All right; take this, and report again if no better ... Next! – Oh, you, Johnson (examines the thermometer) ... Let me see your tongue ... Had much fever? ... Bowels all right? ... Very well; ten grains of quinine."

"Next! ... What's the matter with you?"

"Pain in me neck, sir." (examination reveals nothing).

"Are you well in yourself?"

"Just fairly well, sir, but – " (whispers).

"What? ... Five days? Good gracious, man whatever are you thinking of? ... Orderly! ... " (instructions follow).

"Next! ... Well, what's the matter with you?"

"It's me head, sir."

"What's the matter with it?"

"Pain, sir." (Victim looks bright and well, and answers the usual questions with a negative result . . . Doctor sits down and meditates . . .)

Doctor (suddenly), "Orderly, give this man ten grains of quinine and some phenacetin – and (to the man) *go away*!"

The man departs disgruntled.

The next case is obviously a genuine one, for the man is helped in by a comrade; he is immediately drafted into hospital. During all this time I have been occupied in taking off my bandages and the doctor sees to me last. When he has finished, I hear him say as he slowly and wearily washes his hands, preparatory to visiting the hospital patients, "I have been in this country now for over four years, and I am simply sick and tired of seeing sick men! If only one man would stand up and say he was *well* it would add ten years to my life!"

Unlike this good-natured doctor, I knew of one on the Lindi line who had such a bad temper that one of the men, out of sheer funk, said he was well when he really was not.

"How do you know you are well?" snapped the irate MO. "Are you the medical officer, or am I?"

Outside the medical *banda* the group of sick men await anxiously the arrival of the sick report.

"Light duty!" comments one, with evident disgust as it arrives, referring to his own fate. "Well, it will be so damned light, nobody will be able to see it!"

For two weeks more it was a case of hobbling about the camp. I could neither walk for long nor rest for long, "exercise" resolving itself into walking from resting and resting from walking – in any case the pain becoming unbearable whatever I did. Sometimes I became despondent and felt completely helpless. Sometimes I got the relief of an hour with my friends Thompson and Davies in their little workshop, watching and helping in the interesting work of vulcanising, marred only by the increasing pain that brought beads of perspiration to my forehead.

One night I was turned out of my bed by the invasion of an army of ants that came in a long procession from outside. Climbing one of the legs of my bed, they commenced their formidable attack. I had only just retired, and, turning out, fondly imagined I had vanquished the enemy by applying a liberal quantity of creosote, but they returned to the attack two days later. This time, following with the creosote their track outside, I made sure I had seen the last of them. But at four in the morning they were back again – or at least their friends were, for the advance army had been obliterated. They must have been on the march for hours, for my head – the very hair of my head – my face, and my pillow were swamring with millions of them – small as pin-heads, but none the less unwelcome for that. In the dark, with the aid of a lighted lamp, a brush, and a tin of creosote, in silence (for fear of waking my comrades) I had to remove the whole of my bedclothes and belongings, including a cupboard containing food, out into the open to get rid of the ants that had invaded all these things. To my disgust, during these long and very necessary operations, a snake dropped through the bottom of my bed – drawn there in the first place, probably, for warmth. I could not conceive that I had been sleeping with this horrible thing unconsciously for goodness knows how long! It was in a comatose state and easily killed as I hit it on the head . . . What with the melancholy howl of some prowling animal outside, the ants and the snake, the pain in my legs, the disordered state of my belongings, and the uncertain time of the morning, I did not know whether to go to bed, sit up, sit down, or stand on my head.

I took the snake, which measured three feet long, and threw it away, and then sat down. When the boys awoke and turned to, I was still sitting – thinking . . .

In spite of additional precautions against the outbreak of fire, still another occurred, this to be the worst of the lot.

Quinine parade had been attended. We had seen once more the great African sun go down with magical splendour amid a riot of gorgeous colour: vermillion, orange, and gold, intermingling and spreading gradually over the whole sky. Now a full moon hung overhead. Pipes were aglow, and a chatter of tongues told of men enjoying the ever welcome hour's relaxation, when the work of the day was done, and the almost unbearable heat gone with the sun's downward plunge.

With startling suddenness, and unattended by any cry of warning, we hear the now all too familiar hissing noise, as of the escape of steam, sharp explosions, the shuffling of men's feet hurrying over the ground, and saw the lurid glare getting even brighter. Our *banda* immediately emptied itself as the boys tumbled out and I followed as quickly as possible. The beautiful moonlight was paled by the vivid glare from the fire, which was already assuming alarming proportions.

The seat of the trouble was at a spot about a hundred yards on the other side of the open road that passed right through the centre of the camp. Several *bandas* were already alight and going up into the air in flames. Myriads of sparks ascended and mingled with great patches of flaming thatching that were being carried away bodily on the draught of the roaring vortex. Unfortunately, the wind was in the direction of our own quarters where, already, natives were posted with strange weapons, in the form of twenty-foot-long bamboo sticks, with which they frantically beat out sparks as they fell upon the roofs of the *bandas*. Owing to many natives having been sent away from Ankwabe (since there had not been so much to do) there was a serious shortage now for the work of fighting the flames. It was questionable, any way, if more labour could have had the slightest effect in checking the fire, which was so rapid as to cause us to look on, stunned, as the whole square became a roaring furnace. The camp water, stored in a huge cylinder, and unapproachable, went up in one great cloud of steam;

nothing could save the post office, which quickly became one mass of flames; and then, as the whole tragedy developed, we began to have serious fears for the whole of Ankwabe. It was clear that if once the round hut, a permanent structure which stood in the middle of the road (long before the camp of Ankwabe was ever thought of) became alight, it would form a connecting link between the east and west sides, and nothing could possibly save the rest of Ankwabe. A native was already on the roof, putting out the sparks as they fell, but it was soon obvious that if something further were not done, and at once, the roof would burst into flames with dire results. The sparks were becoming too numerous for the native to deal with, and he was now showing evidence of exhaustion. The saving of this hut meat the saving of Ankwabe, which included many other camping quarters, besides our own, telegraphs (as distinct from the post office), officers' quarters, stores, stock, administration, and the hospital. Realising this, and seeing an ominous streak of thin smoke leaving the roof, the forerunner to a burst of flame, and the helplessness of the native, who was now slipping down the steep sides of the cone-shaped roof, two MT men, Lieutenant Chapman[67] and Sergeant-Major Roberts,[68] clambered with set determination to the seat of danger, hauling great pieces of thatching out and throwing them to the ground. The danger to these men was real and hey knew it as well as we did. At any moment the roof might burst into flame under their very bodies. Early attempts had been made to level the roof to the ground by pulling the wooden supports and knocking in the thick walls, and, although the substantiality of the building defied these efforts, it had left the roof in a weakened condition, swaying to the weight of the men. Seeing this, some one with a voice of authority ordered them to "come down at once." But no heed was taken of this as the men, quite regardless of their own safety,

---

[67] Chapman - unable to trace
[68] Roberts - unable to trace

battled with and tore at the rickety roof. The smoke now got thicker, a cry of alarm came from the interior of the hut, declaring the roof to be alight on the under side. The voice of authority now sternly repeated its commands to the two heroes sweating and struggling overhead, but again they turned deaf ears. They thrust their arms in up to the shoulders and smothered the flames with their bare hands. By this time the fire itself began to die down . . . With a thrill we realised these men were going to win, the voice of authority was stilled, the fire was getting less and less, the sparks fewer; in breathless silence the men completed their work, and then, with one great cheer from all onlookers, natives as well, they slid to the ground, exhausted but elated over the success they had attained, laughing congratulations aside as they hurried away . . .

This was the last fire in Ankwabe, as it well might be. For some days after this the natives discussed the incidents of the fire over and over again, repeating in English the word "quick!" and suiting the action to the word in the manner peculiar to them.

In a country like this, where circumstances and conditions were so trying, it was not an easy matter to retain an even temper. I was saving a tin of cheese, which had been specially purchased for me down at Port Amelia, to be opened one day as a little surprise for my friends. when the great occasion arrived, tea being ready, I prepared to open it with a great show of solemn ceremony, surrounded by a gathering of anticipatory friends, stoic of countenance but greedy of eye. The tin-opener was driven home. Immediately there was a fountain of desiccated matter which rose into the air, to the accompaniment of a hissing sound, covering us all over with a white powder and sending everybody running, and gasping for breath. It was not my fault that the cheese was bad, but by the long and strained silence that followed, and by the way my apologies were ignored, it was implied that I was entirely to blame! With nerves on tension, Thompson was the first to start the row. Carefully avoiding any reference to the tin of cheese, he suddenly said: "It's a poor thing that shirt you are wearing, Campbell," looking at me savagely; "I thought you had given it away to the niggers, long ago!"

I would not be drawn, so Davies was appealed to. To my surprise the little Welshman took Thompson's side, always having taken my side in previous disputes: "Yes, you ask me," he now said, "I say it is dreadful indeed! If he go home in that shirt, his poor wife will think he has gone to the ruin and dogs, isn't it?" Even this quaint English failed to dispel the ruffled atmosphere.

True, the shirt in question was an old thing, the tail and sleeves gone, and very little of the other left, but it was, at least, clean, and in my defence I ventured to make the most of this fact, emphasising the heat of the weather as an excuse. But in spite of all my efforts to save it, the shirt was firmly condemned.

"All right," I said at last, "I will get rid of the offending remnant but on one condition: that I am photographed in it first with my two friends, Thompson and Davies." This brought loud protests, Thompson declaring that he would never let his people at home know that he had been associated with tramps. The use of the plural in reference to tramps brought Davies on to my side at last. He not only agreed to my suggestion, but threatened to dismiss Thompson from the workshop if he did not come into the group (Davies being senior to Thompson). This Thompson declared, would not worry him, but might inconvenience Davies, who, in that case, would be deprived of the extra tot of rum he received regularly from Thompson, who did not usually drink it.

"Indeed to goodness!" yelled little Davies to Thompson, "that will not do at all! *That's what I keep you for!*"

This settled the matter, and the three chums were duly photographed. Thompson afterwards said, as we all three critically examined the proof of the camera's ghastly work, that it looked as if we had got Davies under close arrest. But Davies retorted that Thompson looked as if he had been drinking!

Some time after this, Thompson and Berins were ordered away and went off up the line . . . Five days later, they surprised us with a return visit, when we all had lunch together. They brought the news that Harris, when he left us to go down to Port Amelia, had met with such an alarming accident that, in theory, he should be dead. As a matter of fact, the little pianist was as brightly alive as ever. It appeared that he stepped in front of an on-coming lorry, seeing which, he ran for his life, the lorry after him. It overtook him, knocked him down, and, before the driver had time to pull up, had completely passed over him. We were relieved to learn that it resulted in nothing worse than a bad bruising and a few days in hospital.

Our welcome friends also brought the interesting news that Von Lettow had crossed the Lurio River in central Portuguese East,[69] and had gone to earth to the southward. They themselves were now bound for the same district, and, they informed us, we would probably be required to follow on later. They finally departed with the hope that we would meet again.

So few people were now left in Ankwabe that Davies caused amusement by speculating on what we were going to do in the event of being forgotten and left behind. For some time now we had led the quiet and peaceful life of a sleepy village community.

A few Fords were still running cheerily on the road. They had been so running for years, hardly one capable of being started by the handle; they were simply put into gear and pushed off by crowds of yelling natives. If one got hung up in the blue with the engine stopped, and no chance of a restart by a dash down hill, it was simply a case of having to wait in the hope that something would turn up. It was not at all

---
[69] 1 June 1918

uncommon for men stranded in the bush to have to remain out all night. But lions had become bold lately and some severe frights had ben experienced by such men stranded by the wayside. So an order was issued decreeing that in future no man should be left stranded on the road all night. It was nine o'clock and one of our company had failed to turn up. Having waited long enough, a relief party of two men departed in a Ford ambulance car with the object of finding the man. Imagine their surprise after covering ten miles to see a lion leap out of the bush on the left, and, falling into line with the car, keep pace with it in long, springing bounds. Labouring under the natural excitement of the moment, the driver swerved the car badly, nearly pitching it over in the darkness. As they graphically described it afterwards, when the lion turned its great head to look at them as it raced along, they did not know whether their car was on the road or off it. With the increased speed to outpace the brute, and owing to the bad state of the road surface, a hundred yards of reckless riding was literally in the air. The lion tiring – unable to retain full speed for long – suddenly turned into the bush and disappeared. They found their man barricaded in the front of his car with what slender material there was at hand, the barrel of his rifle comically protruding over the top of his windscreen, and suffering from nervousness and suspense, having had to fire, as he said, at shadowy objects he had seen from time to time in the bush. They returned to camp safely, although it was after midnight before they arrived, waking us all up with an exciting account of their adventures, which was the topic of conversation, needless to say, for some days . . .

All the old crocks had been gathered off the road, suffering from broken axles, broken springs, fractured frames, smashed transmissions, broken wheels, some with no wheels at all, and, at least in one case, no engine. Some of them had met a violent end by being pitched into ravines, thrown off the road, turned upside down, and driven head first into the solid trunks of trees, treatment few self-respecting cars could resist without a shudder – especially Fords. Many were simply worn out. In any case they had all done their bit. In German East Africa, during the comparatively short time I was there, I rode three thousand miles over the most atrocious roads imaginable, so some idea can be gathered of the amount of work these cars had done during a period of some years. It was an impressive sight to see their big brothers, the "Auto" lorries, arrive loaded up with their broken bodies.

One afternoon, near the end of our stay in Ankwabe, as the sun was gradually losing its merciless midday power, strange sounds of a blast from a horn coming from the direction of the virgin forest at the back of the camp drew attention to the arrival of a strange company of fifty natives, all fully armed with bows, arrows and spears, dressed only in skins, and escorting a body of native porters carrying bunches of plantains on their heads. Led by an impressive personage decorated in feathers and lustily blowing the horn we had heard, they entered the camp with much pride and ceremony. By their manner of self protection and general aspect it would have fared badly for any foe, be it man or beast, who would dare to interfere with them. Resenting any intrusion, the guard rested on their weapons, the porters on their haunches, in silence, while the camp authorities bought their plantain. Two hours later, the business concluded and the sun going down, the strange visitors departed the way they had come, with a resumption of horn-blowing as they disappeared into the dark recesses and gathering gloom of the forest. They left behind a deep impression of the mystery of native life in these wild and desolate parts, ignorant and uneducated, crabbed and confined, but displaying, in the orderly nature of their visit to our camp, a desire to rise to something better.

Friday, the 5th of July, was a day of excitement. The camp was practically deserted. We ourselves, almost the last to go, were packed up ready to be off on the morrow. Watkins, the cook,[70] had regaled us with excellent supper. Games and good sport followed, with a double issue of rum all round – in the last connection Davies said he was sorry Thompson had gone. The next day at dawn, with the fresh morning air as an excellent tonic, stimulated by the uncertain nature of the project before us, we left Ankwabe, westward bound for Medo and the Lurio River.

A Corner of Medo—Sunday morning.

---

[70] See p208, from Ankwabe

Chapter 12

Bishop[71] at the wheel, with Davies and myself as passengers, left Ankwabe in a Ford car, happy in the thought that we had at least left some of our troubles behind.

We travelled through typical African country, thick forest land, with an occasional craggy, mountainous rock lying back amid a tangle of undergrowth – deep, silent places, deserted and full of gloom, reminiscent of the mysterious romance of the Rider Haggard genre. The earthen road surface was not so bad, as we passed through bamboo twenty feet high and elephant grass which, although blocking out our view, did not interfere with progress. Burnt-out camping places revealed their empty spaces on the edge of the bush; by the roadside two lorries lay – so much scrap iron; and in a lonely clearing were several graves mounted with little wooden crosses. As we stopped to change a tyre, the gentle "coo-coo-coo-coo-" of the African dove's plaintive little notes running down the musical scale broke the silence and filled one's heart with a strange sadness.

It was past noon when, reaching a higher level where cool and refreshing breezes swept round the hills, we reached Medo. This was a Portuguese outpost, but the *boma* had been burnt down and only an old storehouse remained, together with a collection of *bandas*. Commanded by several rocky eminences it was, like Ankwabe, high and dry and ideal for its purpose, but, also like the camp we had just left, practically deserted. We found an empty *banda*, where the rest of our little company were slowly assembling, and settled down, prepared to spend an idle week-end here, for it was Saturday and we were not due to leave until Monday

---

[71] Bishop - unable to trace

morning.

In the enviable position of being free from any weighty responsibilities nobly born only by those in authority, our life, care-free, was devoted to enjoying ourselves thoroughly. Cars parked, belongings sorted out, sleeping places readied, a good wash and change, and we were a holiday crowd. In a spirit of fun, one of our fellows, urged on by the others, while half-stripped attending to his toilet, with his hair all awry, rushed out to show some half-wild natives who were employed in sweeping up the camp the evolutions he could perform with his false teeth by a dexterous movement of the tongue. Natives are wonderfully impressed by the magic of the white man, and are not sure whether this magic is only self-contained, or whether it is possible for it to be turned in harm against them. Therefore, when our friend, who was not noted for good looks, came running out with horrible grimaces, thrusting his front teeth to and fro with his tongue, they first cowered with fright, then gave one scream and ran for their very lives; brooms went hurtling through the air, and one man who took the open road never looked back, and moreover never came back. Another trick was to persuade an innocent native to hold on to the sparking plug of a car while electric currents ran up his arm, with no effect beyond a twitching of the muscles, while his great mouth grinned as he said, "Yes, Sar, ver' dam good!"

Among the natives at Medo was one who stood out as a clown, creating immense entertainment among his mates. As he grimaced, talked, laughed and skipped about, he had his dusky audience listening intently one moment, and convulsed with uncontrollable laughter the next. Before they could recover, he was at it again. Sometimes he would single a man out, much to that individual's concern, playing gymnastic tricks upon him but, it was noticed, without actually touching him. The pantomime went on continuously, the natives looking upon their entertaining friend as a supernatural being, as indeed they well might.

That he was mentally queer was evident, for sometimes he had an abstracted look, as if he had forgotten, and then, recovering, would play on until he reached a state of physical exhaustion, when he would disappear with a spring and a yell, probably to rest his poor, aching head in some dark hole, only to come out again later to continue the foolery that must go on – directed by a mad brain.

Meeting Sergeant Day, whom I had not seen for some time, he stared at me as if he were looking into the vapoury features of a ghost. "Why, I thought you were dead!" he declared. "Oh, thanks!" I said. "I am keeping very well." He was so obviously affected (having received an erroneous report from Ankwabe after my accident) that I was obliged at last to take his salutations seriously and thank him for his kindly concern for me. It was different from another occasion when I was impelled to speak my mind to a friend who had let me down badly. But he took his gruel so well that it ended in a renewed pledge of friendship over a glass of Eno's fruit salt – the only substitute for a whisky and soda.

The next day we witnessed the destruction of the camp, or

The Lurio River from the north bank.

rather the major portion of it, which was purposely fired in the interests of hygiene, preparatory to evacuation. Dozens of *bandas* blazed up one after the other; the patient industry of many weeks was destroyed in as many minutes. Viewed from the top of an ant-hill, strikingly spectacular was the toppling over of the spire-like roof of one large *banda* in the centre of the camp, to the accompaniment of a thousand explosions as the bamboo sections expanded and burst.

The next morning, in bright cool weather, typical of an early spring day in England, we left Medo, a convoy of twelve cars, for the Lurio River. The open country revealed extensive tracts of sparse bush and thorn-trees, with grassy slopes of meadow land stretching away to the foot-hills in the middle distance, beyond which a range of mountains revealed their misty heads to the open sky. As we travelled along, for mile after mile, through scenery that was ever changing, with no evidence of life except when a few shy natives peeped slyly at us from the narrow confines of their habitations, the cool breeze and welcome warmth of the sun cheered us on our journey. The road, simply a beaten-down track, was hard and even, though obscure; we took a line merely from the worn state of the ground. In one place, where the tall grasses reached to a man's height, a pathway had been purposely made by a company of native troops on the march to the Lurio River, with a view to making it easier for the transport that was to follow on. Bush fires were encountered and for several thrilling moments we rushed through fire and smoke. One car, obliged to stop to change a tyre, was restarted just in time to escape the flames that licked greedily the open track the car had just vacated. It was rather awe-inspiring to see whole tracts of country in the grip of the all-devouring fire; bush, trees, and grasses were eaten up and left behind in the form of ash and dust in blackened wildernesses.

A series of watercourses, fortunately dry, hard, and smooth-banked, afforded us great play as we rushed down one side and tore up the other, and, as these steep dips into the ground were quite numerous, a switchback-like sensation was the result. This wild driving caused the convoy to straggle out and they ever regained formation, which was just as well, for we ran into tracts of thick, dry dust, each car leaving a cloud of it behind.

As the day was closing, and we reached the well-watered district of the Lurio River, stately palm-trees raised their crested heads on high, and, in the mellow light under the trees, a cone-roofed hut was seen, evidence of human life, although of a dusky nature, homely and inviting. At last, with no visible evidence of its close proximity, we came to the banks of the river itself. Here we were told to shift for ourselves, relieved at least with the respite that was ours till the morrow. We were now in the heart of Portuguese East Africa (on the Survey Maps it was a blank). On the thickly-wooded banks were a few *bandas*. Europeans hurried about and the usual number of natives were to be seen. On the placid waters of the river itself, in the gathering gloom of the evening, several natives, hauling laboriously on a rope, were ferrying a car over to the other side.

Taking these matters in at a glance, I turned to where my two friends stood speculating on what they proposed doing. Before we could make up our minds on the subject, Sergeant Fineberg, the recruiter of natives, walked up, much to my pleasure and surprise, and warmly invited us to supper and to share his *banda* for the night. Thereupon we went indoors to find the interior snug and cosy, a native servant preparing supper, and the lamps lighted. After enjoying the excellent meal put before us (we had nothing to eat all day), over a glass of whisky and with pipes full charged, we listened to all the news. Von Lettow had crossed the river a little higher up several weeks before, making, to it was thought, for Kilimane – a Portuguese port as far south of the Lurio as the Rovuma was north. He was causing a good deal of embarrassment to everybody but himself, and a new British base was being opened at Mozambique (or Lumbo, which was on the mainland, Mozambique being an island) for further operations against him. Troops were moving in from that district to co-operate with those marching down from the Lurio. He (Fineberg himself) with his great gathering of natives (there were hundreds) would be crossing the river on the morrow, as we ourselves would do. Then, as we should be the last to go over, the weighty ferry would be dismantled.

Changing the conversation to matters personal, our interesting friend lamented the loss of his dog, a little fox-terrier, which had been eaten by a crocodile on the day of his arrival. It had accompanied him throughout all his adventurous travels, and was slaking its thirst in the river at the time when it was seized. He felt the loss of his little friend keenly, and was not satisfied until he had shot several of these reptiles, which were to be seen basking on the mud banks in the middle of the river a little higher up the stream. From the body of one was abstracted a bracelet as worn by local native women – evidence of a more sinister tragedy.

We crossed the river the next morning, and found Berins there. He told us that Thompson had not come to the Lurio after all, but had gone back to Port Amelia. Fineberg followed over almost immediately, with his long retinue of natives, who were singing. For a long time after they had disappeared southward we heard the murmur of their weird and barbaric chant, floating back through the air like the distant sound of falling water, we stayed here the whole day, many taking advantage of the plentiful supply of water to bathe – but not in the river!

Next morning we were off through thick bush and forest, which became more dense as we progressed. Thick clusters of tangled creepers hanging down from overhead almost obscured the path. The roots of trees, gnarled and twisted, crossed the track, and rocky boulders threatened to overturn the cars. Once more we encountered a series of watercourses, over which we "switch-backed" with renewed thrills, while some strange birds whose span of wing was as wide as the road itself followed, sweeping up and down after us. For hours we kept in view, and approached ever nearer, the fantastic shape of a huge rock that towered high above the level of the surrounding forest trees, and at noon came upon it, a sheer wall of rock ascending a thousand feet above the puny cavalcade that wended its lonely way round the great base. Thereafter, country was entered that reminded one of the wild mountain scenery of North Wales (the home of my two friends) as we passed between rocky mountains that bared their great heights to the light of the sun, on the topmost edges of which huge boulders poised giddy as if suspended in mid-air, the whole noble prospect overpowering us with its solemn silence and sense of remoteness.

In the late afternoon we stopped, Davies, Bishop and I, for respite, in the middle of fertile valley. On the hillside was evidence of a Portuguese outpost, but of life we saw none, neither was there any sign of the rest of the convoy, which had straggled. After an acceptable break of one hour the journey was resumed, still with no sign of a living soul in the still heat of the afternoon. We had not proceeded far, however, before we realised that the car was pulling badly, and as this got worse we alighted and an investigation took place. I think the trouble can best be described by quoting the remark of one of the party: *"The damned engine's trailing on the ground!"*

We tied it up with rope, after which all went well – not exactly well really, but five miles an hour was better than no progress at all. Darkness found us still struggling along, through thick bush country again, with the aid of a solitary oil lamp that afforded a feeble outlook on a dark and mysterious world.

It was two hours after sunset – past eight o'clock – when we saw fires ahead on the open road, denoting the presence of the forward part of our convoy. Overtaken by darkness, they had decided to stop for a while, and after supper were reluctant to move on again. We found them enjoying a pipe. Greeted by their cheery voices we were glad to pull up, tired, and ready for something hot to drink and eat. Several of the cars were still unaccounted for and failed to turn up until the following day. Under the impression that the convoy would remain where it was until daylight, many turned in. They were fast asleep when the "start up" was called, much to their disgust. The sergeant in charge, becoming uneasy and unable to reconcile his mind to the situation in face of the order to reach his destination in one run at all costs, had decided to go on. So out we got, and went on into the night, driving in the dark behind the feeble light given out by one or two cars that happened to possess oil lamps that would light. In strange country, encountering several forked roads, it was not surprising that we lost our way. We came to a stand on the edge of a swamp at 3 a.m. in utter darkness, where we were. Although not a sound was to be heard, and no challenge of any lonely sentry had startled our ears, we guessed we were not far from our destination. As a matter of fact we had overrun it. We did not know this at the time, but fearing it, very properly halted.

While the only three among us who seemed to have any further interest in life were discussing the situation, we were startled by the abrupt appearance of a stalwart and half-naked savage who seemed to have sprung from the bowels of the earth. Actually he had emerged from the dark bush at the side of the road. This man, who looked like the devil, stood at our side, sour-visaged, glaring with suppressed anger as he clasped his long spear in his right hand, the butt to the ground, the broad blade glinting wickedly in the faint light of the flickering lamps.

We affected not to notice the aggressive attitude of our strange visitor, but could not very well ignore his presence. Giving the name of the place we wanted to go to, in a friendly manner, we were startled by the rapidity of the man's response. He spoke in guttural tones, long and angrily, an imposing figure as he stood to his full height of well over six feet. His eyes flashed and his nodding head emphasised every angry remark as he intimated, very forcibly, his displeasure with our presence. Having apparently satisfied that he had effectually cursed us to oblivion, he awaited, stiffly silent, the result of his imprecations, a result which, one would think who believed in magic, would be sufficient to cause us promptly to fade away. Instead of this we called up our faithful Swahili boy to interpret the language we had heard, but, as we suspected, he understood as little as we did, and, as the savage spat across the boy's face, we refused to have any more parley with him and promptly turned away. When we looked again this Mephistophelian apparition had vanished.

Uneasy with the course events had taken, we nevertheless decided to stand our ground, and turned in. We slept with one figure in the trigger guard and one eye open, so to speak. In this way, the misery was added to by hordes of mosquitoes that came in from the swamp and attacked us vigorously as we were afraid to entrammel ourselves too much with mosquito netting. Hence the remaining few hours of the night were spent in wakeful wretchedness.

Before the first streak of dawn had time to chase away the fleeting shadows, and while the mist still hung heavily over the marshes, we started up. There was no evidence of the dusky brave of Satanic personality of the night before in the empty bush and low marsh land around us, and turning, we motored back to the top of the hill. Here among the *bandas* of the camp of Nampula (as the place was called) we obtained the information we wanted, turned off sharp left down the side of a ditch, and finally found our depot on the edge of a swamp, in fact a continuation of the swamp we had just left, a place allotted to us by the inconsiderate Portuguese with a studied disregard for the consequence to our health. Though reeds and bushes abounded, the ground was hard and dry, and would stand the weight of the cars and camp equipment;

but another hundred yards farther on lay the stagnant water. To make matters worse, it rained a fine drizzle the whole of the morning and well into the afternoon. Although duties were light, consisting merely of erecting a few bell-tents and fulfilling our own requirements, we were tired for the want of sleep, and disgusted with the fact that we were forced to camp on the edge of a swamp. We could not understand the OC,[72] who had left the Lurio River twenty-four hours before we did, agreeing to such a place for a camp, no matter what was said, and especially as he himself was a medical officer (for we were still with the Ambulance Corps). However, the camp was moved on to high ground some time later, but not before the mischief was done and many of our boys lay in hospital with fever. I had left by then, determined not to stay in such a place if it could possibly be avoided. I slept only two unforgettable nights there, when the mosquitoes came out in battalions and would have literally eaten us alive had it not been for the protecting nets. The noise of their wings kept us awake, tired as we were, with a drumming as of ten thousand humming-tops.

Following up my intention to avoid sleeping here if possible, I reported to the OC to be allowed to go on the line, a request that caused some surprise, as the men were supposed to be resting, but was granted, nevertheless. Taking out a car and following instructions I called at the local hospital – a big and rather muggy allocation of native-made huts – loaded four native patients and went off down the open road, I hardly knew whither.

One wound on my leg had not healed, and it was really problematical whether I could drive or not, but to my relief I found I could do so without undue discomfort. But, as luck would have it, my car collapsed when twenty miles down the road, the back axle having broken. Transferring my dusky patients (who couldn't understand why I had stopped!) to the

---

[72] Possibly Captain WB Walker, he was OC for last diary entry of 18th MAC, June 191 although he is not listed on the CWGC database as having died.

first available vehicle going down the line, I felt relieved of further responsibility regarding them, and awaited eventualities regarding myself. Several more cars passed down the line, but they were of no use to me; I was awaiting the possibility of one coming the other way. Then, who should turn up but Bert Shaw in his "Auto", but he too, unfortunately was going in the wrong direction. His face was still dirty, but his smile as clean as ever as he pulled up his heavy vehicle and saluted me in his usual cheery manner: "Hi, hi, Cammy!" With the likelihood of my having to remain there all night, Shaw handed me a portion of his own rations, which he could ill spare, and then, with good wishes and making excuses for necessary haste, he jammed in his gears and sped away. I stood and watched his car grow smaller and smaller as it rolled away and swayed, like a top-heavy battleship, across the open, scrubby plain, until out of sight. I reflected how much better off the world would be with more men in it like Shaw.

I had lit a fire, made tea, and had resigned myself to the inevitable, when I espied a belated motorist in the far distance coming my way, tearing along at great speed. He grudged the very short time it took me to pack up and get on board. In such desperate haste was he to get into camp before dark that he swore the whole of the way. We got caught up in the dark after all, but reached camp eventually.

Badly situated as the camp was, I was thankful to turn in. During a continuous thirty-six hours I had only had three hours' broken sleep and two scanty meals.

The next morning, with a devout wish never to see this infernal place again – we were bitten all over in spite of nets – I left with Dick Burrows[73] (the depot mechanic) with a spare axle for my car, and in the company of two other fellows on a similar errand. As we rode along through the keen morning air it was so refreshing in contrast to the

[73] The only Burrow(s) listed on CWGC who died in East Africa in 1918 is Cecil N Burrow, M2/149228, Army Service Corps, 626th Motor Transport Company, died 22 July 1918, buried Lumbo British Cemetery, Mozambique (WO 372/3/195460)

atmosphere of the swamp that we could not resist giving expression to feelings of liveliness, calling to the accompanying noises of the car and its engine as we raced along. Bursting into song as men are wont to do on such occasions, we laughed and joked about things we would have scowled at the night before.

With a loud and unnecessary "Whoa!" we pulled up where our friends' car was and, after helping to put things to rights, we bade them good-bye and proceeded, arriving in due course where my own car stood. We fitted the new axle, a job that took us till late afternoon, but it was a job we were well satisfied with, and we thought ourselves justified in enjoying a strong mashing of excellent tea when the OC turned up, leading his convoy, and coming to a halt opposite us. We were not slow in tinkering about as if the job were not yet completed, and the ruse succeeded. Before departing, however, the OC gave me a definite order to get down to rail-head before dark, an order impossible of fulfilment, even if I started right away. We were getting rather disgusted with this officer's excessive zeal, which led to nothing that was any good. The mistaken policy of giving the sergeant an order to get down to the swamp camp from the Lurio River in one day at all costs was now apparent – it fagged the men

"... certainly the coolest place in the whole country"

out, and we lost twelve hours of time. My first impression of this fussy little officer was of a short, stout man dashing into our *banda* at Ankwabe, roaring like a bull, and demanding to know why all the men present failed to jump up and spring to attention when he arrived. The men were all sick cases and I lay helpless, with both legs bandaged up. When the true situation became known to him, he did have the good grace to mumble a few words of apology. It was said he was fresh out from England with an experience limited to attending patients in a civilian capacity, which, if correct, would account for a good deal . . .

"When we get this job finished," said Burrows knowingly, when the officer had gone, and sipping his tea with self-satisfaction, "there will just be time for you to get to Mkonta, the next station, a delightful place, where you will be very comfortable at our depot there. In any case you would be very unwise to attempt to get to rail-head to-night."

This pleasant hour, amid the vast solitude of Africa's scrubby plains, joyously imbibing tea and irresponsibly chatting on many things, cussedness of things in general and OCs in particular, is a halcyon yet sad memory. Poor Dick! His last concern was for my welfare as he stood watching me and my renovated car out of sight. I shall always remember the tragedy of that early morning ride when the four of us – happy, care-free comrades of a common cause – went flying over broad African plains, singing for the very joy of life, lapsing into wholesome and irresponsible laughter when some fancy or mood moved us, unconscious that the shadow of death was with us, its icy finger on the shoulder of our friend – Dick Burrows.

I went to see him before he died, three days later. He lay on a bed of straw, in the clutches of blackwater fever, in the muggy little hospital of *bandas* on the hill above the camp in the swamp. He opened his eyes to my touch – glazed, vacant eyes, with no understanding. I wanted him to speak to me, to be Dick Burrows again, but there was no response – only a closing of the eyes and a silence – as if he wished it so. He lies buried out there in the middle of the wilderness, a stout-hearted friend, a cheery comrade, dying for his country as bravely thus as on the field of battle.

The irascible OC himself succumbed later, so in humble commiseration I forgave him for the unintentional troubles he brought upon us, which, after all, sprang from an honest desire to do his best.

Emerging from between two long lines of fruit trees, I arrived at Mkonta, to find it the neatest thing in native villages I had ever seen. Well-made huts, long, roomy and cool, stood back under the shade of the trees, while dusky natives, freed from their daily toil, lounged and squatted on the open verandahs, lazily staring as I went by. In the centre of the village was an open space of great extent, as space goes in such places, and in the middle of that an open well, the source of the village water supply. Over the well, supported on stout wooden props, and approached by a ladder, was a substantially-built round tower with pointed roof of heavy thatching. This curiously placed structure over the well, containing an ordinary door entrance and windows, was probably the village storehouse for grain, but it appealed to one as immensely suitable as a municipal council chamber – for situation, certainly the coolest place in the whole country.

The first favourable impression of Mkonta was somewhat marred by the general appearance of the inhabitants. Portuguese white guards lounged about armed with old pattern muskets of the hammer detonator variety, which they trailed about in the dust. With the inevitable cigarette drooping from their lips, they presented a grotesque appearance in uniforms that for pretension and age might have belonged to naval officers of Nelson's time, assuming a swagger, nevertheless, that made them look the more ridiculous. In this respect a Portuguese *safari* of fifty native porters was a still greater curiosity. As they passed along the road in single file, some wore trousers without any shirt, others a shirt without any trousers. There was cast-off clothing of great variety; frock-coats and evening dress, green with age; lounge suits; no suits at all; pyjamas; nightshirts, long and trailing; and, most amusing of all, a grave-looking porter was dressed only in boots, an army tunic, and a top hat! Where a hat was worn, as in this case, the load was carried on top of it.

In this village I saw the most grotesque evidences of Portuguese supercilious pride and humorours streaks of native pomp. In the latter connection one nigger stalked about the place with all his monetary wealth tied to the long hair of his head through the holes in the centre of the coins, consequently giving a rich jingle at every movement – a perfect personification of a perambulating money-box. The *tout ensemble* was completed by a walking-stick, a kaleidoscopic fancy waistcoat, a bicycle chain for a watch-guard, a one-tailed coat, and – bare feet. Needless to say, he was the envy of all his fellows.

A striking contrast was a gang of twenty emaciated and wretched native victims of a crude and merciless Portuguese administration, crouching on the pavement tied together by the neck with what appeared to be telegraph wire – a strange use for the latter. The usual armed guard of cigarette suckers stood limply by. In fact, these somnolent guards of so-called white justice were to be seen everywhere, and were held in awe by the servile natives.

I found the local depot of our unit in the grounds of the hospital of *banda*s among the pineapple plantations on the side of the hill. I knew the sergeant and the twelve men stationed there, and they gave me a warm welcome, inviting me to their mess where supper was already prepared. In sympathy with my complaint against the camp in the swamp, they encouraged me to leave and join them, the very thing I desired.

Under the pale light of the stars, enjoying our pipes in the open after supper, we heard once again the mysterious call of

A Native Dancing Woman (caught unawares adopting an attitude of contempt).

the *ngoma* drums. From the distance came the barbaric chanting of the multitude. Fitfully among the dark shadows of the night we could see the glare of the *ngoma* fires. Of one mind, drawn by an irresistible impulse, we surreptitiously left the camp. After a difficult walk of an hour through the bush – for it was not policy to carry a lantern and we frequently tripped up in the dark with oaths and suppressed laughter – a scene of unsurpassed savagery presented itself. We watched, unseen, the caperings of the simple blacks, men and women, dancing round and round a huge fire in an endless circle, eyes dilated, lips pouted. They worked themselves up into a frenzied excitement, their dark bodies perspiring, limbs pulsating to the rhythmic beat of the drums. Wilder and louder grew the chanting, the women becoming hysterical, the men half crazy, until at last the time arrived when we thought that to stay longer was to pry too closely into their private life . . .

Next morning I was off down to the rail-head, on a good hard road surface. It was thick jungle nearly all the way, through which the road must have been hacked yard by yard. Arrived at Monapo, as the place was called, I found it to be the end of a twenty-eight miles single-line railway from Lumbo (Mozambique) on the coast. It was from here troops were operating inland against Von Lettow. Several regiments of black troops were billeted in *bandas* spread along the south side of the main road, overlooking the endless expanse of forest that stretched away like a great green carpet to the far horizon. The impressive grandeur and mystery of these wild and far-reaching stretches of dense countryside in their silent solitude, deserted and unknown, were now added to by the fact that hidden away somewhere in their depths – no one knew where – were the elusive Von Lettow and his merry men, scheming no one knew what! In addition to the British troops there was a large number of Portuguese, great quantities of stores, in some cases stacked twenty feet high, and much liveliness; everybody's nerves were on strain; the south side of the camp was trenched, wired and barricaded, with every vantage point manned by armed men.

On one of my return visits to this place I was delighted to find Alex de Bussy, quite by accident, in charge of the sergeants' mess, into which he invited me, and we had lunch together and exchanged all the news. The reader may be conscious of the customary method and order of army discipline. It was just as well so. It would have made difficulties more difficult, trying situations more trying, and would have put men into hospital sooner. And the very fact that men were left, more or less, to their own individual responsibility resolved itself into more work, higher efficiency and greater satisfaction to all concerned; indeed, turned duty into pleasure. Commissioned officers themselves could not exactly fraternise with the men, but they did the next best thing, and, altogether, we all got on very well indeed. It was because of this that de Bussy and I found ourselves taking lunch together in the sergeants' mess. I learnt all the latest news obtainable of Von Lettow.

It appeared that Von Lettow had marched through Portuguese East Africa from the Lurio River south until he had reached Kilimane, and had succeeded in completely routing the Portuguese garrison there. It was reputed that he was even now on his way back towards this line, but exactly where, nobody knew. Any part of the line was open to him, as it was impossible to hold its entire length, though it was fairly clear to anyone that the vulnerable Monapo, with its great quantity of stores and its important strategical position, was a temptingly good prospect.

What we did not know, however, was that his operations at Kilimane had resulted in a greater success than Von Lettow himself could have hoped for. Desperately short of ammunition, clothes, food and medical stores at the time, he was now able to supply himself with more of these commodities than he knew what to do with, including 350 new rifles, three light machine guns, and seven heavy guns, all intact. In his book, Von Lettow says: "Unfortunately, it was not possible for us to get away the whole stock of excellent wine we had captured. After a sufficient quantity had been set aside as a restorative for the sick, the rest had mainly to be drunk on the spot. The risk of wholesale jollification that involved was gladly taken, and everyone was allowed to let himself go for once, after his long abstinence." (*My reminiscences of East Africa* by General Von Lettow-Vorbeck; published by Hurst and Blackett).

Events moved quickly after my meeting with De Bussy at

Monapo. For several more days transport was busy dashing up and down the line when, suddenly, all available cars – ambulance cars as well – were ordered to be in readiness to take 500 troops and attendant carriers up the line, which was by direction a little south of west. It transpired that, during the past week, troops had been sent down from Mozambique to meet Von Lettow, but they missed him in the dense bush, and the extraordinary situation arose of the two forces marching away from each other. On finding out their mistake, the British troops retraced their steps, hurrying to make up for lost ground, but it was too late, and, exhausted and lost, they failed to come into touch with the enemy at all. It was on receipt of definite information that Von Lettow was at Namirrue, a lonely outpost on a hill, midway between Kilimane and Monapo, and that he was overwhelming the little garrison there, that the sudden move by swift motor transport was decided upon.

On the 22nd of July our little company of twelve Ford ambulance cars from the camp in the swamp, with their red crosses blacked out, left rail-head with as many native troops as we could possibly carry, with porters, and all necessary equipment. A noisy, jabbering, excited lot of passengers they were too – one would have thought they were out for a glorious picnic instead of a dangerous enterprise. Anyway, one thing was quite certain – it was a fine day for it. A grand motor ride had an irresistible appeal to these darkies, who realised with voluble satisfaction the ease of covering in a few hours distances that would otherwise mean several days' heavy tramping.

Leaving at daybreak, and passing *up* the line, we were astonished to see companies of barefooted, black Portuguese Askari marching *down*. It was said that this was an agreed arrangement, but it was hardly considered fair, and opinion was expressed, with some heat, that they ought to march on until they drowned themselves in the sea!

Passing through the well-kept village of Mkonta, and on to

Nampula, where still lay the camp in the swamp, we joined up with such a large number of fully laden cars that, although I had no opportunity of counting them, there must have been a hundred, all Fords. The troops were officered by Europeans, who were feverishly anxious to get their force up the line as speedily as possible. So severe was the mental strain under which these leaders, usually cool-headed men of mature age and undaunted experience, were suffering, that one irate officer, quite oblivious of the impracticability of the remark, shouted to one of the drivers, during a lull in the progress of the cars: "Why the ell don't you come on?" and then: "Oh, all right," going off as if waking from a dream. As we slowly rounded the Portuguese barracks, we came to another involuntary stop due to the road not being suitable for motor transport. We were laughed at by the few Portuguese whites, who came out in shirt sleeves and stood, hands in pockets, sneering while the usual cigarette was stuck into unshaven faces. From the portals of their ramshackle mud – and – plaster fortress they watched the cavalcade struggle with almost unsurmountable difficulties for a cause that was as much theirs as ours if honour counted for anything. But we got a laugh back at them when a squad of their own native guard came on parade, a dozen all told, standing in a row like a comic crowd in a pantomime: short ones, tall ones, fat ones, thin ones, some bandy-legged, and others knock-kneed. Some wore boots and some didn't, and all the clothing was a misfit; no two caps were alike, and they were worn at different angles; consequently all looked absurdly ridiculous in their exaggerated effort to be smart.

Good progress was made once we got into the open country, the faster cars passing the others and disappearing ahead. Some attempt had been made to keep close formation, but this, owing to the variable performance of the cars and the awful dust, was soon found to be impracticable, so, notwithstanding orders, the convoy straggled. In fact, so drawn-out did it become, that by the end of the day, when we reached a place called Chinga, high up among the rocky hills where the air we breathed was like champagne, I arrived with no sign of any other member of my own convoy. Discharging my passengers, who alighted with whoops and yells after the manner of joyous schoolboys on holiday, I had some difficulty in finding the corner allotted to the members of our little company among such a multifarious crowd, all two busy preparing their own sleeping places, lighting fires, and getting food, to bother about anybody else. After a time, I found our own camping place on a rocky eminence with fires lighted under the stars that now began to show up in the sky, and with plenty of water on the boil. Several more cars were still due to arrive, and eventually turned up after experiencing the same difficulty of location as I had. There were many camp fires burning that night at Chinga, and many minds speculating, with hopes and fears, on the morrow, as black and white lay down to sleep, officers and men, side by side . . .

We were astir at three o'clock, and on the move again long before daylight. Like a living black snake, the writhing convoy wormed its way through the dark bush in a direction due south, crawling along over a track that was now no longer than a hard surfaced road, but merely the virgin soil, for mile after mile, hour after hour. During the whole of this time we were surrounded by bush and forest trees, holding on to the open track until we could go no further. Then, silently and on serious business bent, the troops alighted, and, in the light of the midday sun, disappeared into the dark forest. A few minutes more, and a long string of empty transport cars rested for a while before returning the way they had come. In due course our own little section of twelve cars returned together to the camp in the swamp.

Like the calm before the storm, the atmosphere for the next two days on the line was electrically charged with hope and fear – hope that this time determined and concentrated effort would be rewarded with success, and fear that the troops would not be strong enough to deal effectively with the indomitable Von Lettow, and that, once again, he would get the better of the situation . . . Quickly the news arrived that Von Lettow had been checked. But this was not exactly the truth. What really did happen after our dusky passengers had left the transport was a stealthy movement by them through the thick bush, executed with commendable rapidity and followed by a quick engagement with the enemy. The Germans, however, recognising the weakness of the force they had to contend with, attacked with their full numbers – early three to one – with the unfortunate but perhaps natural result that the British troops suffered a severe reverse, and were scattered through the forest.

This news was, however, unknown to us at the time. All we knew was that the enemy had been "checked." But reading between the lines, the worst was feared. Our doubts were justified when, after a while, the disastrous details began to dribble through. Thereafter, the gravity of the situation revealing itself, the whole Mozambique line was in a state of intense excitement, for no one could tell just where and when Von Lettow, like the devil, might appear.

A Portuguese Redoubt built into a dead ant-hill and large enough to hold twelve riflemen.

Chapter 13

After the exciting event of motoring the five hundred troops into the forest, transport and ambulance work on the line became normal again. I successfully broke away from the camp in the swamp and became attached to the little section at Mkonta. Healthily situated on the high land among the pineapple plantations our camp in the hospital grounds was pleasant enough. Left to ourselves we were, more or less, our own masters. Every morning after breakfast (the food here was excellent and plentiful) I took my complement of patients off down to the rail-head, returning in time to attend to my car (ready for the next morning) before darkness fell.

On the line there was plenty of incident to keep one interested. In the more secluded parts the natives, all armed with spears, could be seen, if one had watchful eyes, peeping from the dark recesses of the bush, and later a few would come out and stand, half afraid and half in anger, watching us pass to and fro. With their tortuous, narrow mentality, they hardly knew whether to accept us as friends or foes, and although they had no newspapers or telegraph wires, they nevertheless learned all the news in their own way. The Portuguese government owned the country. They leased it to the Portuguese prospectors, and they exploited the natives. When the Germans entered the country, the government were their enemies, the prospectors adopted an attitude of neutrality, and the Portuguese Askari refused to fight. Then the British invaded the country, friends of the Portuguese government and friends of the Portuguese natives as well. But the Germans also avowed friendship for the natives, and spoke of themselves as their deliverers from the Portuguese yoke. How could the British be friends of the natives when they were chasing the Germans to kill them? And were they not also friends of the hated government? The natives concluded that the magic name of Von Lettow meant freedom for them. It was not to be wondered at then, that the natives, getting bolder, were throwing spears at the passing cars of the British motor transport.

Of the women folk we saw very little. If we did happen to meet one or two, they stood until we had passed, like shy children, their backs to us, their eyes to the ground. On the other hand, a large group of women labourers, working on the repair and upkeep of the road surface, took no notice whatever of anything but the heavy work they had on hand – one shy glance, perhaps, at us, and then on with their work again. Well endowed by nature, half naked, some with the additional burden of having to carry a baby, slung pick-a-back, they were indeed a hardy lot. With limbs like navvies, one imagined that neither a blow from their fists nor an embrace from their arms was to be courted. Some of the babies, too heavy to be carried, hung suspended from the lower branches of adjacent trees. To me the brightest side of native life lay with the little children, not young enough to be frightened, not old enough to be suspicious. They made friends at once, joining whole-heartedly in any fun that was going, giving vent to roars of laughter, loud and continuous. Little boys, like other little boys of a more enlightened race, were never happy unless they were doing something, if it were only to balance an empty jam tin on the top of their woolly heads; indeed they practise this balancing trick from the very moment they are able to walk – both boys and girls – and this, presumably, helps them to attain perfect poise, and certainly gives them gracefulness of carriage. These little children would play at being grown up, making fires, cooking food, fighting wild animals with bows and arrows and spears, struggling with supposed foes, or running away screaming from an imaginary lion. The whole day was theirs in which to play and act, for there were no schools to attend, and no lessons to learn – only the lesson of the wild bush and forest, and the lessons from the tales their mothers told.

In carrying patients – who were nearly all fever cases, although there were a few wounded coming down the line – care had to be taken to bump them as little as possible when travelling over the bad surface of the improvised road. In some instances, not only were the patients bumped but the cars themselves turned over. Keenly anxious as we were to avoid bumping, I am afraid they were painful journeys to many. It was almost impossible to drive on for hours and hours without sooner or later coming to one big bump that would eclipse all the others; the poor patient would then probably experience something he would remember for the rest of his days. I took a European officer down to rail-head one day, and the poor fellow was so ill he hadn't the strength to complain of the bumps he kept receiving – only to moan. Even with the greatest care these bumps were unavoidable, but, without warning, one particularly bad one threw my patient out of the stretcher he was lying on, into the air, and back again, giving my heart the biggest thump it had had for some time. The poor man gave one groan and then lapsed into silence. I stopped the car and the engine, got out quietly and spoke to him. He bravely said, as well as he was able, that he was satisfied I was doing my best. In this way did we get the best out of each other.

I was astonished to see that my patients one morning included the imperturbable Bert Shaw. He was as pale as a ghost, and, from a desire to find him not so ill as he looked, I hurried up to him with a cheery, "Got you at last!" but it was no use. His smile had gone, his cheeriness vanished, and there wasn't even the slightest suspicion of acknowledgement of my sally. Seriously now, I helped my friend into the car, where he lay, like a limp rag, on the stretcher, and, silently and slowly, we had a miserable journey. As I left him in hospital he held my hand for a long time, and would not let go until he was able to murmur one word: "Thanks!"

At Monapo the discontent that had been fomenting between the various factions at last resulted in a free fight. Anything was used, from bayonets and spears to sticks, and before law and order could be restored, big Portuguese stores and *bandas* had been burnt to the ground. The British Askari could no longer withhold from the Portuguese Askari a few home-truths they had been dying to convey for some time, and this started the row.

One day I was taking some sitting-up cases down the line and felt so unaccountably happy on this particular morning that my patients stared at me with some astonishment. From an inexpressible feeling of well-being I sang as I navigated the car dexterously between the rocks and through the shallows. "How the 'ell can you be happy in a God-forsaken country like this beats me!" declared one, with envy. He little knew it was merely the forerunner to collapse – neither did I! On the return journey a feeling of depression came over me. I suddenly began to feel afraid, as if the shadow of some unknown evil were dogging me. The sensation of physical and spiritual oppression grew over-powering as I neared the journey's end. It bore me down under a leaden weight as I parked my car, crawled inside under the hood, covered myself all over with blankets, and, trembling like a leaf but feeling ridiculously heroic, muttered: "You can't get me now, you devils!"

I was awakened by the rays from a hand lamp. It was night. I felt a hand on my neck, and a quiet voice was saying: "All right, leave him like that till morning!" It was the MO himself, and a sergeant holding a lamp up. I spoke "Hello, who's that? What do you want? . . . Oh, very sorry – didn't know it was you, sir. Yes, I'll be all right till morning – quite all right, till morning!"

In the morning the sergeant came and had a peep at me and, before I could say anything, went off without muttering a word. "That's funny!" I said, talking to myself. "Why didn't he speak? Time I was up – lots to be done – can't afford to be lying here – broad daylight! Why I turned in all standing last night! Ha, ha! that's funny! I might at least have taken off my boots and my tunic!"

Jumping up from the improvised bed, I prepared the car for patients in the usual way. It was too late for breakfast, so I made up my mind I would get some fruit along the line. But the sergeant came along and told me I was to remain in camp that day – doctor's orders. How absurd! No spare hand to drive my car; in camp idle all day; patients badly needing cars to take them down the line. The doctors were not always right. Can't drive my own car? I would show them!

I found the tent of a friend, convalescent from fever, and happy to have me for company. We were as merry as sandboys as we prepared a special dish of bacon and eggs for breakfast over a jolly little fire of our own, laughing over the folly of a too pessimistic doctor who was giving a man a holiday when he did not want it and never asked for it! Well, I never had the chance to express an opinion on the delectable quality of the fried bacon and eggs, for without realising it, I collapsed, so suddenly as to be talking one moment and speechless the next, with the tent swimming round and round. They sent immediately for the doctor who, on arrival, looked down at me as I lay stretched out on my friend's bed. He gave a few terse instructions and so definitely sealed my fate. In ten minutes I was entering one of the hospital *bandas*, helped by my friend, and feeling very much like one of my own late patients. I shall never forget the camp boy stopping in his stride, his rough, dark features softened with sympathy as he watched the helpless progress of the *bwana* whom he had known so different.

The hospital *banda*, open at each end, was mean and empty, except for straw beds raised two feet off the ground, and upon which sufferers tried to get what peace they could. When the doctor came, he told me he was sending me down the line on the morrow, but as I had no wish to go, I begged of him to let me stay and get well where I lay. Pleasantly, but more firmly, he emphasised his intention to send me away, adding that I would be much better off on the coast, where there were healthy sea-breezes and better medical attention to patients in the tented hospital.

I remember very little of that day, except for the faint noises that came to one's ears from outside, as on a hot summer's day in rural England when one lies down on the edge of the cornfield, and with closed eyes, hears the sounds from the village in the hollow. After dark the orderly came and took my temperature. He departed in such haste that, suspiciously, I looked at the record book and so learned that my temperature was 105 degrees. He returned at once with a drink for me, which I think was brandy and milk, and then left me, smothered with blankets, to spend a lonely and wretched night in the claws of the fever fiend.

For hours I found myself watching the stars through the open ends of the *banda*. Not a soul came near. In the quiet stillness of the night I listened, fascinated by the call of wild animals in the distance. Once there was a heavy *s-s-swish, s-s-swish*, as a big bird flew slowly overhead. "Bury me deep" Bury me deep!" I heard myself saying. "*S-s-swish, s-s-swish*, deep, deep! *S-s-swish, s-s-swish!* down, down! to where the evil influence of this terrible country could not reach – say six feet – not shallow, no, not shallow! – six feet at least, or ten; ah, that would be better, ten!" In this state of mind I had to listen to the ravings of a man near to me which culminated in his getting out of bed and giving vent to an outburst of frightful invective against God and man, the devil and the Kaiser! He then went out into the night. I slept after this, waking with the first streak of dawn, just as the orderly himself arrived, his kindly attention so welcome. The doctor followed, and left orders for me to go down the line at once. I was in such a weak state that I was then glad to go, and I was driven, as I had driven many others, down to the hospital at Monapo, in an ambulance car. Blessed with a fairly strong constitution, I stood the journey well, arriving at Monapo to find that fires were raging still, and men were running about saying: "Those damned Portuguese again – three fires in four days!"

Together with several others, I was lodged in a tent that stood very near to the edge of the camp by the wire entanglement. There was so much excitement over the hourly expected visit of Von Lettow, the will-o'-the-wisp of Africa's wild bush, that troops were standing to arms in the trenches and on the earthen ramparts day and night, and alarms were frequent, especially at night, during the few days I was stationed there. Amongst the reports, rumours and alarms, information came to hand that a white Portuguese had been caught red-handed setting fire to the camp; our allies were reputed to have actually set fire to their own stores. But with all the rumour, doubt and misgiving, one simple incident occurred regularly every morning: it was the deliberate action of a bare-footed nigger who stole silently into our tent by the pale light of dawn and picked up all the cigarette ends. He then disappeared as mysteriously as he had entered.

Those of us who were well enough to withstand the journey were now permitted to leave by train for Lumbo on the coast.

Sitting in an open truck, twenty all told, we rolled away over the rickety rails, while the antiquated engine puffed sparks all over us, threatening our prompt extermination by fire. We passed the time watching one another break into flames, to the ironical cries of, "Fire, fire!" Sometimes the extinguishing efforts savoured of a personal assault! When the engine rattled downhill in order to gain sufficient impetus to scorch up the next rise, the fireman furiously plied the furnace with generous quantities of wood fuel; thereby causing an alarming increase of fire and smoke that smothered and nearly chocked us. But we did not fare so badly as a company of negroes in another truck behind us. Their shrieks and yells as glowing chunks of charcoal hurtled through the air and fell on their naked bodies suggested the agonising cries of the tortured in Hades.

To add to the glorious uncertainty of this journey, we stopped at a timber mill for more fuel! After this, our existence wasn't worth talking about. With rumblings and shakings a wooden trestle bridge over a river was crossed with a good deal of risk to the bridge. Arriving at last at our destination comparatively intact, we were thankful indeed that this exciting railway journey was over, never again, we hoped, to be repeated.

In passing through this particular stretch of vast and thickly-wooded country, with its evidence of timber industry as seen by the presence of several saw-mills, its potentialities of future money-making were obvious to the most casual observer.

On the train was the white Portuguese under arrest for setting fire to the camp at Monapo. He had occupied the only other carriage, a covered saloon next to the engine. He had been free from the discomfort we had to suffer! We saw this worthy alight full of swagger, dressed in a bright-coloured shirt, open at the chest, broad-brimmed hat worn at the back of his head, and a cigarette stuck nonchalantly between his grinning lips.

There seemed to be particular sympathy for the German cause in this part of the world, and a marked antipathy to anything and everything British. This was unaccountable, but a good deal was clear if, as it was said, many of the principals in the country were of German origin. As we lay in hospital later, we were annoyed by an incessant whistling from railway engines that lasted all night, with some of the blasts continued for needlessly long periods. The effect of this annoyance on the nerves of patients can best be imagined. It was quite unnecessary, Lumbo being only a small settlement of a few bungalows and the railway terminus, with no important traffic. We were, of course, quite convinced that the noise was intentional, and made purposely to annoy. It was too distracting to be treated with the contempt it deserved. Protests were of no avail, and it was only when our authorities threatened drastic action (and we had some idea of its stern nature) that the abominable nuisance stopped . . .

A weary trudge up the slight rise bought us to the tented hospital on top of the cliffs, facing the sea. Each tent contained twenty beds, and was ventilated by health-giving sea breezes. It was surprising to learn that there were no fewer than two hundred and forty patients in this fine hospital, where indeed there seemed to be not a soul, so quiet and still were the surroundings, except for the gentle rustle of the palm leaves. With silent tread a sister walked through our ward; it was heartening to see a white woman again with her sad, kindly eyes, and with a consoling smile on her wistful, pale face. With the peace that was ours, soothed with comfort and content, we rested.

The next morning curiosity took me to the edge of the cliffs to view the prospect. The bay was fringed with coconut trees, from between which a few straggling buildings and huts looked out over the water. Lining the shallow beach, barges discharged stores from a steamer which, in company with a British cruiser and a hospital ship, lay at anchor in the deep waters. Beyond, and almost blocking the broad entrance to the bay, was the elongated island of Mozambique, its ancient town and fortifications just discernible. For five hundred years the Portuguese had held this stronghold, and were still its undisputed masters; surrounded by water, it had been immune from attack by the wild natives of the mainland and fortified against foes from the open sea. Within a short distance native fishermen in their boats hauled rhythmically at their nets. Beside me, the double-roofed marquees of the hospital lay spread out among the nodding palm-trees, and beyond that, where the land fell gently away, was the place we knew as Lumbo, composed of a few mean buildings. Beyond that again, as if with a desire to smother the little settlement out of existence, were the close confines of the mighty forest.

During my stay in hospital, hardly a day went by but alarming news reached us of the doings of Von Lettow. At one time he was at Monapo, blowing the place to pieces. A little later rumour had it that he was marching on Lumbo, and, to add colour to the gossip, feverish haste was made to complete the trench digging and the erection of barbed-wire entanglements. Somehow or other thoughtful men could not persuade themselves that Von Lettow would attempt to come either to Monapo or Lumbo – it was too much like entering the lion's mouth. Against this assumption, however, was the attitude of the Portuguese, hostile to our cause and passive in face of the enemy's threat.

Many of my friends were in this hospital, including De Bussy (very poorly), Bert Shaw (who was getting better), and our genial Ankwabe cook, Watkins. During convalescence we would watch the new patients arrive, more dead than alive, staggering up the hill into the hospital, dragging their sorely depleted kit-bags after them through the dust. In extreme cases motor transport was requisitioned. We knew that the majority would be all right again in a few days – as we were – but some were not so fortunate. And now they lie out there in line with the swaying palms, under the shade of the mango trees.

To spend a week in this hospital was indeed to know a haven of rest – only the gentle rustle of the palm fronds overhead and the sigh of the tropic wind broke the stillness. Protected as we were from the heat of the midday sun – when to venture out from the cover of the double-roofed marquees was to be instantly scorched – we enjoyed the refreshing coolness of indoors, the luxury of light pyjama suits, and the clean, tidy bedding on which we lay, to read, talk, and rest.

A pleasing feature was the marked solicitude of native servants. Always respectful, never spoilt, they could not do enough for the white *bwanas* who lay sick. They would even go to the extremity of making personal sacrifice if they thought it would win our approval. For instance, one day sister thought it was time my beard came off, so off it came. There was nothing remarkable about this; but the next morning our native orderly arrived with all the hair of his head off. Up to this thrilling moment our dusky servant had been looked upon as a very fine example of a living gollywog, so woolly had been his head with a shock of hair to eclipse anything we had ever seen. As he stood respectfully at attention, with bald head and expansive grimaces, looking first at me and then at the astonished sister, his appearance provoked everyone to roars of laughter.

At the end of ten days I felt that the hospital, heavenly enough to sick men, was no place for anyone feeling at all fit. So, recovered, I resolved to ask the doctor for my discharge, an unusual course. He listened to me with raised eyebrows, exclaiming, "What's wrong?" with such emphasis as to startle me. On hastening to assure him that nothing was wrong, and that, on the contrary, there was every reason for patients to be thankful and grateful for all the kindness and attention accorded them, he handed me my discharge with the card marked "ten grains of quinine daily for three months."

On leaving hospital I went into details. That is not to say I fell to pieces. "Details" was the name given to the camp for those temporarily out of employment before rejoining their unit. The first question I was asked on arrival there was, would I sing at the next concert? I could have sooner wept! But the concert took place and I sang the "Bandolero" – I felt more like a very over-ripe tomato! However, the audience passed it and they were the only ones that mattered. I remember later, when at the top of my form, rendering popular chorus numbers with a good, rollicking swing in them, I was called on four times. They were happy days, and no one more happy than those who could give entertainment to others. These Saturday night concerts took place in the YMCA *banda*, a clumsy, open-air thatched arrangement capable of seating accommodation for several hundred troops. The YMCA, notwithstanding great difficulties under trying conditions, contributed extensively to helping to make life more endurable for all ranks during East Africa's little war. On the night of my first concert at Lumbo, as I stood under the stars and looked through the open sides of the *banda* at the sea of flushed faces — there were troops in hundreds, officers from ships and army units, sisters and nurses from the hospital, and the usual crowd of curious natives at the back whose dusky faces were a study as they gaped and gasped — it was indeed an ideal and fascinating setting for the "Four Indian Love Lyrics" which the very capable little orchestra was rendering, with a feeling attuned to my own . . .

Troops had been receiving mail in a shockingly slovenly manner, if at all. Heaps of letters lay unsorted and uncared for. On my own suggestion I was granted permission to set this to rights, and for days I dealt with thousands of letters, newspapers and parcels — though precious few of the last name needed "sorting", as they had passed through far too many hands between the post offices in England and the little camp at Lumbo. It was pleasurable work, and I could not rest until it was completed, which took about a week. It brought its own reward when I constantly received the grateful thanks of boys who had had no news from home for months. Sacks full of mail were sent up the line to the boys there, and occasionally I found letters addressed to myself. Once the work was completed it was not difficult to continue with the system I had inaugurated, and delivery of the mail after this became regular.

  This work and my recent engagement with the concert party brought me to the notice of Sergeant Millane[74] of the MT Stores, whose influence resulted in my drifting from details to his office, a double-roofed marquee, coolly inviting, full of records, dockets, beetles and tobacco smoke. Into this office came the OC himself, sealing my fate: "Sing for us as

---

[74] Millane - unable to trace.

you did on Saturday night, Campbell, and you are here for as long as you like to stay!"

I soon found that life in the MT Stores camp was very different from having to rough it up the line. I had guessed this, of course, from the beginning, but had preferred the up-country experience anyway. Now I was glad of an opportunity to see life at the base and welcomed it. We were a small company of twenty-five men and two commissioned officers. We saw very little of the officers and they bothered

Lumbo.

The "Office."

us less. Sergeant Small[75] came from Rhodesia, another NCO hailed from South Africa, and Corporal Marmont,[76] like Sergeant Millane and most of us, came from that "tight little island – God bless her – away up in the clouds," as an Englishman who had been thirty years in South Africa once described our homeland to me. We were indeed a light-hearted crowd, happy in our work and in one another's company. We lived in square-shaped tents, two in each, my "half-section" being H___,[77] a cheery young fellow from London town, who was fond of showing me how well he could sing by kicking up an infernal row in my ear every night after indulging in rather more than his fixed portion of rum. "You needn't think you are the only one who can sing!" he would say. "Listen to this!" And away he would go. The diversion, as such, would have been delightful had be been able to realise, as painfully as I, that he sang down his nose, and dropped his voice to a guttural "ah" at the end of each line. One night he said, "Well, damn you, then I'll sing to myself!" if possible, that was worse, but it wasn't possible.

Work in this camp consisted of receiving, sorting out, and sending up the line, as required, all spare parts for motor vehicles, from a black axle to a spring washer.

While we were in the comparative comfort of the sun-proof office, the majority of the company had the terrific heat in the open to contend with as they superintended the loading and unloading, by natives, of material that constantly passed through the camp. All hands turning immediately after dawn, we of the office staff had the special privilege of ejecting all the unwholesome insects and reptiles that had gathered in the office (such as it was) during the night. In spite of carefully sealing the tent overnight, they got through the merest cracks, or tunnelled under the sand. To find a creature like a crab bedded down comfortably on your

---

[75] Small - unable to trace

[76] Marmont - possibly Philip JN Marmont, M2/033875 Army Service Corps (WO 372/13/120995) or Albert J Marmont, DM2/163827 (WO 372/13/120985)

[77] Is this Percy Head? see page 246

blotting-pad, to discern a creepy, belegged, horn-backed thing like a miniature octopus affectionately embracing your ink-bottle, to see their relations on the canvas sides or suspended from the roof, and to feel some slithering, slippery thing dart suddenly from between your legs and disappear into your favourite rest corner, had the effect, by constant repetition, of giving everyone "the jumps."

In spite of the bush having been cleared for hundreds of yards around, right up to the edge of the forest itself, these pests came amongst us. Great care had to be taken to see that none of these reptiles became concealed in our beds before turning in. Quite frequently, and in broad day-light, we would see a snake, five or six feet in length, leave the confines of the surrounding bush and make straight for one or the other of our tents – why, we could never tell – and disappear swiftly within.

A hue and cry would be raised. The boys would at once race up armed with thick sticks, and a general battle would ensue. So lightning-like would be the snake's ten-feet leaps to escape (while making no effort to get away from the tent itself) that usually the whole of the furniture was turned upside down before the elusive creature met with its ultimate death.

Scorpions were much more to be dreaded, being secretive, hiding away in bedclothes, in the folds of our wearing apparel, and even in our boots. However, we exercised a natural caution, and there was little chance of a lurking scorpion being overlooked. With a terrifying yell one of our fellows woke the stillness of the night. He was a notoriously careless fellow, otherwise he would probably have found the scorpion that lay concealed in his bed and subsequently bit him. Fortunately he escaped, with a few extremely painful days laid up.

I must confess that we sometimes took an inherent delight in watching these horrible, shrimp-like creatures (shrimp-like except that they have claws like a lobster and their tails turn upward) hoist with their own petard. We would imprison two or three of them on the ground within a circle of burning petrol and cruelly watch them sting one another to death.

After the day's work some of our evenings in camp were of a boisterous nature. After "rum up" a lot of us would gather in a tent and make enough noise to waken the dead. One night, when the row was at its loudest, we were conscious of the red face of the OC peering at us through the clouds of tobacco smoke from the open flap of the tent. He was so gratified at our high spirits that he went away to return immediately with a welcome bottle of whisky . . . The gentleman with the guttural "ah" sang louder than ever . . .

NCOs and men messed in one common tent. Each had a personal boy (native servant), or one servant between two, to perform domestic duties and otherwise attend to personal wants, paid for out of our own pockets. We also subscribed to augment our rather meagre camp fare, buying eggs, chickens, sweet potatoes and fresh fruit; one hundred deliciously ripe bananas would cost only fifteenpence, a chicken a like price, and other food in proportion. As a newly elected treasurer of the mess (presumably a nomination with Scottish associations had an alluring prospect) I had to account for the buying in and the spending. But this was no sinecure. At the end of the first week I found I had spent *seven thousand reis*, a sum at first sight to suggest that we were rapidly heading for "the ruin and dogs" as our Welsh friend used to say. As a matter of fact, in English money, it amounted only to about three pounds ten for the whole crowd! Our white Portuguese cook did the actual buying from the natives as they were too shy to come into camp, he having to go out to their habitations and barter with them there. But he, swarthy rascal, could never balance his accounts correctly, mistakes being always in his favour. But apart from his natural weakness, he was an excellent cook. His delicious fruit salads will live in the memory of all who were so lucky as to share in these delectable dishes in that out-of-the-way little camp in Portuguese East Africa. They simply swam in milk. With all his evil reputation – and he was even said to exchange our modern rifles for old pattern "gas-pipes", and a little hard cash, from the unscrupulous Portuguese at Mozambique, crossing to the island by boat in the dead of the night – he nevertheless won his way to our hearts, like a woman, through the cooking pot . . .

An amazingly unexpected thing happened one morning to all my music. I had left it in the form of a bundle on my bed and was working in the office. Suddenly a roaring wind like the whirl of a thousand propellers brought us hurrying out. There, high in the sky, going round and round on the apex of a whirlwind, was my precious music in a hundred loose sheets. Astonished, I stood looking on at this sight, the little white specks disappearing quickly, accompanied by a cloud of dust. H___ and I ran to our tent to find it (the only one so affected) collapsed, and all our things strewn about and lying buried under a deep covering of sand – an astounding and discouraging sight.

Although miles separated some of the sheets of music – which fell to rest on barbed wire, in native camps, on the open road, and in the hospital grounds – so thorough was the search that a surprising and welcome proportion was ultimately recovered.

Another distraction, in this case of human origin, every morning was the insistent clanging of an alarum to awaken the camp. The contrivance used hung suspended from the branch of a tree in the form of an iron hoop, just within the shadow of our tent, and was struck regularly and violently by a native with an iron bar, at 5.45 precisely. It did not trouble my snoring half-section, H_____, whom I had to rouse to the dawn of each day by artificial respiration. On me the effect of this daily musical call was different. I would not have minded so much if the alarum had been gradual, but the wielder of the iron bar, after the simple manner of the native, took a fiendish swipe that sounded as if a badly cracked bell had been struck by a thunderbolt. This made me nearly jump out of my skin, to lie, trembling and bathed in perspiration, listening to a succession of lesser strokes that lasted some considerable time. The mental effect on me was to make me anticipate the wretched performance by exactly three minutes every morning. Because the dusky operator arrived barefooted I could never tell to the very moment when the thing was going off, and, when the crash did come, it was like receiving a shock from a galvanic battery. I soon began to lose my whole night's rest through this and lodged a protest with the OC, expecting little satisfaction.

However, the next morning, lying awake as usual, waiting for the crash, I listened with mixed feelings to the faintest little tinkling sounds that emanated from the direction of the iron hoop. With a desire to find out what manner of creature was this – be it man or devil – who could perpetrate such jokes in the cold dawn on poor suffering souls, I arose and took a peep around the corner of the tent. He was indeed a typical native "boy", his sombre features gradually relaxing into a grin as he saw my blank expression!

As I could not be assured of peace from such a versatile artist, I shifted my quarters to the far corner of the camp.

In charge of the YMCA, which had our blessings for the comfort it brought to body and soul, were Captain Sandacock[78] and Lieutenant Milton.[79] Poor as the opportunity was for them to keep up supplies, the troops at Lumbo seldom wanted for a variety of tinned stuffs, potted meats, sauces and such like. Notepaper and pencils were in great demand, and every encouragement was given to the boys to write home frequently. Divine service, held two or three times during the week, and on Sundays, was always well attended

---

[78] Samuel Sandercock, 4th Class Chaplain, Army Chaplain's Department attached Royal Army Medical Corps (WO 372/17/156688; WO 374/60228);
https://m.facebook.com/Small-Town-Great-War-Hucknall-1914-1918-117600881609310

[79] Milton - unable to trace

and appreciated. There were many interesting and frank discussions, even on such a subject as swearing; swearing as a habit, swearing on occasion, or swearing by accident. Was it really wicked or not, and had it a value as a stimulant? These discourses were sincere and homely, and sometimes amusing, but our clergy-officers were jolly good fellows and wished only to come from everything. They organised the Saturday night concerts and took a concert party on board the hospital ship *Gascon*,[80] which lay in the bay. We enjoyed the excursion immensely, including the discomfort of having to wade ashore in three feet of water at 1 a.m. amid laughter and an exchange of good-natured banter.

The water hereabouts was shallow, the beach shelving gradually to deep water. There was no landing-stage for the heavy barges to unload stores they were bringing ashore from the ships. It was therefore a common sight to see many hundreds of natives in long lines, wading through the water, bringing these commodities to dry land. But these natives were all as naked as when they were born and it mattered not to them that they had a quarter of a mile to walk to the storehouse and a like distance back again. The simplicity of the native was a delight. Having to go down to collect half a dozen Fords off the barges, once they were ashore, I allowed my "boys" to amuse themselves trying to start them. Instead of pushing the starting handles home, they merely turned them loosely in their sockets and did that vigorously. Obtaining no result, they turned faster and faster, finally falling in a heap on the ground, exhausted. Nigger-like, the performance was followed by yells of derision . . .

Again I went down with fever. All the livelong day I lay, bathed in perspiration. The boys gathered round and the

---

[80] *Gascon* was built in 1897 in Belfast with a tonnage of 6287grt, a length of 430ft, a beam of 52ft 2in and a service speed of 12.5 knots. Owned by the Union Castle Line, *Gascon* became a hospital ship on 25 November 1914 able to carry 434 patients. Her first task was transporting survivors of HMS *Pegasus* sunk in Zanzibar Harbour on 20 September 1914. *Gascon* returned to normal service on 15 February 1920.

thermometer did the rest.

So, once more, I found myself in hospital, fairly comfortable, and everybody kindness itself. The days were easy, the food light, and peacefully the hours passed slowly by. I used to lie awake at dawn and listen to the deep-throated roar that came from a thousand natives turning-to for their day's work. I cannot express what deep mystery lay hidden in that wild, barbaric yell that greeted the first streak of dawn. I used to lie and try to anticipate the gracious moment when we should leave a country like this for ever. Men fell ill, got better, and fell ill again. One of our hospital dispensers was a man with every opportunity to keep well; he never went into the sun for a moment without a helmet; yet the sun got him, penetrated his brain and sent him mad. I heard his dreadful cries and the scuffling of the men holding him down. Exhausted and limp, he was carried away to the *Gascon*, and so, in due course, out to sea. The country would turn any man mad, or kill him by degrees if he waited long enough. I was reading an authority on the country who wrote in glowing terms of the glorious sunshine. Glorious it certainly was and weirdly wonderful the country, but with all its great possibilities, it was no place for a white man. The white Portuguese themselves, swarthy and inured to a hot climate, showed unmistakably the physical effect of living in the country, in the sallowness of their complexion, the jaggedness of their temper, and a general appearance of debility and extreme lassitude.

During convalescence I was privileged to hear two very interesting addresses: one on snakes, the other on the problem of the African native.

Trooper Arthur Loveridge[81] left England before the war to secure a representative collection of African snakes, and was on this work when war broke out. He joined the East African forces and mixed the work of war with the business of snake-

---

[81] Arthur Loveridge, 714 East African Mounted Rifles (WO 372/12/145432); *Many Happy Days I've Squandered* (1951); Carl Gans, "In Memorium" in *Herpetologica*, Vol. 37, No. 2 (Jun, 1981), pp. 117-121.

lifting as circumstances permitted. He spoke from the front of the platform in the YMCA reading-room, and had with him at the moment sixty snakes of different species – there were 1700 different species altogether, he explained. Some of the snakes he let loose, much to our discomfort, for they got out of hand, and began to crawl among our legs. One thing that had puzzled us he now made clear. We had often seen what we thought were snakes wriggling along the ground with four little half-grown stumps, two just behind the head, and two near the tail. These we learned were not snakes, but skinks, a branch of the lizard family. Once upon a time these four little stumps were properly developed legs by which they propelled themselves along, but now, owing to the tendency to crawl on their bellies, had become atrophied. Some day, he averred, they would entirely disappear. This may be true but is probably open to question.

Some of the snakes he had freed remained motionless, head erect, and eyes – fiery little orbs of rich colour – fixed on one or the other of us. So steady and prolonged was the magnetic stare that a distinct feeling of uneasiness crept over those who had to withstand the ordeal. It was difficult, explained our naturalist, always to distinguish dangerous snakes from harmless ones among so many different species, and it was equally difficult to tell to what degree a snake might be dangerous – it was certainly impossible for a novice to do so. Among the snakes present there were deadly poisonous ones (we gave a shudder and moved uneasily) and some perfectly harmless ones. In one part of Africa the small boys had a clever way of dealing with the most mighty of snakes, the python. A farmer, say, has been troubled by the loss of some of his stock. Small boys are put on the watch. A goat is seen to fall, seized by the leg by a waiting python lying cunningly hidden in the long grass; the deadly coils are twined round the struggling body, crushing the victim to pulp and stilling its piteous cries for ever. The time for action has not yet arrived. From their hidden vantage-point the watchers see the prey devoured, and then, and only then, stealthily follow up the track of the python as it retires, with equal stealth, into the shade of the surrounding bush. But it does not go far. In the first convenient shady spot, the sluggish creature now comes to rest, to sleep and digest its meal. Eager for revenge and the reward that will soon be theirs, the boys follow up and wait. They know that, sooner or later, the reptile, satiated and overcome with lassitude, will yawn in its sleep. At this moment, with remarkable dexterity, they thrust into its open jaws a stick, pointed at each end, and the python is caught.

The other address, by Captain Sandacock, was of a personal character, inasmuch as the subject had to do with the native and our treatment of him. This was a matter that more closely affected many Dutchmen, or South Africans as they preferred to be called, who sat among us. The padre spoke well, though admitting that he lacked personal experience to any great extent among natives, which admission led the kindly man on to dangerous ground. It was admitted that nobody could know the native better than those who had to live with him and deal with him all their lives. These South Africans averred that to teach the black man that he was a brother of the white man, and that the white man's Christian religion said so, was, to put it forcibly, not only wrong but wicked. It caused no end of trouble in South Africa, they declared where natives made use of this doctrine for an excuse not only to demand but to take equal rights and privileges with the white man; indeed it did not end here, for the vices of the white man were copied with dire consequences, principally to white women. Cases were cited in detail which hushed the audience. The discussion, which took place in the recreation hut in the hospital grounds, waxed sultry. Some of the Dutchmen got up and walked out, and we were all relieved – and particularly the padre, who was distinctly getting the worst of it – when the meeting was rather abruptly brought to an end . . .

When I left hospital and returned to camp, I found that De Bussy had floated in from "details" and had become one of our company. He must have found the same hospitable current that I did, for he was also known to Sergeant Millane; at any rate, he was heard to say, *"Meredith, we're in!"* a cryptic form of expression that conveyed much.

The *Salamis*.

". . . . I shifted my quarters to the far corner of the camp."

Chapter 14

The military situation during the latter part of July and early August gave the gravest concern to all British troops on the Mozambique line. After his great success at Kilimane, and the routing of the troops sent down against him through the forest, Von Lettow succeeded in subjugating the garrison at Namirrue. After this he took a rest for several days. He then started on his anticipated march to Monapo. It was then that all the alarm took place and Lumbo dug trenches and put up barbed-wire defences. He got one-third of the way, whereupon, doughty man as he was, he realised the hopelessness of the task before him. Scattered British troops were reforming and closing in on him. Monapo and Lumbo were too dangerously near the coast, well held, and in the apex of a triangle, and, tempting as the project was, it was too daring. He turned on his tracks and retreated, with the same methodical thoroughness as he had advanced. For two hundred miles into the west, far into the wilds of Portuguese East, he retired by forced marches.

When the news of his disappearance reached us we again lapsed into that phase of stagnation that always followed the disappearance of Von Lettow. Excitement died down, work slackened off, and everybody began to look at everybody else as if asking, "Well, what's to be done now?" And nobody knew . . .

On resuming my duties in the office I found that owing to depletion in the ranks due to illness we were very much behind in our work. It was not always fever or the sun that sent men into hospital. Corporal Mamot[82] and Pye,[83] two of

---

[82] Mamot should be Marmont.

our company, were both in hospital with poisoned feet caused by jiggers. The jigger is a flea-like insect that lives in the sand. She, for it is the female that causes all the trouble (as usual, from some points of view), gets into your boot, or at any rate gets on to the foot, burrows into a tender part, usually under the nail of the big toe, and there deposits her eggs. Irritation and inflammation set in; then, discovering what's the matter, you engage a native – see that he is skilled to the work – and, with the help of a needle (not a rusty one), he extracts the bag of eggs. If the operator is unskilful and the bag is broken, then look out for trouble, and septic poisoning, which might result in the loss of the toe-nail, the toe, or even the foot. I had often heard the expression, "Well, I'm jiggered!" but never thought it would apply to me! I had no less than eight taken out of one foot in twenty-four hours, all carefully extracted without a single mistake, by my boy – "Blanco," I called him, for he was the whitest black man I ever knew.

"Blanco" and I got on very well together. He used to make excellent tea, at least I thought it was until one day I happened to see him *boiling* the brew. However, right or wrong, it proved excellent drinking, and so I said nothing, but let him carry on in his own way. Our fellows thought a lot of my tea; there was no one in the camp who could make tea like it, and I received a commission to provide tea for the boys every night. One night, for some reason, the tea was not forthcoming, and as there was no obligation on me to provide it, nothing was said; but when I turned in, I found a rifle in my bed (to shoot myself with, I suppose), a bayonet (in case the former miscarried), and a note to the effect that they (my disappointed friends) wished me good-bye, and a soldier's farewell.

Next morning I unearthed a mess tin for the brewing of tea, a hair-brush, and several other articles which had escaped my attention.

---

[83] Pye - unable to trace.

I took care that the tea had an extra boiling that night, in the hope of revenge, but the unsuspecting victims pronounced it the best brewing yet! The man who provided the milk declared it to be his milk that had improved the tea so wonderfully, but one might expect anything from this hardened individual (Corporal Fairchild, by name),[84] whose fertile mind had conceived the idea of providing paint-brushes for the camp by snipping off chunks of my hair. "Camels' hair brushes from Cam'ell's hair," he used to say, playfully, taking off another chunk. He it was who strongly objected to my old bamboo pipe, albeit a sweet smoke, that had taken the place of my little broken briar, filling the stem from time to time with bits of iron, copper wire, and match sticks. On my threatening to cut off the supply of hair, so to speak, in the future, if this outrage were ever repeated, he promised reform, admitted my tea was good, and all was well again . . .

Another lively insect living in the hot sand, but unlike the jigger, minding his own business, was the ant-lion. In appearance not unlike a wood-louse, though much smaller, this little animal excavates a cone-shaped pit in the sand, digging himself in at the bottom, where he waits, ready at any moment to seize with his powerful pincer-like jaws any unlucky insect – usually an inquisitive ant – that happens to tread on the loose and treacherous edge of the pit, and slip in. once an insect finds itself sliding down the steep sides, it has extreme difficulty in obtaining a foothold in its efforts to climb out again; the victim of this ingenious trap might be on a fair way to regaining the edge, but in such a case it receives a shower of sand, thrown up by the now anxious ant-lion. Odds are against the luckless insect, which cannot stand the maddening showers of sand that smother and blind it, and, exhausted with the futile effort, it sinks to the bottom of the pit, to be drawn underground by merciless claws to a dark and certain death. Sometimes an insect slips over the edge,

---

[84] Fairchild - unable to traace.

to fall headlong to the bottom, to an end swift and sure. I have seen insects fall in and get out again, but not often; the odds are all in favour of those terrible onslaughts of sand, which increase in volume as the struggling insect's endeavours to escape appear to be succeeding. Any foreign matter lodging in the pit by accident is immediately ejected. Interested to know what would happen in the event of one ant-lion getting into another's trap, I tried the experiment. Immediately there was a battle royal. They seized each other and the sand flew in all directions, the antagonists going round and round in the cramped space in the bottom of the pit in a whirl of conflict. Sometimes it ended by the intruder being thrown bodily into the air, to escape immediately, only too glad to do so; or the contestants disappeared to continue the fight underground, when the sand lifted in convulsive little upheavals. In the latter event one could generally tell when the battle was over by a movement of dry sand just below the surface, denoting the rapid retreat of the defeated one.

Berins was a patient in the hospital and came to see me. Davies, my little Welsh friend, was another who paid me a visit and gladly accepted the invitation to share food with me, bringing the news that Von Lettow was making north, to German East again, that all the troops were coming down the line, and that some of them were being drafted into the Lindi district again. Sergeant Fineberg also looked me up. (By the way, we never saw anything of him or his band of natives after they left the Lurio River, although we were on the same road – striking evidence of the extensive and dense nature of this wild country.) Seeing me again, he pressed me to visit him at his own habitation, a thick-walled, whitewashed, loopholed pirate's lair. I went one evening to find my host in good form, surrounded by a cosmopolitan crowd of rough white men, used to the "bossing of niggers". But, with all their roughness, they were fine, hardy men, ready to feed with you, fight with you, or get thoroughly drunk with you, for as one of them said, "What the 'ell's the use of doing a thing, unless you do it well?" Before supper was over, they were out on the road, quelling a fight between native troops and Indians. We could tell by the row that it was quite serious, and several casualties resulted, but, in due course, when our friends returned, supper was resumed as if nothing had happened.

Sergeant-Major "Pete" – he was known by no other name – the roughest diamond of the lot, took pleasure in reminding me of the memorable New Year's Eve at Massasi, when the sentiment of "Merry and Bright" made a lasting impression upon him, and, as he and Fineberg were the principals in this strange company, I was indeed well at home. A musical evening followed in the courtyard of the building, with the aid of the piano borrowed from the YMCA; Parkinson was the pianist, and Mounce the fiddler. Songs were sung, differently and indifferently, everybody joining in when they should, and sometimes when they should not. With unlimited quantities of *vino tinto*, the Portuguese wine, honours were drunk, and men were drunk. So convinced were our friends that work was now over in East Africa that they were determined on enjoying themselves prior to sailing for an unknown destination. Although the future was still obscure, they were certain the campaign was at an end, and this was the spirit of the evening.

From September right through October we found matters getting quieter and slacker. The days were long, sunny, and peaceful, the nights starry and still . . . Only the jackals howled to the empty sky, and made us turn uneasily beneath our mosquito nets . . .

One evening we visited an Indian farmer. The farm, including the out-buildings, was completely surrounded by a prickly pear-hedge, twelve feet high, and far too thick for any prowling animal to force a way through. Entrance was by a heavily barricaded door extending to the top of the hedge.

The live-stock was secured every evening in sheds built on piles, standing rakishly high above the level of the ground. A large number of bullocks and goats had to climb laboriously up a crazy plank to enter these night shelters, after which the plank was removed. Hundreds of fowls departed in the same way except that their abode was still higher in the heavens. On the occasion of our visit we saw all these things done, after which our dusky and dour-visaged host – careful to have us understand that he owned the lot – begged to be allowed to retire, which he did after making a courteous bow. It was now dusk, and we saw him carrying his lighted lantern to his own apartment within a building something like a miniature castle, as he pulled up the "drawbridge" after him. Just as if all these precautions wree not sufficient, he kept a pack of ferocious dogs, whose snarling and barking now hastened our depature. It was typical of the sort of existence one had to live out here, and, if he made any money at it, we thought, he was richly entitled to it.

Another night was spent in a visit to a great *ngoma*. After a walk of two miles through the bush we came to an open space where hundreds of natives, both men and women, were dancing round blazing fires in wide circles. At an improvised drinking stall, *pombe* was being consumed in reckless gulps. The wild, almost fanatical chanting, the glare of the fires, and the familiar rhythmic beating of the drums, drew us nearer to the pulsating, naked dancers, who squirmed and twisted, and called to the open stars above, and sang to the music of the hollow drums below. Dusky young maidens smiled with flashing eyes and a liberal display of white teeth as they performed the shimmy – the real shimmy. Their shapely, smoothly-rounded, quivering limbs shone like polished mahogany in the glint of the fires. If there was the slightest suspicion of the glad eye for the white visitors, it was discretely received. Some very elderly women, passive onlookers no longer, joined in the throng amid encouraged shouts, and for a space at least, with laughing faces, were youthful again. The men, of more excitable temperament, leaped into the air, and some broke away to perform wild, spinning dances by the edge of the roaring flames . . .

It was a shame to spoil a gathering of this kind, but nevertheless, before we could realise the purport of it, from the darkness of the surrounding bush sprang a large posse of native police with great cries and a blowing of whistles; and instantly there was a terrific uproar! A quick application of sand put the fires out, in the darkness it was impossible to tell friends from foes as everybody yelled and fought. In the resulting confusion we were lucky enough to escape a resounding crack on the head. We got out of the mêlée as quickly as possible, thanks mainly to a friendly Somali, who guided us through the bush . . . it was because these natives had not first asked permission to hold the dance that action had been taken to stop it . . . we heard their angry cries from the bush, long after, rising to the vast, starry dome above, like a long-drawn-out wail –

"Curses on the Police! Curses on their fathers and mothers, and on their children, and their children's children! Curses on the Authorities, and all their relations – their children and all their children's children! Curses on them! Curses on them!" (Literal translation)

As we turned weary heads on our pillows that night, we wondered who had justice on their side, the white interlopes, or the children of the forest . . .

There was little chance for walking excursions, owing to the thick bush and the long reaches of the forest, but one Sunday Sergeant Small (the one from Rhodesia, who was used to this kind of country) and I took a tramp of five miles along a cart-track – heavy walking over the rough surface, but enjoyable nevertheless – until we came to an important Portuguese fruit plantation. Here we found a pretentious building that was as difficult to get into as a fortress. But we managed to attract the attention of the foreman of works, and win his favour, though he seemed frightened beyond our understanding of his Portuguese master. Shown into the courtyard, we saw tons and tons of fruit being crushed, for the making of wine, by a large number of native women. Strange and primitive it all was; the women were extremely embarrassed, for they rarely, if ever, saw new-comers the whole year round. We were not invited into the place where they made the wine (which was disappointing) but we received permission to stroll over the huge plantation at will.

Although we had not been privileged to sample the no doubt excellent quality of the wine, the fresh air and exercise had imbued us with a natural exuberance that gave rise to boyish pranks. We playfully pitted our skill at spear-throwing against each other. (It was the fashion when walking to carry these handy and useful weapons in place of the conventional walking-stick.) Some passing natives, fascinated by this unusual exhibition on the part of white men – they had probably never seen such a sight before – watched us until we had disappeared. They might well be amused; we could never imagine the stoical Portuguese in playful mood. We intended to visit the place again and to carry a camera with us next time, but before we had an opportunity to do so, a row broke out, several people were wounded, one of our own Askari killed, and some inoffensive passing motor transport fired upon. So, after that, the project was off!

My bent for taking photographs brought me to a sad pass one day, on the horns of a dilemma – more literal than metaphorical, for the dilemma was an oryx. The only time I had seen this beautifully graceful creature was on our first arrival in Lumbo, when I was told it was a "tame" buck. Tame or not, he was now so dangerous that no one would venture near him, though this was unknown to me. I saw this noble creature on the outskirts of Lumbo, and, eager for a photograph, approached for a close-up. It was a "close-up" all right! He lowered his head and came for me, not at a rush, but quickly enough to prevent my escape . . . Here was a nice predicament! I had to hold on to his long sharp-pointed horns to avoid being impaled. I felt I had not sufficient strength to compete against this animal, which was as big as a horse. I tried gently relaxing my hold, but, as I did so, pressure became greater and warned me of the danger of letting go. This strange antagonist seemed glad to match his strength against mine, and to have at last the opportunity for a fight, for which he had probably been thirsting for years. I was at my wits' end to know what to do . . . Even with my six feet of bone and muscle I felt unable to resist the increasing pressure that was forcing me to the ground. Looking round – wildly, I admit – for some means of escape, I espied a garden surrounded by a fence. If only I could get behind that fence! I allowed the brute to force me – indeed I had little option – tottering like a drunken man, backwards. Sideways now, towards the gate, nearer still – another yard – I was there! With a quick movement I released my hold, darted within, shut the gate, and stood perfectly still. I knew the futility of moving away from that fence, which was frail and of no great height. The enemy, seeing now a barrier between us, after recovering from his surprise, jumped high into the air and, for a moment, I thought he was going to leap the fence; but I remained close up to the gate, standing motionless. And there we were, staring at each other over the top, my heart thumping like a steam hammer, his eyes glaring with anger and disappointment. It was some time before a party of Askari, seeing the fix I was in, came to the rescue, the beast making a noble picture as he slowly approached the new intruders in challenging attitude. But the numbers were too many for him, and a formidable ditch barred the way. After due deliberation, and in the face of increasing difficulties before a fusillade of heavy stones, the creature suddenly bounded away and we saw him no more. The photograph was lost, leaving me alive, so to speak, to the possibilities of what an excellent picture we might have made!

We left Lumbo at ten o'clock one Sunday morning for what

proved to be the most interesting of our excursions, chartering a boat and sailing across to the island of Mozambique. Stepping ashore in the heat of the midday sun, not a soul was to be seen. The foreshore, with its innumerable native sailing craft laying idle, and fishing gear spread out to dry in the hot sun, was deserted. Climbing up the sloping footway, we entered the narrow, winding main street, hot as an oven and silent as the grave. Coated in white, the thick-walled, centuries' old buildings shimmered in the fierce rays of the sun. Doors were closed and windows barricaded. High above the narrow pavements coloured sun-blinds protected the windows of the upper stories, giving relief to the surrounding whiteness. Even our rascally cook from the camp, whom we had enlisted as guide, was at a loss. The whole place seemed wrapped in the slumber of centuries. Indeed, it required little imagination to believe it a city of the dead, except for those tell-tale sun-blinds. As a matter of fact, it was the midday siesta, and we found accommodation, eventually, where light refreshment was obtained, the Portuguese attendant, though civil enough, careful to let us know that, although he had no objection to our presence, neither the Germans nor the British were welcome in his country.

A walk to the far end of the island brought us to the ruins of the old fort, founded (as still plainly inscribed on the well-preserved portals) by the great Portuguese navigator, Vasco da Gama, in 1502. Still sturdy and gaunt, its old, weather-beaten battlements frowned over the waters as they had done since those far-off days when that first intrepid voyager from Europe landed and built this distant bulwark of empire. Along the wide parapet the old muzzle-loaders still stood, nozzles to the open sea, deserted, groggy at the knees, and now half hidden among the gloom of these ancient ruins – disturbed only by the occasional boom of the sluggish waves breaking listlessly on the long sloping shore – was to conjure up scenes of stirring days of old when first the Portuguese hoisted their flag there, and ventured into the mysterious forests of the mainland.

We turned from this silent evidence of the ancient glory and power of Portugal to the wretchedness of the natives living in humble abodes close by, a community to themselves. But fist impressions here did not invite closer inspection, and we departed.

The early days of November found Lumbo nearly empty. The YMCA had gone, nearly all the hospital was cleared away, and, I believe, by this time nobody was left up the line.

The last regiment of King's African Rifles had rushed, whooping and laughing, naked, into the sea, to march back, refreshed and very smart in their clean shorts and tunics, proudly led by a young (very boyish) English officer, his pale face and slim figure contrasting strangely with the grim bearing and big black limbs of his dusky company as they sang in the quick, barking fashion peculiar to them:

(translation) – England has enemies,
So have we!
England is fighting,
So are we!
We are British soldiers – Ah!

These fine British Askari – whom we could not help but admire – had gone. Members of our own company had departed, and the MT Stores camp was practically empty of personnel and material . . .

Sitting alone in my tent one dark evening, quietly writing, I was startled by a long, piercing scream. After a few tense moments it was followed by another. With a succession of further screams which now appeared to come from the direction of the car-track at the back of the camp, I hurried there with a hurricane lamp, to behold a hulking savage in a ferocious temper – indeed the foam was dripping from his thick, pouting lips. Before him stood a young woman, not a third of his size, sobbing bitterly. Her only garment, which had slipped to the ground, she now drew about her as, in piteous and frenzied tones, she appealed to me for help. She told her story in rapid and excited words, occasionally angrily interrupted by the man. But, ignorant of their particular language, I felt nonplussed until the arrival of the native police who, perhaps fortunately for me, were soon on the scene. With the help of their Swahili interpreter I gathered the hideous truth: the girl had been bonded to mate with the man, whose very presence she loathed. She would not go with him peacefully, so she was forcibly being carried to his camp in Lumbo. He would tolerate no interference as he was entitled to her under their peculiar rules and laws, and he even now appealed to the police for assistance, so that, in opposition to my strong objections, they could not deny him. With the help of the police she was thereupon dragged away, her piteous screams rising excruciatingly on the still night air, until distance merged them into the other faint noises of the night.

Later, when I was on my way back to camp from Lumbo (where I had been for the latest wireless news, which was a nightly custom), I was shocked to see this same girl stretched out, face down to the ground, in a native camp. She was crying out in her helpless agony while stern and sullen-visaged savages looked on. She was being cruelly beaten, and I was alone – it would have been more than my life was worth, and useless also, for me to attempt to interfere. When at last her wailing died down, and the body lay unresponsive to the lash, the thongs binding her wrists and ankles were untied and her tortured, limp body was picked up – tenderly enough, maybe – by her lord and master, and carried away to his tent in grim triumph.

They do not put this type of picture on the cinema screens for the edification of the young ladies of England who are so enamoured of sheikhs – it would be as well, perhaps, if they did.

Suddenly, like a nightmare dispelled by the light of a glorious dawn, revealing a way to a new-born hope, came the cry: *"The* war's over!" The news that flashed like magic from the battlefields of France, thrilling millions, trickled silently over the wireless to a few men holding aloft hurricane lamps in a desolate little outpost on the lonely coast of East Africa's wild domain.

A great stampede followed. Men, with some excuse, nearly demented, ran in circles. The news flashed to all quarters of Lumbo; a few rockets soared into the sky, rifle fire crackled in jubilation and the sky was bright with the glare from fires in various camps. The natives, easily excited, now had good reason to become more so. We still had a small army of Swahili natives with us, and, with the whites of their eyes gleaming in the firelight, they begged confirmation of the news: "*Germani kwisha?*" "'*Dio! 'dio!*" In high glee they stoked the fires higher, giving vent to wild yells. On returning to our own camp, *bandas* that were no longer required were fired, though this was no excuse for our misguided camp boys to set fire to our one and only lavatory! "What the hell did you want to do that for, you blithering idiots?" was shouted to non-understanding ears, and we had the mortification of watching the flames vie in intensity with those from the burning *bandas*. The mentality of the native is often beyond understanding, but when the Indian store close by was fired, they probably had a shrewd method in their madness. The unhappy owner came running out in great alarm, and it was only by the efforts of the white men in the camp that the building was saved. He hardly deserved it, for his prices were always high and his nature, like that of most Indian traders, was mean. His livestock had to be set free to escape the flames, but they met with an equally disastrous fate (from the owner's point of view) when they fell an easy prey to the delighted natives, who gleefully absconded with their prizes into the dark night. Many fowls, in evading the grasping clutches of the excited natives, ran straight back into the flames, to roll over at once and shrivel up – before their time!

The next day, leaving three men only in charge of what remained of the camp, we left Lumbo once and for all, embarking on the *Salamis*, which was decked out gaily in bunting from stem to stern. After a brief call at Kilwa Kisiwani we arrived in due course at Dar-es-Salaam.

We landed in a veritable downpour and semi-darkness. For at least two miles we marched beneath the dripping coconut trees to the main base MT camp – Sea View Camp, as it was called. It was a hot, steamy, sticky ordeal. It took us two whole days to recover from this thorough soaking and generally to settle down – thankful that there were no other duties than attention to our own needs.

In the depths of the Coconut Plantation.

Chapter 15

Duties at the base MT workshops necessitated a daily trip by Ford trolley. The ride took us for two miles through the coconut plantation by which, except on the seaward side, Sea View Camp was surrounded – as pretty a journey as one could wish for. So jolly and fair-like were these daily excursions that we dubbed the little Ford line "The Scenic Railway".

Dar-es-Salaam was a general re-union place for all ranks. Some familiar faces were missed, and these, alas! we should see no more. Subsequently nearly all my friends disappeared one by one into hospital again. Then the mysterious epidemic of influenza broke out; we lost thirty-seven men in one week. The little cemetery on the outskirts of Sea View Camp became filled up and had to be extended, and the number of deaths – one hundred and thirty-six – was pitiful and also alarming, for we never knew whose turn it would be next.

Indians, natives and Chinese went the same way, with a difference only in the method of burial. We saw the gleam of a funeral pyre far away on the beach at night, with dark, lithe figures in attendance, watching the cremation of their friend. In the heat of the midday sun, a running, mourning, hysterical cortège carried the body of some dead native to a grave, a screaming, crying retinue of women running behind. I preferred the quiet dignity of our own funerals – the solemnity, the muttered prayer, the Last Post, and the sharp salute.

And then, when we thought there was no hope for us, and that we were all going to be wiped out, the epidemic gradually waned and, after a while, ceased.

In the meantime 900 troops left Dar-es-Salaam on the

Ingoma for the Cape and Europe. As the steamer slowly left harbour, bedecked with flags, a salute of guns speeded her on her journey, and envious eyes followed her out to sea.

A free Sunday gave four of us the opportunity to hire a native boat and explore the high reaches of the harbour, sailing round the wrecked German steamers, and climbing the steep hills ashore to enjoy the scenery revealed from this vantage point, becoming conversant with the local natives, visiting their habitations and wandering through their humble plantations. In the terrific heat of midday we enjoyed the luxury of sustaining drinks from the unripe coconuts, which were plentiful.

In the evening we met Harris, the pianist, and Bunn, subsequently all dining together at the Africa Hotel, on the open balcony. A big crowd of troops took dinner or indulged in cooling drinks. It was pleasant to be in a state of civilisation again, talking in subdued, quiet tones, at tables with clean, white linen, waited on by people who acknowledged one's existence with the prefix "Sir". Somebody was playing the piano to indifferent ears when we arrived, but, after dinner, it wasn't a case of indifference when Harris took his place; crowds came in from the street, and the blocked pavements had to be cleared by the police. A little man, with an excitable temperament, Harris was undoubtedly a pianist of distinction.

When the visitor first arrives in the harbour of Dar-es-Salaam, he is fascinated with the charm and fairy-like appearance of his surroundings. To a mere human looking from the deck of a ship there is revealed a vision that a speck of dust has settled on a diamond. The speck of dust is the ship, but the diamond is the beautiful harbour, reflecting in its waters a million suns that cast a radiance over the surrounding palm-covered beaches, accentuating the vivid colours in the kaleidoscopic view of the straggling little settlement nestling beneath the coconut trees – a memory that will live with him his life through.

Once ashore, he will pass under the flamboyant trees which in the season gladden the eye with a profusion of scarlet bloom. Keeping in the shade – for it is terrifically hot – he will spend an hour, or maybe two, in the seductive, spice-laden atmosphere of the Indian shops that are to be found on both sides of the main street which runs parallel with the whole line of the harbour front. One may buy almost anything Eastern here: exquisite Indian jewellery, precious stones, rare models of quaint design and origin carved beautifully in ivory and gold, and such prosaic objects as an elephant's foot as a footstool – if such a thing appeals – lions'

A Street in Dar-es-Salaam.

A Street in the native village of Dar-es-Salaam.

and leopards' skins direct from the hunters, rhino horn and hide. Hundreds of pounds may indeed be spent in this way on a small number of articles.

There is a quiet solemnity and ease in the movements of the cosmopolitan crowd. Here, until quite recently, the swarthy Arab slavers held undisputed sway, plying their callous trade with a blind indifference to any interest, but their own. Now the natives move freely about. Well-to-do Indian shopkeepers and stout Indian and Greek caterers rub shoulders. Bronzed Colonials from all parts and a few khaki-clad British soldiers, hard-visaged and sun-tanned, take the place of the one-time ubiquitous German. Buildings, some pretentious, some mean – government buildings, humble bungalows, hotels and native eating-dens – reflect the dazzling light of the sun in splashes of colour, bright reds and blues, in tiling, facing and decorative lining. Cool retreats from the heat are seen on open stone balconies, airy verandahs and roomy courtyards. Behind lattice-work fences are to be discerned beflowered terraces, pretty tea-gardens and green tennis-courts. Then two miles way there is the native quarter of Dar-es-Salaam, which might appeal or might not.

For myself I was only too glad to make an excursion that way as soon as I had the chance. The town was four or five square miles in extent, its outer edge fringing the open road that leads into Dar-es-Salaam. The huts were of mud and wattle with thatched roofs, and some of the more pretentious had a verandah overlooking the street. The streets were ankle deep in sand, from which coconut trees sprang up in abundance, in fact, in some cases, the long slender trunks protruded through the roofs of houses to spread their lofty fronds above. Natives were dressed scantily: with the majority, a loin cloth was sufficient; a few wore the white robes of gentility; but all the little children – the bright spark of this dark life – were naked, chubby and pot-bellied, but full of life and fun, ready for a feed, fight or a good cry. The women, taking more pride in appearance, wore robes of gaudily-coloured cheap prints – one was clothed from head to foot in a Union Jack! Also, unlike the men, they were bonny, shapely, and decidedly clean; for charm of manner, grace, and good looks many could take full credit.

On regaining the town I met one of my chums of the *Port Lincoln* days, Thomas,[85] whom I had not seen since we parted on landing at Lindi. Over a cup of coffee in the Africa Hotel I listened to the exciting account of his subsequent adventures. Drafted into a company of Pioneers, he went with them up to the Lemasuli River and cut a path south-west for a distance of eighty miles. Here natives saw white men for the first time, and white men saw natives for the first time with nothing on, both sexes being quite naked. They didn't begin to dress till they saw the white man in trousers! But trouble followed the little band of hardy workers. For the purpose of their road-making, native labour was recruited wherever possible. After recovering from their first fear, the natives were only too anxious to oblige, falling on their knees and praying to be allowed to help. But, easy as this was, it was not so easy to prevent their taking fright and running away on the slightest suspicion of anything unusual. The Wireless Corps attached to the Pioneers used donkeys, and these donkeys were tracked by lions which, not content with taking a donkey occasionally, turned their attention to the natives, snatching them away in the dead of night. These silent and uncanny disappearances resulted in so many desertions that the headman was called upon for an explanation. He declared in distress that the white man's medicine was spiriting his men away. No amount of assurance that lions were the cause was of any avail. So traps were set and men spent uncomfortable nights in the branches of trees, without seeing a lion and without trapping anything except jackals. These creatures often indicate the presence of lions, whose constant companions they are,

---

[85] Thomas - unable to trace.

following them about. At another time and place a lion was seen crunching a dead zebra with a great circle of jackals looking on, hungry-eyed and motionless; sometimes the circle would imperceptibly close in a little, but not so little that it was unnoticed by the king of beasts, who stopped feeding and, with a series of snarls, sent them back to a respectful distance. When he had eaten his fill the jackals' turn came.

Eventually the Pioneers convinced the natives that lions were really the cause of the trouble. Proof was forthcoming in the discovery of a native who had been badly mauled by a lion. He was dead and his body torn to shreds, but why his body was left uneaten no one knew. On a further search of the surrounding bush human remains were found with deep indentations of lions' teeth in the skulls. After this indisputable evidence the prestige of the white man was reinstated. Unlike the experience of transport men, who found the noise of their vehicles driving all game away, the quiet and slow-moving band of Pioneers encountered any number of wild animals browsing in herds on the open meadow lands, and sometimes ran into bigger game in the form of buffalo and elephants. One day, with an elephant offering a target that could not be resisted, it was fired upon. Wounded or enraged, or both, the great beast charged. The valiant sportsmen now had recourse to "rapid fire" with a vengeance, and the animal, fortunately for them, collapsed only a dozen paces from where they stood. This meant plenty of food for the natives, who lost no time in sharing up the meat. What was left was buried, but was dug up a week later by other natives and devoured with relish!

The simple native thinks the white man a wonderful being. He looks upon him as one devoid of fear – he has never seen a frightened white man. My experience at the MT depot taught me a good deal. When work is to be done the native will see the white man tackle it boldly, and master it quickly. Not so the native; he approaches the work gingerly, and with a lack of confidence. This is the reason for the use of the *kiboko*, a whip composed of a strip of hippo hide, a cruel thong cutting deeply into the flesh if crudely wielded. This whip, unhappily, has to be used more or less on the uncouth bush native rather than on the semi-educated town worker if any progress is to be made at all. I never saw the *kiboko* used in Dar-es-Salaam, but had on occasion to raise my hand to one or two natives for crass stupidity and impudence. It had the desired effect at the moment, and any risk of subsequent bad blood was prevented by a cigarette and a lecture.

On the Lindi line I saw a white man (I regret to say) use the *kiboko* on two native porters with heavy loads on their heads who were *walking* instead of *running*. It was no affair of mine, but I wouldn't thrash an animal as he thrashed those men. Inquiries confirmed my suspicions. He was notorious for an uncontrollable temper. Here was a case of a man carrying the *kiboko* who was not fit to be in charge of natives in any capacity. Another man, a South African, at Lumbo, took a running kick at a native who at the moment was in the very act of handing me a chit from the doctor, excusing him from duty, a vivid example of some white men's impatient ignorance. He slunk off without a word to the distressed native, or the courtesy of an apology to me. Because the native accepts this brutal treatment silently, it follows not that he does not think deeply. Some day, this may be revealed unexpectedly. On the other hand, by reasonably kind treatment the ordinary native can be instilled with an affection towards his white *bwana* that places a sometimes unworthy gentleman on a divine plane. For instance, a NCO of the King's African Rifles once told me that his black comrades at one time really believed that their white officers went up to heaven every night and came down again in the morning!

Natives stood and stared at wonder at machinery working. They sat and closely watched the white man turn a handle in a box that gave out a clicking noise and threw out a brilliant light, transforming a plain white sheet into real life – a strange life of another world. At Sea View Camp they gathered in hundreds at the back of the screen of the open-air cinema, there to watch the pictures, which could be seen as clearly that way as from the front — reversed, of course, but that did not trouble the dusky spectators. As the scenes changed, their noisy comments were gloriously irrelevant to the subject. Their laughs, squeals, and shouts were so grotesquely out of place that the white company invisible on the other side of the screen were irresistibly swept into peals of laughter themselves. In those humorous pictures — not seen so much now — which used to depict a great crowd of people running and falling over one another, the natives yelled aloud, jumped up, waved their arms about, and laboured under the greatest excitement. In scenes where well-behaved people in evening dress moved about in elaborate drawing-rooms the clamour dropped to subdued whispers and intense gazing. In those gloomy diversions when what is known as "sob stuff" wracked our hearts, so misguided was the interpretation by the dark and more keenly sensitive section behind the screen, that they stood up and fought each other!

". . . I waited twenty minutes at a water-hole and succeeded in getting a good picture."

In addition to the wonders of the cinema, the natives were dumbfounded by such magic as the voice of the gramophone, the wireless, and the powers of electricity. Great ships came in from mysterious places beyond the waters, and, in like fashion, disappeared again into the unknown. When the first aeroplane rose like a giant bird from the crest of the hill opposite, and droned its way into the sky, can it be wondered that the natives completely lost their heads? Curiously enough they ran round and round in great circles, and, with their eyes glued skywards, collided and fell headlong. It is not surprising, therefore, that they should imagine that white men had divine power over life and death. They knew that the white man could, by the mere pointing of the "evil eye" (that glittered from the centre of a little black devil-box), strike a person into a motionless attitude, not materially, but in spirit certainly, which to their mind was much worse, for the material would die, but the spirit would live on, for ever subject to unnatural and evil possibilities in its helpless, mundane state. They shunned the camera as one would shun the devil. This made the obtaining of good photographs very difficult. Caution had to be exercised, or otherwise the production of the little "evil eye" had the electrifying effect of scaring the subject away in panic. Women were the worst subjects, their high-pitched screams distinctly embarrassing as they ran away. If they were encumbered with children they hid them under their garments, and covered up their own faces. These experiences were so disappointing that for a long time I gave up hope of obtaining really good results, though on one occasion I waited twenty minutes at a water-hole and succeeded in getting a good picture.

During my relatively short experience with the natives I liked them for their guileless, innocent manners, and got on with them very well. I never swore at them, had only to reprimand them on occasion, cultivated their confidence and respect, got more work out of them than even some of the old hands could get, and personal boys never parted from me without some show of emotion. "Blanco", my Portuguese boy, shed copious tears when I bade him good-bye...

The weather in December became overpoweringly hot, and, except for a few hours of cooling downpour, the sun shone intensely all day. The flies became veritable plague in the camp, and those who could avoid them by clearing out did so, though they might miss their meals, which did not matter as both the food and the cooking in the camp were unappetising. One jolly old character who really did make a visit to the cook-house worthwhile was "Jock" – Charlie Crichton fra' Dundee.[86] In his fifties now, as he would say, he had been a cabby of the old school; a typical Jehu of the whip and whipcord, hat a-cock, flower in the buttonhole variety. He had to drive one of "they" taxis now for a living, and a poor game it was! In "the guid auld days" he was never short of a nice cigar and a shilling in his pocket, and mixing with the gentry. But the best taxi-driver today could not come a "patch" on him in the heyday of his youth before motors were thought of. "Och no! They can never have *them* days," he would conclude with a chuckle. The last time I had seen Jock was when they were trying to make a soldier of him on Salisbury Plain, which, as he himself declared, was an "eempossibility" as he was too old in the tooth.

On the Plain, MT men were engaged in digging away a hillside to make room for a railway extension. This "navvy work" lasted all day and every day, including Sundays, enhanced however by glorious weather. Light-heartedly the men chalked inscriptions on wheelbarrows and lorries: "The Bulford Express", "Sit and Watchit", "Johnny Walker – still going strong" (that was mine), "Convict 99", "Load not to exceed One Ton – Daily", and "Six days shalt thou labour and on the seventh put a jerk in it!" A very honest sort of man, who had been a chauffeur in gentlemen's service, and who took his new position very much to heart because his wife cried and sent him sorrowful letters so that he was "sent to

[86] Charlie Crichton - unable to trace.

the beer" as he termed it, introduced me to Jock.

"Ah've never wor-rked in ma life," declared the new acquaintance; "always got good money lookin' for it! Ah'm a hackney cair-riage driver in private life and always had a gentleman's life of it; they canna mak' a navvy o' me now Ah'm gettin' auld man! Just tak' it easy, and dinna fret yersel'! Ah'm no worryin' aboot the wor-rk masel'; Ah've a guid job at you railway siding where Ah'm doin' vera well as a *sleeper* – that's all! We're navvies – just His Majesty's Navvies! It's no bad job – moving one corner of Salisbury Plain to another; and after the war we'll just set it back again. Ah joined as a motor driver, but all Ah've seen of motors is them passing me. Och, but we're all right – we're goin' to be fine!"

I never expected meeting him in the cook-house at Dar-es-Salaam. "Ou aye, but ye never know y'luck. Maybe Ah'll be giving ye anither surprise – some day," pointing downwards with his thumb. He always supplied me from a special dish which nobody else ever saw, and the operation was accompanied with a wink that was never acquired in a common cook-house.

When possible, Percy Head,[87] my genial half-section, and I took food at the Hotel Kigoma, going there from the depot nearly every day for lunch, served in the cool atmosphere of the stone balcony. This place will be remembered by the thousands of black troops who took advantage of the excellent catering of the popular Greek proprietor. Although it was two miles out of the town, we would return there sometimes in the evenings for dinner, for we were honoured with special privileges and the use of the piano, kindly considerations appreciated by those musically inclined.

In the middle of December another large draft had left for home, and it seemed that we should be there for some time longer – over Christmas anyway.

Sea View Camp, as its name implied, overlooked the sea,

---

[87] John Percy Head, M/203796 Army Service Corps (WO 372/9/114093)

spread out along the top of the cliffs, coconut trees having been cleared away to provide the site. Along the foot of the cliffs, Percy Head and I had many pleasant rambles, exploring the caves and backwaters for miles. We could walk straight into the sea for nearly half a mile without getting wet above the knees, so shallow was the water. At high tide it came up to the cliffs and we bathed in it from an iron ladder fixed in the cliff face. During our long rambles the treasures of the seashore were disclosed to us in all their variety and beauty. Fish of the most gorgeous colours – rich vermilions, vivid greens, silver and gold, variegated, striped, or of one colour – were a delight to behold; in shape ranging from delicate, translucent featherweights, to globe-fish of the appearance of well-seasoned footballs. Where the sea had eaten a way under the cliffs the dark caverns were full of interest; in the transparent pools little fish like gudgeon were as much at home out of water as in, hopping out on to the flat bare rocks when playfully chased by our spear-heads. On the shallow East African strand there was a perfect galaxy of sea-shells, seaweed, corals and living animals of

"Where the sea had eaten a way under the cliffs."

fascinating variety. On the return to camp, our black boy used to abstract the hermit crabs by the dextrous handling of a piece of string as a trap.

Just before Christmas an important personage who had been known to us in name only was to be seen basking in the sun on the verandah of a quiet little bungalow, overlooking the harbour of Dar-es-Salaam – "the Haven of Peace". This was our erstwhile and elusive enemy, Von Lettow. This valiant henchman of the German cause had worked his way right up from Kilimane back to German East, and round into Northern Rhodesia, no doubt greatly amused over the vain effort of the thousands of pursuers wo had attempted from time to time to capture him. There (in Rhodesia) he was planning a resourceful campaign that was going to be extremely embarrassing to pursuing troops with lengthened lines of communication, and to that sparsely inhabited province. He was cycling on ahead of his company when the news, brought by a British motor-cyclist, that the war was over, and that the Fatherland had agreed upon the "unconditional surrender of the German East African forces", gave him just cause for an expression of personal opinion!

The conditions of peace, however, forced upon him an acute realisation of the desperate state of the Fatherland. With heavy heart but still unconquerable spirit he strongly protested against the laying down of arms and was himself allowed to retain his sword. Travelling to the railhead on the edge of the Great Lakes, they entrained for Dar-es-Salaam, the black members of the party starting another little war on their own when, on being put behind barbed wirer at Tabora, they too realised the true significance of the new situation. The European section of the company reached Dar-es-Salaam in due course, to receive every consideration. The German strength on surrender was 155 Europeans and 1168 Askari, in addition to the usual number of porters and attendant women.

An account of the actual fighting that took place in this

campaign is not within the province of this book, but in case the reader should be under the mistaken impression that there was little excitement in this direction I may refer him to the numerous books that have been written from the point of view of the professional soldier. Meanwhile it might suffice if I quote an extract from the writing of Captain Jones[88] which appeared in a copy of *The Frontiersman* some time ago:-

"Both sides played a game of hide and seek, neither gaining much advantage, though occasionally they would blow up the line. It was easy to do this because there was thick bush up to the right-of-way. A mounted infantry corps was formed, the Fusiliers finding a squadron. They were mounted on mules as the neighbourhood was bad for horses. They were badly ambushed one day, among the killed being our sergeant ... Lieutenant ____[89] was also killed, being awarded a posthumous VC for his gallantry on this occasion. He could have been saved but he refused to move, saying that possibly his presence as an officer would save the other wounded from being murdered by the native German troops. His action was without avail because they were all shockingly mutilated, their heads being battered out of all shape. Our people got their own back, when they wiped out a whole German patrol of nearly a hundred men. In this, Lieutenant _____[90] who had got away in safety from a previous engagement,[91] and who was a noted elephant-shot in Rhodesia, killed thirteen Germans without changing his position . . . I am sorry to say he was himself killed near the close of the war . . . A portion of the Battalion . . . inflicted heavy defeat on the German force which was advancing to cut the line at _____. It was thick bush country with occasional open spaces . . . They held their fire until we were close enough to them, and then opened about five maxims and 800 rifles. They were up above

---

[88] William Price Sutton Jones
[89] Wilber Dartnell, killed 3 September 1915 at Maktau.
[90] Likely Frederick Courtney Selous, killed 4 January 1917 at BehoBeho.
[91] Bukoba, 21/2 June 1915.

in rocks, while we were lying down in the open . . . and we gave them rapid fire, then a mountain gun opened on them and that fixed them. They started to retreat at dusk . . . The next day we found sixty-three dead in the trench . . . Our casualties were only ten . . . I think we were lucky to escape as we did, considering the position they caught us in. We were in waterless country and water was sent out to us in kegs, on donkey-back. They were petrol kegs which had not been aired and the water was undrinkable, which was the very devil, because some of the men were nearly crazy with thirst."

General Von Lettow must be given credit for having attained his object, which, from the first, was to keep as many troops engaged in the futile campaign in East Africa as possible; but it was difficult to see any justification for his complaint that six weeks was a long time for him to be kept waiting in Dar-es-Salaam before he was permitted to leave for home, in view of the length of time he had kept the British authorities waiting for him! However, he departed in due course, and Dar-es-Salaam and the country knew him no more.

On Christmas Eve, Head, the brothers Tarrant[92] (who gave us the lively ghost scene on New Year's Eve at Massasi), Harris and myself motored off to the Chinese camp to fulfil an engagement we had there with the white NCOs. It was a good thing they sent a motor as we should have become hopelessly lost in the extensive plantations through which we had to pass to get there. We were received with a great show of warm hospitality. In the roomy *banda*, decorated lavishly with flowers, palm-leaves and paint, with tables set for forty diners, were prominently displayed terse inscriptions as follows:

      WELCOME TO CHINATOWN
    SERGEANT: WHAT OF THE NIGHT?
      DOWN WITH THE CHINESE!

---

[92] Tarrant - unable to trace.

DOWN WITH DRINK!
A MERRY XMAS TO ALL
BUT

The afterthought expressed in the one word "BUT" was an inference clear enough to us away from home, and although we had an excellent evening (which was carried on into the early hours) there was more than one lonely soul with thoughts drifting to a far-off spot where the phrase "A Merry Christmas" meant a little more than the mere words implied. To all outward appearances we were, nevertheless, a merry crowd.

Christmas Day started hot as blazes as usual. At 8 a.m. it was so sultry as to provoke an uncomfortable feeling of gradual suffocation. Up in the highlands we never felt the heat so humid or the sun's rays so fierce. Here on the coastal belt it was terrific. We all tried to make Christmas Day a success. We started well with a good breakfast and lazed exceedingly well too in the tents all morning. My restless soul prompted a busy morning packing up my collection of accumulated curios, which I despatched for home. In the afternoon three of us braved the sun and explored the coastline for miles, paddling about more or less in the cool water the whole of the time. We were ready for the really excellent dinner the camp provided on our return, and a concert followed in the evening. After that a hectic week of dinners and concerts to most of which we, as a musical party, were invited. A great event was a dinner given at a local hotel to the whole of the members of Sea View Camp (about 500) by the commissioned officers – a gracious compliment emanating from some fertile brain with a kindly sense of proportion in things, and, needless to say, greatly appreciated.

The best evening for our own little party of four entertainers was the last, when we had the honour of providing the musical programme for the Post Commandant and the senior members of his staff and friends, and all question of rank being laid aside for the time being. Thus ended our Christmas festivities.

Then, startled by the unexpected arrival of a case of Scotch whisky with the Commandant's compliments, we four started all over again.

Some time later on, from the darkness without, I heard my name called. "Billie!" shouted one of the boys, "I'm in the wrong tent!" Investigation proved that he was in the bottom of the trench.

A Last Impression of East Africa : the lonely symbol of the white man's only faith and hope, Christianity. (From the foreshore, Dar-es-Salaam.)

Chapter 16

The days of our sojourn in Africa were now manifestly numbered. Taking a last opportunity, De Bussy, Head and I wandered down to the open market-place of the native village of Dar-es-Salaam. The heterogeneous crowd of swarthy vendors and customers were bargaining with a great clatter of tongues and exaggerated gesticulation. On the stalls were laid out quantities of food in the form of cooked fish, live fish, dead fish – very dead; raw fruit, mashed fruit, and worse fruit; villainous-looking cake in bulk form, slab form, and some of it in the form of dry rot; sweetmeats, and meats that were far from sweet, and various other mystic concoctions of sordid flavour and beyond our simple tastes – or desires. There was little else but food for sale, over which hung a pungent odour from which there was no escape. In making purchases it was as well to stick to good, wholesome fruit that required *peeling*, a wise precaution in any circumstances. Through the cosmopolitan crowd of hungry, bustling mendicancy, and avaricious bargainers, swaggered a trio of conceited niggers, blatantly proud of the fact that they sported lemon-yellow boots, vividly striped open-necked shirts, real hard "straw-yards" worn at a jaunty angle of forty-five degrees, and a little more, polished ebony walking-sticks, duck slacks, and buck cigars. With money in their pockets to jingle these very fine fellows not only looked the whole world in the face – but the sky as well . . . Mohammedan women, closely veiled, glided by, their big, dark eyes sparkling at the strange white men over the top of their yashmaks . . . A procession of wailing women drew our attention – but nobody else's – as they passed along at funeral pace. They moaned and sometimes broke into a painful chant – at least it was painful to us, and perhaps also to them – led by a small boy carrying a palm leaf much bigger than himself. The principal figure among these sorrowing females was one led by the arm and entirely enveloped in a black shroud. She was a *bibi* going to the waters to be ceremonially cleansed after the death of her husband.

Only occasionally was Dar-es-Salaam favoured with a visit from a touring company of actors. Incidentally, we gave a performance ourselves, a quite nonsensical show which included a number of very common or (amateur) garden conjuring tricks, to a perspiring, packed house of darkies and other impressionable specimens of humanity. When we made a mistake, and crashed the tables and chairs on top of us, our appreciative audience nearly tore itself asunder with vociferous delight.

As I was saying, it was seldom a show was given in the town, and on the day of our perfunctory patrol of the native market, a touring company of Indians from overseas were performing at the local theatre. We spent a thrilling evening there; the place – a big, straggling barn-like structure – was packed from floor to ceiling. In the gallery patrons could not rest content to sit patiently for the rise of the curtain, but must needs press forward, many thrusting their arms and legs through the iron grille – without which most of them would have tumbled into the swagger seats below. Later, when the players became entangled in the intricacies of the plot, the galley patrons, out of sympathy, became further entangled in the grille, and made such a clatter with their tongues as to create an impression that the gallery was not a galley at all, but a big monkey house. In the swagger seats referred to all the rich Indian merchants of Dar-es-Salaam had congregated. Their noisy chatter added to the general din and interruption that never ceased during the whole of the evening, sometimes even overwhelming the voices of the performers on stage, who, incidentally, appeared to be quite inured to such conditions. Loud and angry protests, one against the other, went unheeded. Waiters laboriously climbed over the laps of people in and out of the auditorium. Bottles of soda water were eagerly brought to them by perspiring patrons, the proceedings punctuated by an insistent and irritating succession of pops and gurgles.

Ignorance of the language did not debar us from understanding the play. The story was like this:

SCENE: *A beautiful garden in India*

A foolish man has gambled away all his money to an ugly, avaricious old villain. Having nothing left but his own pretty daughter, he wagers her. To his dismay, and the conster-nation of his numerous friends looking on, the die is cast against him. Uttering heartrending cries of despair, the ruined father, accompanied by his commiserating friends, takes his sorrowful departure, leaving the daughter alone with the heartless villain. An impressive effect now is the alternative praying and singing by the girl (for deliverance) to the accompaniment of weird Eastern music (off stage) and the distant rhythm of tom-toms. Slowly, and with a gratified leer, the remorseless old villain begins to disrobe his newly acquired treasure. The victim makes no resistance to this proceeding, but redoubles her efforts in prayer and song. Relentlessly her garments are removed, one by one, until it is realised by the audience, with subdued intensity, that her last bit of flimsy raiment is to be removed. At this critical moment her prayers are answered. A holy man arrives by air. That is to say, he floats in on the back of a huge bird whose entry is controlled by a couple of very stout wires. With a great cry, Wickedness (in the form of the old villain) flies before Goodness (in the character of the new arrival).

(*interval*)

In the second act the girl is caught again in the evil meshes. This time, rescue seems out of the question. But the hero of the piece, the true lover of the girl, appears on the scene just in the nick of time, armed with a weighty bludgeon. With this weapon he slays not only the villain, but everybody else he sees. In fact, long before the end of the play, the stage is full of dead bodies. However, peace comes to the hero and heroine at last, and the final scene shows the man burying his hands in the blood of his numerous enemies, and smearing the mess (which is a real mess) all over the long, flowing tresses of his lady love, a customary proceeding on an occasion of this sort which has the effect of overwhelming the lady, satisfying the man's ambitions, and convulsing the already noisy audience into further paroxysms of excitement.

So ended the play. From the European standpoint, the acting was lifeless and lacked sincerity. Undoubtedly, it contained tense qualities, duly appreciated by the Indian section of the audience, and, altogether, the play was enjoyed and metaphorically swept the audience off their feet.

As January advanced there was no apparent hurry on the part of the authorities to bring our stay in Africa to an end. The men, becoming unsettled, discussed the situation thoroughly, marched in a body to General Headquarters, and stoutly requested a definite date for evacuation. Everything was settled amicably. A promise was given that men would be sent away as soon as ships became available, and this was carried out. A speeding up of work at once commenced. It simply amounted to parking the cars and making a scrap-heap of the wrecks. This did not take long, and one afternoon we left the MT depot for the last time. Our work was done.

With a view to turning inaction into activity, even if it were only of a temporary and mischievous character, "Cookie" (Cook) and I constructed a barber's pole with the familiar spiral colouring and stuck it up outside the tent with the following announcement:-

> HAIR CUT
> AND A CUP OF TEA
> 25 cents

We had lots of fun with this, for when once a customer was

in our hands we did not allow him to escape. Cookie was a hefty chap, and I ran him close. When the unsuspecting customer was once seated in the chair, with his back conveniently against one of the upright tent-poles, it was the work of a moment to tie him up and so convince him there was no withdrawing from an appreciative circle – crowds more came running in when they heard the fun – chunks of hair, grown long with neglect, came away copiously with the aid of a serviceable pair of scissors (without much regard to symmetry it must be admitted), after which a wet shampoo was given, whether required or not, by the simple expedient of a sharp tug at a cord that released the contents of an inverted water-bottle on to the victim's head. His swearing and spluttering were silenced by vigorous rubbing until the hair was dry, and a good brushing completed the operation. By this time the kettle was on the boil. With a refreshing cup of tea in one hand and a mirror in the other, the customer was graciously invited to acknowledge that he had never had such a hair cut in all his life. And with equal grace there came the prompt reply amidst roars of laughter that, "By G___, he never had!"

All our customers paid the 25 cents charged. We had trouble with one or two, but even they admitted that the tea was excellent and the hair cut could have been worse – but not much – and paid up. It was a jolly time, and the boys took it all as good sport.

One evening no fewer than five strangers arrived for a hair cut. They stood together inside the tent, asking who the barber was, staring at each one of us in turn. Cookie was out. We roared with laughter, and they obviously wondered what on earth there was to laugh at. It took us some time to persuade them that it was a joke. They referred to the sign outside, and we referred them to the appliances for torture within, whereupon they beat a hasty retreat, declaring us all mad.

After that we took the sign down.

Just on the eve of our departure, Percy Head, my half-section, and De Bussy both fell ill with a return of fever, were taken off the draft and left behind.

On the 9th of February I found myself penning the following lines from the YMCA in Dar-es-Salaam:

"There is not a soul about. The fact that work is finished, that it is Sunday midday and the heat like a furnace, accounts for this, and everybody is indoors and probably fast asleep. It's as lonely in here just now as in an empty barn in the middle of a summer's day in rural England. I cabled you yesterday that we were leaving for home. Tomorrow or next day we go on board. I packed up this morning and am all ready. I am so excited the time does not pass quickly enough! We are all fed up with this awful country and the conditions under which we have had to suffer. I have prickly heat bad enough to drive me crazy, but I don't mind so long as I can get away. I anticipate my return home by dreaming I am there every night . . . The following is a list of some of the things I have sent home: Skins of cheetah, dikdik, and leopard; native pipes, ebony walking-sticks, bows and arrows, spears, two musical instruments, model sailing boat and carved wood images, sea-shells, coral and ivory ornaments. I hope you will get these things all right . . . The next intimation you will receive will be a wire to ask you to meet me at the station!"

If my reader will bear with me a little longer, imagine with what joy we fell in in the early, very early, morning of the 11th of February, and marched with airy tread from Sea View Camp, for the last time, to the placid waters of the harbour of "the Haven of Peace." My black boy would insist on marching with me, carrying my kit-bag, to the landing stage, where he stood with wistful eyes, watching until I saw him no more. We boarded the *Salamis* soon after daybreak, and at midday put to sea. We called in at the Island of Zanzibar and left the next morning. On resuming our voyage we lost two men, who were buried at sea.[93] After a few

[93] Pioneer Benn Southward (Rothery), C33 South African Pioneers, South African Road Corps, died 18 February 1919 aged 38 (CWGC); Albert Victor Lindsay,

pleasant days at Durban, during which we visited old friends, we boarded the *Marathon*, of the Aberdeen line, and left for Cape Town. We found this fine ship a welcome change from the *Salamis*, and greatly appreciated our new quarters, which were roomy and comfortable. There was also a plentiful supply of good food.

An unfortunate order for an unnecessary fully-armed twenty-four hours' guard for forty-two men and two NCOs caused a good deal of resentment. The guard refused to fall in. There was much shouting and booing. The men eventually got their own way, and a more reasonable arrangement of an unarmed picquet was substituted. After this, all went smoothly. The weather was gloriously fine, sunny and cool. As we rounded the south coast of Africa, albatross swept majestically over the long, tumbling waters.

Arrived at Cape Town, we enjoyed twelve hours' shore leave, leaving the next afternoon with a grand send-off by many people who had collected on the quay – the event seemed to command a good deal of attention. As we glided away to the open sea a hundred little white specks waved good-bye from the landing-stage, the ship's siren screamed a return farewell that echoed and re-echoed from Table Mountain's lofty sides, the engine-room telegraph rang out "Full speed ahead," and once more we began to be conscious of the ocean swell and sea-breezes.

On the 4th of March we neared the Equator, the voyage a pleasant one, the weather hot and fine, but the heat tempered by the ship's progress. Conditions for the troops could not have been more desirable. There was a feeling that as the war was over, and work finished, all the privileges of ordinary passengers might be assumed. This was allowed after the execution of all necessary duties. Musical evenings and sports were indulged in, providing agreeable entertainment and good fun for everybody.

M2/227135 Army Service Corps, died 18 February 1919 of malaria, aged 28 (CWGC).

Two more deaths occurred among the troops, and the subsequent ceremonies were very sad.[94] The 14th of March saw us at anchor off the island of Teneriffe for a while, and, finally, in very cold weather indeed, we reached Southampton on the 21st. In twenty-four hours I arrived home in a blizzard – a contrast from the weather we had left behind in East Africa! But the happy event lost none of its warmth because of the snow and sleet of dear old England.

There is no doubt that in the long and trying experiences just concluded certain impressions were left on the mind that were, to say the least, confusing. The complex problem of life is not to be understood by mortals, and sometimes, out there in the Wilds, we wondered what we were doing and why we were doing it. There seemed to be such a waste of time, energy, life and material. All to what purpose? Because we poor humans are not perfect, we suffer, and in our suffering turn upon each other, adding to the punishment.

Perhaps some good will come from the turmoil that rent East Africa from end to end. More progress was made in opening up the country, and in ascertaining its possibilities, in this way during this short time than could have been gathered in twenty years of peace-time effort. Evidence of minerals in plenty was found, coal and gold having since been worked in places unknown before the war. Untold wealth lies buried under those far-away hills with their thick covering of forest and jungle, untouched as yet by the hand of man. Some day they will give up their secret; but I am still to be convinced that it is possible for white men to exist in many parts – the heat, the one great, deadly enemy, always there, day after day, with little variation.

Our own share in what might more readily be termed an exploratory campaign rather than an aggressive and hostile one, at least from the point of view of motor transport, with its trials and difficulties, starvation, heat, disease, and disappointment, will never be forgotten. Happy was the man

---

[94] Unable to trace.

who could take this life with a light heart. He saw the funny side of it. What were we trying to do? To catch Von Lettow! It became a standing joke – a grim one perhaps, but a joke all the same. To catch Von Lettow in Portuguese East Africa was about as hopeless as trying to catch the devil in hell. We laughed at the very thought of it – the desperate, frenzied, almost hysterical efforts to achieve the impossible. I can never lose the impression of what that harassed officer of Askari shouting, "Why the hell don't you come on?" – highly desirable but impossible. Most of the boys were philosophic enough not to take this life too seriously, and it was this spirit coupled with the conviction that our efforts were futile, that produced a form of humour of which the following are examples –

> *Officer (to new arrival)* – "Have you no putties?"
> *Man* – "No, sir,"
> *O* – "Or tunic?"
> *M* – "No, sir."
> *O* – "Or belt?"
> *M* – "No sir."
> *O* – "And no spine-pad?"
> *M* – "No, sir."
> *O* – "Well, get your hair cut!"

Orderly Sergeant – "Put that light out there."
Private – "That is not a light, sergeant, it's the moon."
O.S. – "Don't care a damn what it is – *put it out!*"

18 Motor Ambulance Convoy, War Diary May 1917 ~ June 1918.[95]

Confidential.

On 15th May 1917 I [Captain WB Walker, RAMC] took over command of 18th MAC from Captain Frazer RAMC [became OC Transport Lindi Detachment] and was ordered to equip the unit in view of the unit being posted to Kilwa for clearing purposes.

From 15th May till June 1st I was engaged in equipping MAC for duty elsewhere this consisted in getting all cases into as fit a condition as possible also refitting of MAC cars with stretcher blankets.

On 1st June I received definite instructions from IGC and DDMS that it was proposed to send an advanced section to Kilwa as suitable transport for full unit was not available.

3rd June I proceeded to Dar-es-Salaam with a consignment of cars and camped in the main Detail Camp. The remainder of the unit was transport in lots of 5 to 10 cars by the Railway to Dar-es-Salaam.

16th June last contingent of cars together with workshop and office arrived at DSM in charge of Capt [RA] Humphreys DSC [WO 372/24/75861; WO 372/24/31910]. The idea of an advanced section still engaging attention of AQM (L of C) as transport not available.

[95] TNA: WO 95/5371 part 2; ounctuation as per War Diary

18th June	Orders received to load up with 23 cars and no of personnel required, on *Umtata* and on **19th June** Personnel 34, cars 32 and native porters 16 were embarked on Umtata under my charge.
20th June	left via Zanzibar for Kilwa.
24th June	arrived at Kilwa Kisiwani.
24th - 30th June	time taken to offload my cars.
30th June	starts clearing from Nigerian and other parts of L of C Kilwa.
July 1st	Clearing chiefly from Ngerigeri [6 miles from Kilwa towards Chemera] and Beaumont's Post [near banks of Magaura River, near Humbo] together with various other posts such as Mtoli Umasi also clearing sick from Railway Station (Kilwa) to hospital of Europeans, Indians and Native forces.
July 1st - 11th	various small consignments of cars arrived from DSM together with personnel and equipment.
11th	workshops arrived with Capt Humphrey.
July 1st - 19th	Clearing sick from Beaumont's Post, Kilwa, Minasi Rumbo-Kilwa, Mtoli-Kilwa, also from 19th Stationary Kilwa to HS *Neuralia* Kisiwani.
July 20th	Casualties reported at Lutchakana so went out with convoy personally and cleared 20 wounded.
July 21st	More wounded reported (about 600) and evacuation to take place via Kirongo. Left at 6 o'clock with 16 MAC and arrived at Kirongo about 4.30 p.m. – Too late to proceed further. At 9.30 p.m. wounded began to arrive by supply column so I personally examined all wounded as to their fitness to proceed Kilwa. Those **too**

July 21st cont.	serious I took off cars and placed in hospital. Serious cases were transferred to my cars and remainder allowed to proceed after medical comforts had been administered.
July 22nd	Reported that very serious cases at Mtanduala requiring evacuation by MAC so I left at 8 o'clock with 6 MAC and arrived at 1 o'clock - road was extremely bad both as regards sand and chuck holes – returned Kirongo same day.
July 23rd	Returned Kilwa with all remaining seriously wounded and this cleared L of C to Kilwa of wounded resulting from fight around Narungombe.
July 24th	I was admitted to hospital with Catarrhal Jaundice.
July 24th – 31st	clearing sick only.
July 24th – Aug 22nd	Lieut Mitchell RAMC [unable to trace] took over temporary command during my absence
Aug 1st – 22nd	clearing sick from Narungombe and intervening posts also some from Tchemeri. New Road to Narungombe opened via Mnasi supposed to be 16 miles shorter than via Kirongo. Heavy rains fell during this period which damaged roads considerably.
Aug 22nd	Took over command from Lieut Mitchell RAMC.
Aug 22nd – 31st	clearing sick per usual; various reports were sent to Lt Col [Thomas H] McDermott [WO 372/12/207788] ADMS Ref Sanitation of Camp. Duties of MACT Reports on Cars
Sept 1st – 4th	Nothing unusual

Sept 4th	Camp and cars inspected by Surgeon General
Sept 4th – 13th	Usual clearing of sick from Division and from various units around Kilwa to HS *Neuralia*.
Sept 13th	advanced section in command of Lt Mitchell RAMC reported at Mtanduala consisting of 15 cars with 18 personnel and 8 African porters.
Sept 15th	left with all remaining MAC (20) excepting those requiring attention in workshop. Also all available drivers including sick. Ssayino [?] camp I believe to be one of the most unhealthy the unit has yet experienced and was only surpassed in sickness by Morogoro and Dar-es-Salaam. In these three camps we lost most of our old personnel from invaliding to South Africa. Found Mtanduala to be very healthy indeed no malaria.
Sept 15th – 30th **Sept 18th – 20th**	clearing casualties from Mchambia to Mtanduala (new) and from there to Kilwa. Urgent demands were made from now till end of the month in casualties and sickness.
On 20th	a wire from PC Narungombe arrived stating that 200 casualties expected by supply column and that 106 sick porters were in hospital leaving as accommodation for wounded. Sent Lieut Mitchell RAMC to superintend clearing from Narungombe with all available cars and cleared the post that evening.

Sept 20th – 30th

Personal remarks

Clearing from Kilango Ndessa Lungo and Mssindyi to Matamduala and Kilwa.

The number of patients cleared from 13th September till 30th was 1,200 (European and Coloured Troops). There were three officers including myself (with MAC) two of which were RAMC and MT and all went out on convoy. The result was that all then went sick with sun and malaria after a short time.

In my opinion the MAC in a country such as East Africa ought to be attached to the Advanced Clearing Hospital in order that the onus of clearing should not fall on a few medical officers but could be taken in turns by the Medical Officer of the Clearing Hospital.

After a few weeks with the MAC the officers were either admitted to hospital or were unfit to go on convoy and this might be guarded against if heavy work such as is entailed by the MAC were more divided over a greater number of officers.

The Clearing Hospital would be at the advantage of being more mobile instead of being **dependent on Railway or S&T**.[1]

Signed: WB Walker, Capt RAMC, OC 18th MAC,
30th Sept 1917

Mtanduala October 1st & 2nd	On the **1st** a few cars cleared the remaining sick from Narumgombe which was closing down as a post on the 3rd.
2nd.	A conference of OCs medical units was held ref moving medical units to Nahungo, and on same day 20 MAC proceeded with Lieut Mitchell RAMC and conveyed some 50 personnel (Advanced Clearing Hospt) and stores to Nahungo.
3rd	These cars returned with sick & wounded Nigerians.
4th	8 MAC left for Kisiwani with wounded fit for the journey (the rest were sent by tractor). On same dates –
and on **5th**	cars were clearing Missindye, Kahindi, Nahungo.
Sept **6th – 10th**	MAC were clearing from the various posts – Kahindi, Nahungo, Mawrengye, Missindye, Kilwa, Han Force HQ Camp & Kissiwani, on an average 30-35 MAC were engaged daily and were divided up amongst different posts according to requirements.
10th	I proceeded with advanced Section to Lahungo as Columns were too far from Rail-head. There were 8 MAC.
12th & 13th	I increased the number of MAC to 15 MAC and clearing proceeded with greater ease – chiefly forward of Nahungo on Nos 1 and 2 Columns.
Nahungo **13th**	Col Gunter ADMS ordered the remainder of 18 MAC to proceed to Nahungo

and on the **14th**	the remaining 20 MAC fit cars proceeded to Nahungo. The workshops under Capt Humphreys ASCMT remained to repair unfit MAC.
14th – 18th	now clearing from Ruponda, Nakiu and Luale.
On **17th**	12 MAC cleared from Mnero to Nahungo chiefly sick.
18th	Workshops arrived with remainder of the cars. Clearing Ruangwa, Mbemba, Lukuledi & Ruponda.
19th – 23rd	Clearing from Nos 1 & 2 Columns on the Ruangwa and Ruponda routes also from Chingwea and Lukuledi back to Mtanduala (distance between Lukuledi and Mtanduala is 135 miles).
	As our forces were coming back from Lukuledi to Ruponda and a number of sick and wounded had to be cleared after Lukuedi Fight (1 Column) cars were sent at 4.45 a.m. to Lukuledi & these returned on 24th having got there in time to take back sick and wounded.
22nd	I was admitted to Hospital Lieut Mitchell RAMC took over temporarily.
24th – 31st October	Clearing from Chingwea, Ruponda, Mnero, Jumbe, Ruangwe, back to Nahunga & Mtanduala. Average number of cars daily – 30.
On **27th**	I was discharged from Hospital at Nahungo.
	October was most difficult month of Kilwa area. Distances longer, Roads poor & a greater number of sick and wounded than I had experienced previously.

	On the whole, the number of cars were sufficient to meet all emergencies, and sick were seldom held up for lack of medical transport.
Nahungo **November 1st – 2nd**	Advanced section left for Mnero with Lieut Mitchell RAMC.
2nd – 8th	Chiefly clearing Division of sick.
Mnero **8th**	I made Mnero my Head-quarters with 30 MAC cars
8th – 11th	Clearing from Ngaga, Ruangwa, Lukuledi, Ruponda and Chingwa.
12th	Camp was inspected by S. Gen Pike AMS [TNA: WO 141/31 See Pike Report – www.gweaa.com/medical], 5 MAC left for Column 1 wounded and 10 for Ndanda to bring back lying German sick wounded to Mnero.
13th & 14th	Col Gunter ADMS ordered forward Advance Section to Lukuledi. My unit was now divided up as follows: Workshops Nahungo, my Headquarters Mnero, and an Advanced Section at Lukuledi with Lieut Mitchell RAMC.
15th	I inspected camp at Lukuledi – stopped for night and proceeded to Ndanda next day and got orders to make my Hqtrs at that place shortly after my arrival.
16th – 17th	All available cars were ordered forward from Mero and a guard was left with unfit MAC.
18th	No petrol obtainable so clearing was stopped.
18th – 25th	Clearing Tschiwata & Muriti of sick & wounded Germans.
25th	Workshops arrived with Capt Humphreys in charge.

25th – 30th	Clearing Newala, Luakala, Narombo & Massasi back to Ndanda and Mtama.
Owing to rapid movements of troops this month, workshops was unable to keep up with Head-qtrs, but after arrival at Ndanda the mileage for clearing decreased and work was not so heavy as in proceeding month, so that towards end of the month more cars were available.
Ndanda December	Early in December the 29th MAC proceeded to Massasi & took over clearing forward from Massasi this unit was responsible for clearing Massasi to Rail-head.
Cars were sent on detachment 6 Lindi, 3 Mingoyo, & Mtama for local work.
Ndanda January 1918	Nothing of importance. Still clearing Massasi to Mtama with Head-quarters still at Ndanda.
15th	10 MAC were ordered to proceed to Lindi (on detachment) but had to return to Ndanda as road was impassable about this time a mild outbreak of typhoid occured in the unit but ceased after personnel were innoculated.
31st	Lorries left for Mtama & Lindi as heavy rains threatened and all heavy vehicles were being ordered to Lindi.
February 4th	Rail-head opened at Mkirwa & sick were taken on to Mtama per Tractor. The runs now were Massasi to Mkwira.
WB Walter, Captain RAMC, 18 MAC

Ndanda March 4th	Railhead arrived at Ndanda and on **5th** cars of this convoy stopped running. 29th MAC [War Diary WO 95/5371/5] took over clearing Massasi – Ndanda. Only local work was done from 5th.
22nd	Sixty personnel left for Lindi en route for Durban Rest Camp. 30 of these were taken over by S&T and were employed on loading up derelect MT cars also on road work between Ndanda and Massasi.
On 9 April	only 10 of original 60 were sent on leave South – majority of the above 60 MT had been over 2 years in EA and ought to have had leave in SA.
Ndanda 1 April 1918	Thirty MT drivers of those awaiting transport to Durban on Recouperative leave were ordered by Med Staff to report to STO [Senior Transport Officer] for duty in Lindi area.
9 April	Ten NCO of original 60 were allowed to proceed to Durban.
24 April	Med Staff wired Hand over all MT personnel except 5 MT drivers and necessary staff to STO. Only local work performed during the month.
Ndanda 1st May 1918	No clearing for this month and necessary workshop repairs were undertaken on some of the cars.
7th May	20 Ambulance cars were sent to Lindi under instructions from Med Staff for embarkation at Port Amelia.
On 22 May	these cars were shifted.

1 June No clearing work was done owing during this month except local post work as MT drivers were all attached to STO. Repairs on cars continued.

WB Walker, Capt RAMC, o/c 18 MAC

Mechanical / Motor Transport Companies in East Africa

No 18 Motor Ambulance Convoy (MAC) formed part of 618 Company Army Service Company (ASC).

The units[1] which served in East Africa include:

Unit No	Function	Dates [War Diary ref]
570	Served Lines of Communication (LOC), absorbed into 648	Formed Sept 1915 - June 1917
599	Base Depot & Repair Unit	Formed 1915 [WO 95/5378/1; WO 95/5378/2; See also William Terrell, *With the Motor Transport in East Africa*]
618	Motor Ambulance Convoy incl	Formed Jan 1916
	No 18 MAC	[WO 95/5371/1; WO 95/5371/2]
	No 19 MAC	[WO 95/5371/3; WO 95/5371/4]
622		Mentioned in WO 95/5378/6
631	Ammunition column for 38 Brigade Royal Garrison Artillery	Formed 8 Jan 1916 [WO 95/5378/4; WO 95/5378/5]

[1] Info from Long Long Trail, Army Service Corps, Mechanical Transport Companies and War Diaries

632	Ammunition column for Royal Marine Artillery Brigade	Formed Jan 1916
633	Column for 134 (Cornwall) Heavy Battery	Formed Jan 1916
635	Lines of Communication (from Brigade Supply Column)	Formed Sept 1916 [WO 95/5378/6]
648	Absorbed unit 570	
699	Lines of Communication incl No 29 MAC	[WO 95/5371/5]
No 1 Auxilliary	Based Nairobi (Mar-Apr 1916)	[WO 95/5378/3]
East African	Consisted of Baganda Drivers	Feb 1917 - Oct 1917 [WO 95/5377/2; WO 95/5377/3]
Rhodesian	Northern Rhodesia	[*The British South Africa Police in the Great War* by John Berry]

Other references

Mechanical Transport (re Re-organisation of MT staff on Voi-Aruscha line)	April 1916 [WO 158/873]
Conveyance of troops to Basra and India, mechanical transport to East Africa and invalids to Australia.	1917 [MT 23/811/5]
MECHANICAL TRANSPORT: Light lorries for East Africa	1917 [MUN 4/3112]
Suggestion that there was a Chinese Motor Transport Company	[Medal card - Driver 564 Hosan Chee WO 372/10/49696]

Index

18th Motor Ambulance Convoy 7, 11
648 MT Co 6
816 Co 6
Africa Hotel 237, 240
Ambulance Corps 186
Ankwabe 6, 10, 150-151, 154-156-158, 160, 169, 170-171, 173, 175-177, 179, 188, 208
Ash 153
Bailey 156
Bandari 136, 141, 151, 156
Beaumont's Post 263
Beira 132
Bell 10, 66-67, 69-70
Berins 155, 160, 173, 182, 225
Bishop 177, 183
Blanco 223, 245
Broncho 156
Bunn 125, 134, 137, 145, 149-151, 237
Burrows 187, 189
Caister House 122-123
Cape 20, 22-25, **35**, 114, 237, 259
Caronia 115
Carrick 145, 148-150
Carriers/porters 60, 80, 175, 190, 195, 242, 248, 263, 265
Chapman 170
Chemera 263
Chinese 236, 250, 274
Chinga 196-197
Clipson 156

Congella Camp 118-119, 152
Cook 256
Crichton 245
Dale 153
Dar-es-Salaam 6, 28-29, 41, 134, 235, 236-237, 239, 242, 246, 248, 250, 253-254, 258, 262, 265
Davies 155, 160, 162, 167, 172-173, 176, 177, 183, 225
Day 152, 179
De Bussy 13, 116, 125, 193-194, 208, 221, 253, 258
Double 152
Dukes 19
Durban 6, 35, 115-119, 122, 125, 139, 259, 271
England 6, 24, 26, 35-36, 43, 47, 62, 75, 81, 86, 116, 118, 180, 189, 204, 210, 218, 232-233, 258, 260
Fairchild 224
Fillsell 6
Fineberg 145, 181-182, 225-226
Fitzpatrick 19
Fober 151
France 234
Francis 123
Freetown 20
Frontiersmen 129, 249
Gascon 217-218
Godfrey 19
Gold Coast 60-61
Green 135, 152

Greenacre.......................... 122
Grosse......................... 100, 123
Hall............................. 144, 155
Harris 13, 19, 134-135, 152, 155, 173, 237, 250
Head..... 246-247, 250, 253, 258
Henderson........................... 156
Hotel Kigoma....................... 246
Humphrey.................... 262-263
Indian people 3, 36, 60, 81, 83, 208, 226, 234, 238-239, 254, 256
Ingoma..... 6, 125, 131-133, 237
Jacobs................................ 123
Jones 15, 41-42, 53-54, 59, 166, 249
Kent............................... 20-21
Kilimane 181, 194-195, 222, 248
Kilwa Kisiwani.... 235, 262-268
King's African Rifles... 232, 242
Knowles............................... 13
Königsberg.......................... 47
Laconia.............................. 6
Lemasuli............. 103, 131, 240
Lettow-Vorbeck (von) 9, **34**, 60, 90, 126, 128-130, 135, 150-151, 154-155, 162-163, 173, 181, 193, 192-194, 198, 200, 205, 208, 222, 225, 248, 250, 261
Lindi 6, 30-31, 41, 83, 110, 112-114, 116, 128-129, 131, 153, 167, 225, 240, 242, 262, 270-271
Livingstone.......................... 72
Lorriman............................. 19
Loveridge........................... 218
Lumbo 4, 181, 189, 193, 205-208, 210, 216, 222, 229-230, 232-235, 242

Lurio 135, 173, 176, 180-182, 186, 188, 194, 225
Lutchakana........................ 263
Mamot................................ 222
Marathon............................ 256
Marmont...................... 212, 222
Massasi 47, 48, 52, 56-57, 59-60, 63, 66, 72-73, 77, 81, 88-90, 96, 100, 105, 226, 250
Medo..... 144, 151, 176-178, 180
Mercer...... 13, 19, 109, 112-113
Merryweather...................... 19
Millane................ 210, 212, 221
Milton................................ 216
Mingoya/o 6, 37, 42-43, 45, 107-109, 112, 270
Mkirwa.............................. 270
Mkonta......... 189-190, 195, 197
Mombasa............................. 28
Monapo 6, 193-195, 202, 204-206, 208, 222
Moore......................... 122-123
Mounce............... 135, 152, 226
Mozambique 3-4, 6, 181-182, 189, 193, 195, 198, 207, 215, 222, 231
Mtama............................... 270
Mumford............................. 14
Namirrue.................... 195, 222
Nampula................... 185, 195
Ndanda 53, 65, 70, 99-100, 104-105, 269-271
Neuralia........................... 263
Ngerigeri........................... 263
Nigeria........................ 60, 263
Nyasa........................... 72, 131
Parker........................... 89, 92
Peach................................. 50
Percy................................ 123
Pete.................................. 226
Pioneers............... 240-241, 258

Port Amelia 131, 133-137, 151, 152, 155, 171, 173, 182, 271
Port Lincoln 6, 13, 19-23, 45, 128, 240
Portuguese East Africa 3, 9, 72, 131-132, 173, 181, 194, 215, 222, 261
Power.................................... 123
Pye.. 222
Rajah..... 10, 67, 69, 70, 90, 137
Raspin............................. 13, 19
Ratcliff................................... 50
Rhodesia 212, 228, 248-249, 274
Road Corps 3, 47, 101, 158, 258
Roberts......................... 123, 170
Robinson.................... 67-68, 137
Rovuma 60, 70, 72, 76, 78-79, 80-81, 88, 90, 96, 98, 126, 129-130, 181
Salamis 7, 28, 30, 235, 258-259
Salisbury Plain...... 49, 245-244
Sandacock............................ 220
Sea View Camp 235-236, 243, 246, 251, 258
Shaw 125, 134, 152, 187, 201, 208
Small............................ 212, 228
South Africa 6, 24, 116, 119, 123, 125, 128, 156, 212, 220, 265
Swahili 32, 37, 48, 66, 92, 145, 163, 185, 233-234
Tafel..................................... 129
Talbot.................................. 137
Tarrant................................. 250
Thomas Cook.......................162
Thompson 14-15, 134, 137, 139, 144, 149-150, 155, 160, 162, 167, 171-173, 176, 182
Tiny.. 15
Townsend............................ 152

Uganda................................. 60
van Deventer...................... 136
Vincent............................... 117
Watkins....................... 176, 208
Wells Camp......................... 89
Wheatley........................ 13, 19
Wheeldin............................ 123
White.................................... 19
Williams............................... 50
Wireless ..88, 233-234, 240, 244
women 56, 72, 95-96, 106-107, 154, 182, 192-193, 200, 220, 227, 229, 236, 240, 244, 248, 253
YMCA 134, 137, 209-210, 216, 219, 226, 232, 258
Zanzibar.. 28, 47, 217, 258, 263

www.ingramcontent.com/pod-product-compliance
Lightning Source LLC
Chambersburg PA
CBHW050242170426
43202CB00015B/2885